Pittsburgh Series in Bibliography

EDITORIAL BOARD

Matthew J. Bruccoli, General Editor

William R. Cagle
Charles W. Mann
Joel Myerson

THOMAS WOLFE

Photo courtesy Aldo P. Magi

Thomas Wolfe
A DESCRIPTIVE BIBLIOGRAPHY

Carol Johnston

UNIVERSITY OF
PITTSBURGH PRESS
1987

The preparation of this volume was made possible (in part) by grants from the National Endowment for the Humanities; the University Research Grant Committee, Clemson University; and the Southern Regional Education Board.

Published by the University of Pittsburgh Press, Pittsburgh, Pa. 15260
Copyright © 1987, University of Pittsburgh Press
All rights reserved
Feffer and Simons, Inc, London
Manufactured in the United States of America

Library of Congress Cataloging-in-Publication Data

Johnston, Carol, 1948–
   Thomas Wolfe: a descriptive bibliography.

   (Pittsburgh series in bibliography)
   Includes index.
   1. Wolfe, Thomas, 1900–1938—Bibliography. I. Title.
II. Series.
Z8980.45.J64 1987 [PS3545.O337]   016.813'52   86-16192
ISBN 0-8229-3546-5

For Richard and Catherine

Contents

Acknowledgments	XI
Introduction	XIII
A. Separate Publications	1
AA. Posthumously Collected Editions	199
B. First Book and Pamphlet Appearances	209
C. First-Appearance Contributions to Magazines and Newspapers	229
D. Keepsakes	257
E. Putative First Appearances of Material by Wolfe	267
Appendix. Principal Works About Wolfe	279
Index	281

Acknowledgments

IN COMPILING this bibliography I have incurred many debts of gratitude: none is greater than the debt I owe Matthew J. Bruccoli and Joel Myerson. They supported this project from its inception and corrected and critiqued every draft. Their patience and guidance made this work possible. All that is good in this book is the result of their diligence.

All of the members of the Department of English at Clemson University have been supportive. M. Thomas Inge and G. William Koon, chairmen of the department, encouraged my work by giving me release time. Robert W. Hill and Frank Day, directors of the graduate program in English, assigned graduate assistants to this project. I wish to thank these graduate assistants: Lewis Arrington, William Atkinson, Leslie Beggs, Leigh Berman, LaVerne M. Christoph, C. Mitchell Lee, Judith Shepherd, Clara Shockley, and M. Kellan Williams. The departmental secretaries, Pearl Parker, Julie Harmon, and Kim Hunter, typed copy. Judy Payne, departmental administrative assistant, helped me keep my finances straight. Betty Moore, administrative assistant in the College of Liberal Arts, helped me handle grants.

The National Endowment for the Humanities, the Southern Regional Education Board, and the University Research Grant Committee at Clemson University provided partial funding for this project. Robert W. Waller, dean of the College of Liberal Arts, and Robert W. Henningson, associate director of university research, helped me obtain this funding.

Many librarians helped me in this project. Marion Withington, Julie Pennebaker, and Dale Simmons of the Interlibrary Loan Department in the Cooper Library at Clemson University went out of their way to be helpful. Jan Gambrell and Michael Kohl of Special Collections were equally as supportive. Others I would like to thank include Alice Cotten, Jerry Cotten, H. G. Jones, and Tucker Respess of the North Carolina Collection at the University of North Carolina—Chapel Hill; Mildred Abraham of the Barrett Collection at the University of Virginia; Philip Banks and Edward Epstein of the Wolfe Collection at the Pack Memorial Library in Asheville, North Carolina; Andrea Brown and Christine Thompson of the Wolfe Collection at St. Mary's College in Raleigh, North Carolina; and Michael T. Ryan, curator of special collections, Stanford University. John Idol, Jr. has been especially generous with his assistance during each stage of this project. Aldo P. Magi and Richard Walser graciously allowed me access to the materials they assembled for their edition of Thomas Wolfe's interviews. John Idol, Jr., and Aldo P. Magi read and critiqued this book in an early draft. Mary Bruccoli initially surveyed the Wolfe Collection in the British Library, allowing me to better prepare myself for my trip there. Joel Myerson, Matthew J. Bruccoli, Charles Mann, and William Cagle vetted this book; it is the better for their assistance.

Ed and Mid Gambrell kindly allowed me into their home so that I could examine their collection. Paul Gitlin, executor of the Wolfe estate, granted me permission to survey the manuscript material in the Wolfe Collections at Harvard and Chapel Hill. Charles Scribner III extended permission for me to survey the Scribners archives at the Firestone Library in Princeton.

I am grateful to Paul Gitlin and Charles Scribner III for permission to quote from Wolfe and Scribners manuscripts in the following collections: Harvard University (Houghton Library), The University of North Carolina–Chapel Hill (Wilson Library), and Princeton University (Firestone Library). I am equally grateful to the following libraries for permission to reproduce photographs of materials in their possession: the Sarah Graham Kenan Library, St. Mary's College, Raleigh, North Carolina; the Pack Memorial Library, Asheville, North Carolina; the Wilson Library, University of North Carolina–Chapel Hill; the Alderman Library, the University of Virginia; the British Library, London; and the Bodleian Library, Oxford University. Matthew J. Bruccoli kindly reproduced the bindings, title pages, and copyright pages of several books in his collection.

Others who helped include Manual and Beatrice Bagtas, Charles and Dorothy Ingalls, and Gerda Veator.

Finally, this book is dedicated to my husband, Richard, and my daughter, Catherine. Their love, good humor, and faith have sustained me throughout this project.

Introduction

THIS descriptive bibliography of the works of Thomas Wolfe contains listings of writings by Thomas Wolfe. It does not list writings about Wolfe, unless they include something by Wolfe published for the first time.

FORMAT

Section A lists chronologically all books and pamphlets wholly or substantially by Wolfe—including all printings of all editions in the United States and Great Britain through 1985. Only entries A 12, *The Letters of Thomas Wolfe To His Mother,* and A 14, *Mannerhouse: A Play in a Prologue and Four Acts,* are inserted out of chronology. In both cases these volumes are editions of previously edited work by Wolfe in which the editors made use of either significantly different editing criteria or copy-texts. In both cases, the titles for these books differ slightly from the titles of the earlier editions. For this reason, both books are listed as separate entries, but have been placed in this bibliography immediately after the entry for the earlier edition. Entry A 12, *The Letters of Thomas Wolfe To His Mother,* although published in 1968, follows entry A 11, *Thomas Wolfe's Letters To His Mother,* which was published in 1943; entry A 14, *Mannerhouse: A Play in a Prologue and Four Acts,* though published in 1985, follows entry A 13, *Mannerhouse: A Play in Three Acts,* published in 1948.

The numbering system for Section A indicates the edition and printing for each entry. Thus, for *Look Homeward, Angel,* A 2.1.a indicates that this is the second title published by Wolfe (A 2), and that the entry describes the first edition (1), first printing (a). Issues are indicated by subscript numbers—thus A 4.1.a_2 is the second issue of the first printing of *From Death to Morning.* States are discussed in the text.

Each entry begins with facsimiles of the title page (with its dimensions given) and the copyright page, followed by pagination information and a collation of the gatherings.[1] A description of the contents follows. In entries

---

1. The chief bibliographical purpose of any quasi-facsimile transcription is to provide all practicable information necessary to enable the reader to compare any individual copy to the transcription to confirm its identity or variation. Because any transcription is a compromise, this book frequently substitutes photographic reproductions. When the use of quasi-facsimile transcriptions has been called for, the following rule has been used regarding the use of type sizes: publishers regularly change title page

for collected works like *From Death to Morning* (A 4.1.a) this description is followed by a list of the titles collected. An asterisk (*) following a title in this list indicates its first appearance in print; a number sign (#) following a title indicates that the material was previously published under this title, but has been significantly reworked; cross references follow material previously published under a different title or refer to later printings. Information on typography and paper includes the dimensions of the printed text, type of paper (laid or wove), number of lines per page, and running heads. 5 ¾″ (5 ⅞″) × 3 ¾″ indicates (1) the height (first from the top of the first line of the text to the bottom of the last line of the text, and second from the top of the running head (or the folio, when that appears above the running head or when there is no running head) to the bottom of the last line of the text) and (2) the width of the printed area. All paper is white unless otherwise indicated. Binding information includes cloth types, description of stamping, end papers, page trimming, page-edge gilding or staining, headbands and footbands. All wrappers are paper unless otherwise indicated. Dust jackets of the first American and English printings are fully described in the text and reproduced in full-page illustrations within the entry. Dust jackets accompanying the first printings of later editions are noted.

Information on publication is drawn from Wolfe's notebooks and letters and from unpublished manuscripts in the Wisdom Collection at the Houghton Library at Harvard University and in the North Carolina Collection at the University of North Carolina–Chapel Hill; the Scribners records in the Charles Scribner's Sons Archives at Princeton University; copyright information (from both published and manuscript records at the Copyright Office of the Library of Congress); contemporary book trade announcements; and the title and copyright pages of the books examined. Dates of book contracts, amounts of advances, and royalty percentages are specified, when that information is available; the earliest listed price of an edition is also specified. The prices of later printings within editions are usually not specified.

Between them Charles Scribner's Sons and Harper published all but one of the book-length works appearing during Wolfe's lifetime. Both publishing houses included coded information on the copyright pages of the books they published to differentiate printings.[2] The only book by Wolfe to be published by Scribners prior to 1930 is *Look Homeward, Angel* (A 2.1.a). The first printing is identified by the absence of information identifying it as a subsequent printing; the second printing by the copyright information identifying it as the second printing (see A 2.1.a and A 2.1.b). Beginning in 1930 and prior to 1974, a Scribners first printing had the letter 'A' on the copyright page, removed or replaced by 'B,' 'C,' etc., in later printings (see A 4.1.a).

---

and copyright page type fonts and style, using larger and smaller fonts for aesthetic purposes. No attempt has been made to identify the size type in these transcriptions. Large and small capitals when used in the same line are always transcribed as such.

2. See Jack Tannen, *How To Identify and Collect First Editions* (New York: Arco, 1976).

Beginning around 1950, this lettering code was combined with information about the month and year of the printing and the printer. This new code consisted of a letter (the printing), a hyphen, a number (the number of the month in which the printing was completed), a period, a number (the number of the year in which the printing was completed), and, in brackets, a letter indicating the name of the printer (see A 3.1.r).

Since 1973 Scribners has used a printing number code. This code consists of sequences of numbers to the left and to the right of two slash-separated letters (see A 4.1.c). Odd numbers appear to the left of the letters, even numbers to the right. The lowest number on either side of the code represents the printing. A post-1970 reprint of *From Death to Morning* includes the following information on the copyright page: '9 11 13 15 17 19 M/P 20 18 16 14 12 10 8'. The letters indicate the binder and the binding (cloth or paper); the numbers indicate that this is the eighth printing of *From Death to Morning* in this series. In subsequent reprintings the lowest number to the right or left of the letters would be removed.

The Harper code is different. Beginning in May 1922, the words 'First Edition' were printed on the copyright page of the first printing of a book and removed from later printings. In addition, between 1912 and 1973, a letter code was used to indicate the month and year of printing; it consisted of two hyphenated letters. The first letter referred to the month and the second letter to the year in which the printing was completed.[3]

In 1962 Harper & Brothers merged with Row, Peterson and formed Harper & Row; all books bearing this imprint were necessarily published after that date.

Beginning in 1973 Harper & Row began using a printing number/year code such as '83 84 14 13 12'. This code, observed in a Perennial Library reprint of *You Can't Go Home Again* (A 8.4.b–f) bearing a 1973 copyright date indicates that this, the twelfth printing in that series, was completed in 1983. This code appears in several Harpers volumes observed on the last page rather than on the copyright page of those volumes.

Some of the conclusions in this bibliography are based on material gathered from the Scribners records, as well as from manuscript collections at NcU and MH and from the inscriptions in copies of books I have observed. I have no reason to doubt the accuracy of this material; however, in cases in which my conclusions have been based primarily on this kind of information, I have referred to or quoted from the source of that information in notes.

Elmer Johnson's *Thomas Wolfe: A Checklist* (Kent State University Press, 1970) lists Canadian imprints of the following: A 2.1.a, the first printing of *Look Homeward, Angel* (Toronto: Macmillan); A 2.4.a, the illustrated edition of *Look Homeward, Angel* (Toronto: S.J.R. Saunders); A 3.1.m, the Sun Dial Press reprint of *Of Time and the River* (Toronto: Blue Ribbon Press); A 8.1.a, the first printing of *You Can't Go Home Again* (Toronto: Musson); A 9.1.a, the first printing of *The Hills Beyond* (Toronto: Musson); and A 9.1.c, the

---

3. Tannen describes this code in detail.

Sun Dial Press reprint of *The Hills Beyond* (Toronto: Blue Ribbon Press). Although all of these imprints are listed in the *Cumulative Book Index*, I have been unable to locate any copies with these imprints; none is listed in *The Canadian Union Catalogue;* none is listed in *The Canadian Catalogue of Books Published in Canada, about Canada, As Well As Those Written By Canadians, with Imprint 1921–1949;* none was discovered in a search of the Canadian Library System's DOBIS data base; none was located in a canvasing of the fifty largest Canadian libraries; and none is held by the National Library of Canada which is mandated to collect all editions of books published in Canada. The Canadian imprints listed in the *Cumulative Book Index* almost certainly represent the attempts of Canadian distributors to protect copyright.

Section AA is a supplemental list of posthumously published collections of Wolfe's work. These collections do not include any material by Wolfe published for the first time. Binding is assumed to be cloth unless otherwise indicated.

Section B lists chronologically all titles in which material by Wolfe appears for the first time in a book or pamphlet. Previously published material is identified by cross-referencing. Previously unpublished material is so identified. Binding is assumed to be cloth unless otherwise indicated. Locations are given for copies examined. Books like Carole Klein's *Aline* (New York, Hagerstown, San Francisco, London: Harper & Row, 1979) in which the source of quotations is not given and in which permission to print previously unpublished material is not acknowledged are included in this section only if the existence of previously unpublished Wolfe material in them is verified.

Section C lists chronologically all first American and English publications in newspapers and magazines by Wolfe. I have used the phrase "incorporated into" throughout this section to indicate short fiction that also appeared in a later work by Wolfe (although the actual creation of that later work may have predated the publication of the short fiction).

Section D lists chronologically keepsakes with material by Wolfe. A keepsake is here defined as a separately printed item in a limited number of copies intended for private distribution, printing previously published material by Wolfe, and not offered for sale.

Section E lists putative first appearances of material by Wolfe. Much of this is in the nature of conversations and reminiscences (interviews in which detail and proximity of publication suggest that the interviewer took notes are listed in section C).

Wolfe served as managing editor of the University of North Carolina newspaper, *The Tar Heel*, his junior year (1918–1919) and as editor his senior year (1919–1920); it is likely that much of the editorial material (appearing on page two of each issue) and many of the news stories appearing during these years were written by Wolfe. All except a few of the articles are unsigned, and Wolfe's signature is affixed to only one article printed during these years (see C 10). Articles and editorials from *The Tar Heel* listed in this section have been attributed to Wolfe by others (generally in reminiscences).

Introduction

On one occasion Wolfe is believed to have served as guest editor of *The Tar Baby*, the campus humor magazine, and to have written the whole issue, "cover to cover, forty-five pages of satire modeled after one of the newspapers in the state."[4]

Materials listed in the B and C sections of this bibliography are not repeated in the E section, even if some of the Wolfe material appearing in them is putative.

An *Appendix* lists principal works about Wolfe.

TERMS AND METHODS

Edition. All copies of a book printed from a single setting of type—including all reprintings from standing type, from plates, and by photo-offset processes.

Printing. All copies of a book printed at one time (without removing the type or plates from the press).

State. States occur within single printings and are created by an alteration not affecting the conditions of publication or sale to *some* copies of a given printing (by stop-press correction or cancellation of leaves). There must be two or more states. See A $5.1.a_3$ for an instance in which two states exist within an issue.

Issue. Issues occur only within single printings and are created by an alteration affecting the condition of publication or sale to *some* copies of a given printing (usually a title leaf cancellation). There must be two or more issues. See A $4.1.a_1$ and A $4.1.a_2$.

The terms *issue* and *state* have been restricted to the sheets of a book. Binding or dust-jacket variants have no bearing on *state* and *issue* as properly assigned.

Dust jackets and bindings. Dust jackets for Section A entries have been described in detail because they are part of the original publication effort and sometimes provide information about how the book was marketed. There is, of course, no certainty that a jacket now on a book was always on it.

For binding cloth designations I have used the cloth grains illustrated in the *Bibliography of American Literature,* ed. Jacob Blanck (New Haven, Conn.: Yale University Press, 1955–). Color specifications are based on the *ISCC-NBS Color Name Charts Illustrated with Centroid Colors* (National Bureau of Standards). Centroid numbers have not been assigned; instead, the generalized color designations have been used.[5]

The spines of bindings or dust jackets are printed horizontally unless otherwise indicated. The reader is to assume that vertically printed spines

---

4. See Don Bishop, "Thomas Wolfe As A Student," *Carolina Magazine,* 71 (March 1942), 28–35, 47–48.

5. See G. Thomas Tanselle, "A System of Color Identification for Bibliographical Description," *Studies in Bibliography,* 20 (1967), 203–34. The use of exact centroid numbers creates a false sense of precision. Lighting, oxidation, fading, wear, and nonuniform dyeing practices make precise color identification difficult.

read from top to bottom unless otherwise indicated. The blank fronts, spines, and backs of bindings and dust jackets are not described.

Pagination for reprintings of Section A entries and for miscellaneous collection indicates the number of the last numbered page in the book.

This bibliography makes use of deposit and inscribed copies to help determine publication dates. Dates given for copies located at BL (the British Library), BOD (the Bodleian Library, Oxford), and DLC (the Library of Congress) are the dates as written or stamped on the copies deposited for copyright at those institutions. Inscriptions and letters are Wolfe's unless otherwise specified.

This bibliography is based upon evidence gathered from my personal inspection and collation of multiple copies of Wolfe's works. Items included in this bibliography that I have not personally examined are labeled "not seen." The symbols used for American libraries are those employed by the National Union Catalog; those for Canadian libraries are those listed in *Symbols of Canadian Libraries*, 9th ed. (Ottawa: National Library of Canada, 1981). The following are additional symbols:

APM	Collection of Aldo P. Magi
BL	British Library, London
BOD	Bodleian Library, Oxford
CJ	Collection of Carol Johnston
CW	Collection of Charles H. Woodell
EG	Collection of Edward Gambrell
JI	Collection of John Idol
MJB	Collection of Matthew J. Bruccoli
NcRSM	Thomas Wolfe Collection at the Kenan Library, St. Mary's College, Raleigh, North Carolina. (This collection includes the collections of John O. Fulenwider, Jr., Theodore Theobald, George W. McCoy, and Egar Wolf.)

The names of less frequently mentioned collections not provided in the National Union Catalog or in *Symbols of Canadian Libraries* are written out in full.

CONCLUSION

This bibliography is not an attempt to indicate the scarcity of Wolfe's works and should not be taken as such. If there is only one location listed, it means that, of all the libraries I visited and corresponded with, only one had or reported having a copy of this book; it does not mean that there is only one copy of that book in existence.

A bibliography is more than just a listing of books; it is also a detailed study of an author's literary career. Readers of this book will find evidence on Wolfe's literary reputation, as measured by sales of his books; Wolfe's income from his books; the popularity of individual works by Wolfe, as measured by separate publications and reprintings of them; the popularity of Wolfe's writings in England; and the textual history of Wolfe's works. Students of American literary and publishing history will find information on twentieth-century reprint firms and Anglo-American publishing relations.

A bibliography is outdated the day it goes to the printer. Addenda and corrigenda are earnestly solicited.

Clemson University
31 December 1985

A. Separate Publications

All books and pamphlets wholly or substantially by Wolfe, including all printings in the United States and Great Britain through 1985.

A 1 THE CRISIS IN INDUSTRY

A 1.1.a
First edition, only printing (1919)

UNIVERSITY OF NORTH CAROLINA
DEPARTMENT OF PHILOSOPHY

THE CRISIS IN INDUSTRY

(CROWNED WITH THE WORTH PRIZE)

THOMAS WOLFE

CHAPEL HILL
PUBLISHED BY THE UNIVERSITY
1919

A 1.1.a: 8⅞" × 6"

A 1.1.c *The Crisis in Industry* 3

Copyright page: blank.

[1–5] 6–14 [15–16]

[1]⁸

Contents: p. 1: title; p. 2: blank; p. 3: text, headed 'INTRODUCTION'; p. 4: blank; pp. 5–14: text, headed 'THE CRISIS IN INDUSTRY'; pp. 15–16: blank.

Typography and paper: 6⅛" (6½") × 3⅞"; 37 lines per page. Running heads: rectos and versos, 'THE CRISIS IN INDUSTRY'. Wove paper.

Binding: Light gray wrappers; front same as the title page, but within double-rules frame. All edges trimmed.

Publication: 200 copies. Published 1919. Not for sale.

Printing: Not determined.

Locations: InU Lilly, MH (3 copies), NcA, NcRSM, NcU (2 copies), ViU.

LATER EDITIONS

Second and third printings; priority not determined (1978)

A 1.1.b
Hillsborough, N.C.: Ballinger, 1978.

Facsimile reprinting. Wrappers. Colophon: '300 numbered copies of this facsimile edition were | printed at The Loom Press, Chapel Hill, in 1978. Ten | additional copies were printed out of sequence for | promotional use. | This copy is No. '. Fifty copies were distributed inserted in a gray cardboard folder with a medium blue cloth shelfback together with signed copies of Richard Walser's *Prolegomena to Thomas Wolfe's A Crisis in Industry;* numbers 51–300 were distributed with a reduced photographic reprint of the *Prolegomena*. Price: $35.00 for numbers 1–50; $10.00 for numbers 51–300. *Locations:* Numbers 1–50: APM, NcRSM, NcU; Numbers 51–300: EG.

A 1.1.c
Winston-Salem, N.C.: Palaemon Press, 1978.

Facsimile reprinting. Wrappers. On copyright page: 'THIS FACSIMILE EDITION IS LIMITED TO 200 NUMBERED COPIES, OF WHICH | 180 ARE FOR PUBLIC SALE. PRINTED FOR PALAEMON PRESS LIMITED BY HERI- | TAGE PRINTERS OF CHARLOTTE, NORTH CAROLINA. THIS IS COPY NUMBER '. Price: $15.00. *Locations:* APM, CJ, MH, NcRSM, NcU.

UNIVERSITY OF NORTH CAROLINA
DEPARTMENT OF PHILOSOPHY

THE CRISIS IN INDUSTRY

(CROWNED WITH THE WORTH PRIZE)

THOMAS WOLFE

CHAPEL HILL
PUBLISHED BY THE UNIVERSITY
1919

Wrapper for A 1.1.a

A2 LOOK HOMEWARD, ANGEL

A 2.I.a
First edition, first printing (1929)

Look Homeward, Angel
A Story of the Buried Life

BY
THOMAS WOLFE

"*At one time the earth was probably a white-hot sphere like the sun.*"
—Tarr and McMurry

CHARLES SCRIBNER'S SONS
NEW YORK
1929

A 2.I.a: 7⅝" × 5¼"

> COPYRIGHT, 1929, BY
> CHARLES SCRIBNER'S SONS
>
> Printed in the United States of America

[A–B] [i–vi] vii [viii] [1–2] 3–162 [163–164] 165–388 [389–390] 391–626 [627–630]

[1–2]⁸ [3–20]¹⁶ [21–22]⁸

Contents: pp. A–B: blank; p. i: half title; p. ii: blank; p. iii: title; p. iv: copyright; p. v: 'TO | A. B. | *"Then, as all my soules bee,* | *Emparadis'd in you,* | *(in whom alone* | *I understand, and grow and see,)* | *The rafters of my body,* | *bone* | *Being still with you, the Muscle, Sinew, and Veine,* | *Which tile this* | *house, will come againe."* '; p. vi: blank; p. vii: text, headed 'TO THE READER'; p. viii: blank; p. 1: 'PART I'; p. 2: epigraph; pp. 3–162: text, headed 'LOOK HOMEWARD, ANGEL! | I'; p. 163: 'PART II'; p. 164: blank; pp. 165–388: text, headed 'XIV'; p. 389: 'PART III'; p. 390: blank; pp. 391–626: text, headed 'XXVIII'; pp. 627–630: blank.

Typography and paper: 5¾" (6¹/₁₆" × 3¹³/₁₆"; 38 lines per page. Running heads: rectos and versos, 'LOOK HOMEWARD, ANGEL'. Wove paper.

Binding: Dark blue V cloth. Front goldstamped: 'LOOK HOMEWARD, ANGEL | THOMAS WOLFE'; spine goldstamped: 'LOOK | HOMEWARD, | ANGEL | [inverted triangle] | WOLFE | SCRIBNERS'. White wove endpapers. Top and bottom edges trimmed; fore edges rough trimmed.

Dust jacket: Two formats have been noted. 3,500 copies of the first printing of *LHA* were distributed with the format 1 jacket; the rest of the first printing and all of the second printing were distributed with the format 2 jacket.

Format 1. Front: divided into three rectangular panels: top and bottom panels have brilliant yellow, medium pinkish red, medium orange, and grayish purplish blue zigzag design; center pale orangish yellow panel has grayish purplish blue ornamental lettering: 'LOOK HOMEWARD, | ANGEL | [rule] | THOMAS WOLFE'. Spine: divided into three rectangular panels: '[grayish purplish blue lettering on pale orangish yellow panel] LOOK | HOMEWARD, | ANGEL | [inverted triangle] | WOLFE | [medium orange panel] | [grayish purplish blue lettering on pale orangish yellow panel] SCRIBNERS'. Back: photograph of Wolfe and biographical mate-

First state dust jacket for A2.I.a

Second state dust jacket with wrap-around band for A 2.1.a

A2 *Look Homeward, Angel*   9

rial. Front and back flaps quote from 'a letter by the author which accompanied the manuscript when it was submitted to the publishers'.

Format 2. The same as format 1, except: back: quotes from a review by Margaret Wallace; front flap: quotes from reviews by Thomas Beer, Margery Latimer, Harry Hansen, and from the *Philadelphia Public Ledger;* and back flap contains biographical material. In the NcU copy a three-inch wrap-around band of black paper printed in white containing a quotation from Sinclair Lewis has been wrapped around the lower third of the jacket front extending over the spine and onto the back reading: "SINCLAIR LEWIS | *says of* | THOMAS WOLFE | 'I don't see why he should not | be one of the greatest world writers. | His first book is so deep and spacious | that it deals with the whole of life.' " This wrap-around band was probably added after initial distribution.

Publication: 5,540 copies. Copyright #A14402. Published 18 October 1929. Date of contract: 9 January 1929. Advance: $500. Royalty: 10% first 2,000; 15% thereafter. Price: $2.50.

Printing: Composed and printed by the Scribner Press, New York City. Bound by the Scribner Press.

Locations: APM (dj 1), BL (23OCT29), EG, JI, MH (6 copies; 2 copies with dj 1), MJB, NcA (3 copies; 2 copies with dj 1), NcRSM (4 copies; 1 copy with dj 1 and 1 copy with dj 2), NcU (3 copies; 1 copy with dj 1 and 1 copy with dj 2), PSt (dj 1), ViU (3 copies; 1 copy with dj 1).

Note one: Penciled notes on a 3×5 card in the Scribners records indicate that "30 printings" of *LHA,* a total of "125,000" copies, were distributed prior to 6 July 1944; however, a memo in the same collection dated 6 November 1947 indicates only nine printings of *LHA.* The notes on the 3×5 card may refer to Scribners printings, cheap reprints, and foreign printings; the memo may refer to the nine Scribners printings in the first edition (three in 1929, two in 1930, one in 1931, two in 1934, and one in 1936).

Note two: An abrigment of *LHA* was published in *Omnibook,* 1 (December 1938), 193–320. See C 98.

Note three: One MH copy inscribed to Aline Bernstein is dated 3 October 1929.

Note four: The identification of the second printing of *LHA* suggests the fragmentary and often perilous nature of the evidence on which bibliographers base their conclusions. The Scribners records contain a TLS sent by Herbert Faulkner West to Scribners dated 14 February 1936 and the carbon of an unsigned TL responding to West dated 18 February 1936. In his letter, West queries Scribners on the second printing of *LHA* which he believes is distinguishable from the first printing only by the second format dust jacket. Scribners, inaccurately, verified this in their response. West proceded to publish this misleading information in his *Modern Book Collecting for the Impecunious Amateur* (Boston: Little, Brown) that same year.

10   A 2.1.b *Look Homeward, Angel*

Review copies: 100 copies of *LHA* were distributed in unprinted tan Kraft wrappers in advance of publication for review purposes (MH [2 copies], ViU).

A 2.1.b
Second printing

New York: Scribners, 1929.

On copyright page: 'Published October, 1929 | Reprinted November, 1929'. 3,000 copies. Published 6 November 1929. *Locations:* CJ, NcRSM, NcU.

A 2.1.c
Third printing

New York: Scribners, 1929.

December 1929. *Not seen.*

A 2.1.d
Fourth printing

New York: Scribners, 1930.

On copyright page: 'Published October, 1929 | Reprinted, November, December, 1929 | February, 1930'. *Location:* NcU-C.

A 2.1.e
Fifth printing

New York: Scribners, 1930.

On copyright page: 'Published October, 1929 | Reprinted November, December, 1929 | February, March, 1930'. *Locations:* NcU, ViU.

Note one: A carbon of a TL in the Scribners records to A. S. Frere-Reeves dated 11 April 1930 reads: "We have sold about 12,000 copies of his [Wolfe's] book to date."

LATER PRINTINGS WITHIN THE FIRST EDITION

A 2.1.f
New York: Scribners, 1931.

Copyright page the same as in the first printing. *Location:* NcU.

A 2.1.g
New York: Scribners, 1934.

Copyright page the same as in the first printing. *Location:* ViU.

A 2.1.1 *Look Homeward, Angel* 11

A 2.1.h
New York: Scribners, 1934.

Copyright page differs from first printing: 'COPYRIGHT, 1929, BY | CHARLES SCRIBNER'S SONS | [rule] | COPYRIGHT, 1927–1928, BY THE NEW REPUBLIC | [rule] | Printed in the United States of America | *All rights reserved. No part of this book | may be reproduced in any form without | the permission of Charles Scribner's Sons.* | [Scribners seal]'. *Locations:* NcU, ViU.

A 2.1.i
New York: Modern Library, [1934].

Modern Library Giant #G16. Dust jacket. Price: $1.25. Undated reprintings have been noted with four variant copyright pages: publisher's note on *LHA* and list of other books in *Modern Library Giant* series; Random House seal; '1957 renewal'; and 'COPYRIGHT 1957'. *Locations:* EG, MH (2 copies), NcA (2 copies), NcRSM (3 copies), NcU, ScU (rebound), ViU (3 copies).

Note one: Scribners records note a second Modern Library printing of 10,000 copies in January 1934 and estimate that 103,000 copies were sold prior to 17 April 1952.

A 2.1.j
New York: Scribners, 1936.

Copyright page the same as in the first printing. *Locations:* APM, NcU.

A 2.1.k
New York: Grosset & Dunlap, [1939].

Dust jacket. *On copyright page:* 'COPYRIGHT, 1927–1928, BY THE NEW REPUBLIC ... CL'. Published 19 October 1939. Price: $1.29. Undated reprint with 'CL' omitted from the copyright page also noted. First printing and later printing noted in brilliant grayish blue binding; later printing, trimmed, also noted in yellowish gray and in orange bindings. *Locations:* EG (dj), MH (2 copies), MJB, NcRSM (3 copies), NcU (3 copies), ScU, ViU (rebound).

Note one: Scribners records estimate 81,000 copies printed in two Grosset & Dunlap printings prior to 17 April 1952.

A 2.1.l
New York: Garden City Publishing, [1940].

On copyright page: '1940 ... CL'. Published November 1940. *Locations:* MH, NcU.

A 2.2.a
First English edition, first printing [1930]

LOOK HOMEWARD, ANGEL

A STORY *of the* BURIED LIFE

BY

THOMAS WOLFE

"*At one time the earth was probably a white-hot sphere like the sun.*"
—Tarr and McMurry

LONDON
WILLIAM HEINEMANN LTD

A 2.2.a: 7¾" × 5"

A 2.2.a *Look Homeward, Angel*

> *First Published* 1930
>
> *Printed in Great Britain at The Windmill Press*
> *Kingswood, Surrey*

[i–vi] vii [viii] [1–2] 3–172 [173–174] 175–382 [383–384] 385–613 [614–616]

[A]⁸ B–I⁸ K–U⁸ W–Z⁸ AA–II⁸ KK–PP⁸

Contents: p. i: half title; p. ii: list of books, headed 'NEW & RECENT FICTION'; p. iii: title; p. iv: copyright; p. v: 'To A. B. | "Then, as all my soules bee, | Emparadis'd in you (in whom alone | I understand, and grow and see), | The rafters of my body, bone | Being still with you, the Muscle, Sinew, and Veine, | Which tile this house, will come againe." '; p. vi: blank; p. vii: text, headed 'TO THE READER'; p. viii: blank; p. 1: 'PART I'; p. 2: epigraph; pp. 3–172: text, headed 'LOOK HOMEWARD, ANGEL | I'; p. 173: 'PART II'; p. 174: blank; pp. 175–382: text, headed 'XIV'; p. 383: 'PART III'; p. 384: blank; pp. 385–613: text, headed 'XXVIII'; pp. 614–616: blank.

Typography and paper: 5¹³⁄₁₆″ (6″) × 3¹³⁄₁₆″; 35 lines per page. Running heads: rectos and versos, 'LOOK HOMEWARD, ANGEL'. Wove paper.

Binding: Dark blue V cloth. Spine: goldstamped 'LOOK | HOMEWARD, | ANGEL | [inverted triangle] | THOMAS | WOLFE | HEINEMANN'; back: blindstamped Heinemann seal. White wove endpapers. All edges trimmed.

Dust jacket: Front, spine, and back printed in red and black against a medium orange background. Front: '[two black rules] | [six inverted red triangles] | [red zigzag line] | [six red sabertooth-like marks] | [black ornamental lettering] LOOK HOMEWARD, | ANGEL | [three zigzag vertical lines—red, black, and red] | [black ornamental lettering] THOMAS WOLFE | [two red rules] | [two black rules]'. Spine: '[two black rules] | [three inverted red triangles] | [red zigzag line] | [two red sabertooth marks] | [black ornamental lettering] LOOK | HOMEWARD, | ANGEL | [red diamond-like decoration] | [black ornamental lettering] THOMAS | WOLFE | [three zigzag vertical lines: red, black, red] | [black ornamental lettering] 10s. 6d. | [black roman lettering] NET | [black ornamental lettering] HEINEMANN | [two red rules] | [two black rules]'. Back: Author's foreword. Front and back flaps: blurbs for *LHA*.

Publication: 3,000 copies. Published 14 July 1930. Advance: £100. Price: 10/6.

Printing: See copyright page.

Locations: BL (15JUL30), BOD (JUL 19 1930), InU Lilly (dj), MH, MJB (dj), NcA, NcU, NcRSM (dj).

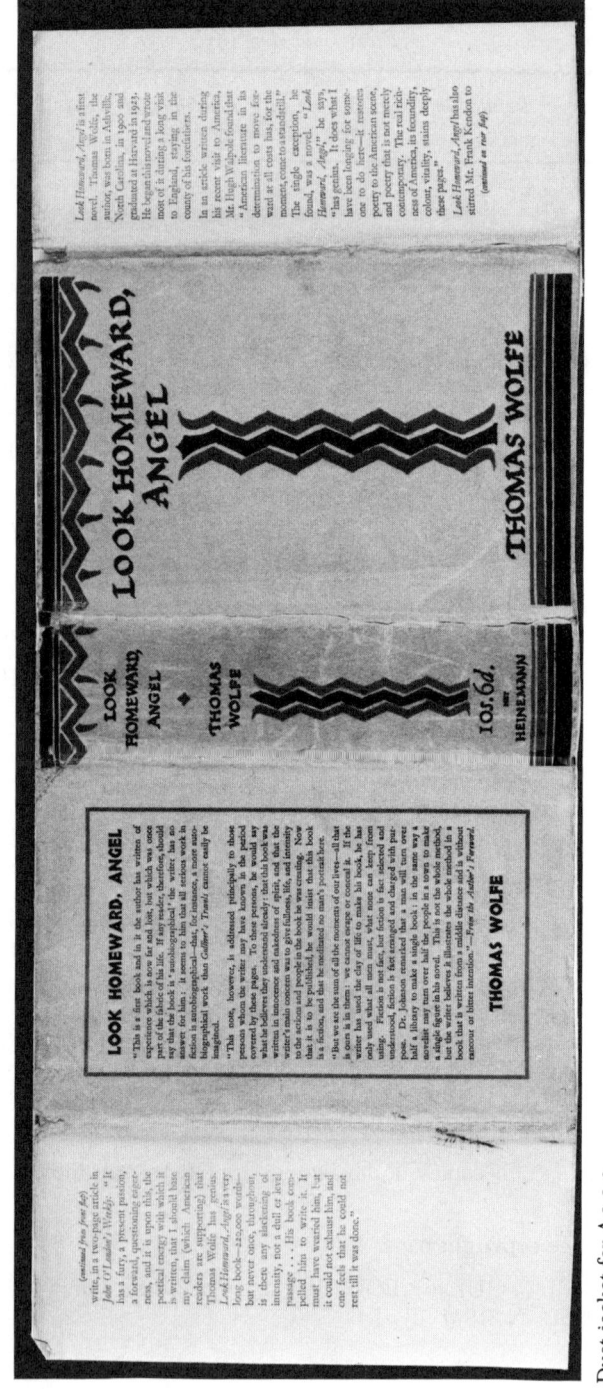

Dust jacket for A 2.2.a

A 2.2.a *Look Homeward, Angel*

Note one: Type slippage has been noted in the folio in some copies on p. 214: the '2' is raised (BOD, MH, MJB, NcA); the '2' is lowered (BL and InU Lilly).

Text: The first Heinemann printing of *LHA* varies from the first Scribners printing in 974 readings, of which 64 are substantive.

SCRIBNERS (1929)			HEINEMANN (1930)
10.3	drooped	[10.19	dropped
13.37	oldest	[14.29	older
14.4	oldest	[14.34	older
27.17	me succour	[28.28	my succour
37.5–31	them. [paragraph] He . . . vexation. [paragraph] And	[38.10–11	them. [paragraph] And
59.10	vine-wound	[61.3	vine-bound
70.19	cholera infantis	[73.18	cholera infantilis
72.20	skreeking	[75.26	screeching
79.27	window	[83.17	wondow
93.25	flatted	[98.14	flattened
94.27	throatiness	[99.17	throatness
98.20–28	abscess. [paragraph] "He . . . disease. [paragraph] One	[103.26–27	abscess. [additional vertical spacing; paragraph] One
141.2	at Dixieland	[149.2	in Dixieland
142.7	hill	[150.10	hills
144.31	older	[153.1	elder
148.15	blonde	[156.25	blond
150.35	all of his	[159.15	all his
153.2–3	sled-/ding	[161.27	sledging
162.34–35	forever. [paragraph] Eugene was almost twelve years old. [end of chapter]	[172.11	forever. [end of chapter]
175.8–10	gutter a slimy gob of phlegm. [paragraph] "Well	[185.29–30	gutter. [paragraph] "Well
184.36	ilk	[196.8	silk
192.22	burnt	[203.24	burned
239.23	sprawled out face downward, with	[254.27	sprawled out face to face, with
239.33	stunk	[255.2	stank
239.34	stunk	[255.3	stank
264.7–13	watch. [paragraph] "The . . . told. [paragraph] His	[280.12–13	watch. [paragraph] His

269.10	taken on	[285.24	taken, years before, on
281.13–32	relief . . . instance. [end of chapter]	[297.29	relief. [end of chapter]
293.11	angel. [end of chapter]	[310.5–312–20	angel. [additional vertical spacing; paragraph] Eliza . . . hand. [end of chapter]
311.15–17	of G. K. Chesterton and E. V. Lucas. [additional vertical spacing; paragraph] "O	[331.23–25	of two famous men of letters. [additional vertical spacing; paragraph] "O
315.19–317.32	read. [additional vertical spacing; paragraph] Eliza . . . hand. [end of chapter]	[336.8	read. [end of chapter]
318.1–322.17	[beginning of chapter] With . . . wind. [additional vertical spacing; paragraph] Miss	[337.1	[beginning of chapter] Miss
322.31	griped	[337.14	gripped
324.0–348.23	alone!" [additional vertical spacing; paragraph] A light . . . earth! [end of chapter]	[338.34	alone!" [end of chapter]
351.7–8	wait!" [paragraph] In	[341.12–34	wait!" [paragraph] They . . . Keats. [paragraph] In
351.34–35	editor. Then, witness of his own martyrdom, he dropped two smoking	[342.24–344.15	editor: [paragraph] "It's . . . knife—" [paragraph] Smiling bravely, Eugene dropped three smoking
386.18–20	name where does it all come from?" she said, grinning tearfully. "I do nothing but mop up after her. Will you	[380.14	name, will you

A 2.2.a *Look Homeward, Angel* 17

386.24–31	months." [paragraph] "Yes . . . laughter. [paragraph] "Hel-en	[	380.17–18	months." [paragraph] "Hel-en
394.19–403.1	for!" [additional spacing; paragraph] Eugene's . . . gold"? [end of chapter; beginning of chapter 29] Before	[	388.23–24	for!" [additional spacing; paragraph] Before [*note—Chapter numbers were not adjusted in the Heinemann edition to allow for this revision. As a result, there is no chapter 29 in the Heinemann edition.]
403.7–404.26	body. [paragraph] He . . . forget. [additional vertical spacing; paragraph] Eugene	[	388.30–31	body. [paragraph] Eugene
405.10	near Mrs. Bradley's but	[	389.18	near Eugene's, but
411.25–28	right! [paragraph] He went to the curb, and vomited into the gutter. Then he straightened, mopping his mouth with a handkerchief. [paragraph] "How	[	396.15–17	right!" After a moment he straightened. [paragraph] "How
412.23–24	his loins were black with vermin. The	[	397.10–11	his body was crawling. The
420.22	April the nation declared	[	405.19	April, America declared
420.30–421.34	movements. The fraternity . . . war. [paragraph] On	[	405.26–28	move-/ments. [paragraph] On
459.28	to-morrow and get	[	446.32	to-morrow to get
466.14	vat of the	[	453.34–454.1	vat o the
479.21	Nobody ever	[	467.29	Nobody's ever

484.5	a Damocles sword	[	472.12	a Damoclean sword
484.18	at all times	[	472.26	at times
486.17–487.28	Music! [additional vertical spacing; paragraph] It . . . Scholar. [additional vertical spacing; paragraph] In	[	474.33–34	Music! [additional vertical spacing; paragraph] In
510.19–20	with un-/laborious fatigue	[	499.35–500.1	with the laborious fatigue
512.13	red and blue	[	501.35	red and white
514.37–516.10	him. [paragraph] He . . . rockets. [additional vertical spacing; paragraph] These	[	504.29–30	him. [additional vertical spacing; paragraph] These
516.17–517.6	month. Three . . . Liberties. [paragraph] At	[	505.3–4	month. [paragraph] At
517.38–518.6	morning. [paragraph] Thus . . . effort. [paragraph] Eugene	[	505.35–506.1	morning. [paragraph] Eugene
521.2–525.5	on. [additional vertical spacing; paragraph] He . . . France. [additional vertical spacing; paragraph] Mr. Finch	[	509.15–16	on. [additional vertical spacing; paragraph] Mr. Finch
527.25	bought by	[	512.4	brought by
561.8	flanged wheels	[	547.12	flanked wheels
590.22–591.6	door. He. . . Utopias. [additional vertical spacing; paragraph] Sometimes	[	579.3–4	door. [additional vertical spacing; paragraph] Sometimes
599.20	Weldon spoke	[	587.20	Weldon, the philosophy professor, spoke
602.20–603.32	more. [paragraph] And . . . path. [additional vertical spacing paragraph] He	[	590.31–32	more. [additional vertical spacing; paragraph] He

A 2.3 *Look Homeward, Angel*

| 604.10–19 | oblivion. Soon. . . street, the car | [591.13–14 | oblivion. [paragraph] The car |
| 624.29 | chance. Apexical summation | [612.11 | chance. Summation |

A 2.2.b
Second printing

London: Heinemann, 1930.

On copyright page: 'First Published, July 1930 | New Impression, July 1930'. *Location:* MJB.

LATER PRINTINGS WITHIN THE FIRST ENGLISH EDITION

A 2.2.c
London: Heinemann, 1932.

Location: MJB.

A 2.2.d
London, Melbourne, and Toronto: Heinemann, [1958].

On copyright page: 'First, published 1930 | This edition 1958'. Published 15 September 1958. Price: 21/–. *Locations:* BL, MH, NcU.

A 2.2.e
London: Heinemann, [1966].

On copyright page: 'First published 1930 | This edition 1958 | Reprinted 1966'. Published June 1966. Price: 42/–. *Location:* BL.

A 2.2.f
London: Heinemann, [1973].

On copyright page: 'First published 1930 | This edition 1958 | Reprinted 1966 | Reissued, 1973'. Price: 60/–. *Location:* BL.

LATER EDITIONS

A 2.3
New York: Editions for the Armed Services, [1944].

512 pp. #0-31. Wrappers. Condensed by Don Wayne. Not for sale. *Locations:* APM, MJB, NcA, NcU.

A 2.4.a
New York: Scribners, 1947.

662 pp. Dust jacket. Illustrated by Douglas W. Gorseline. *On copyright page:* 'A'. Price: $5.00. *Locations:* APM, EG (3 copies with dj), InU Lilly (dj), MH, NcA (2 copies with dj), NcRSM (dj), NcU (dj), ViU (dj).

A 2.4.b
New York: Scribners, [1952].

Modern Standard Authors. First Scribners printing to omit epigraph from title page. Includes an essay by Maxwell Perkins on Thomas Wolfe which originally appeared in the Autumn 1947 *Harvard Library Bulletin.* Twelve full-page illustrations inserted in the 1947 printing are not included in this printing. The illustration appearing on page 247 of the 1947 printing has been removed and replaced with another illustration. Trim size reduced. *On copyright page:* 'Copyright 1929, 1947, 1952'. Price: $2.75. Reprinted in 1958. *Locations:* CJ (1958), EG, InU Lilly (dj), MH, NcRSM, NcU (2 copies), ViU.

A 2.4.c
New York: Scribners, 1956.

Not seen.

A 2.4.d
New York: Scribners, [1957].

Includes Perkins's essay on Wolfe. *On copyright page:* 'AA-9.57 [H]'. Published September 1957. *Location:* DLC.

A 2.4.e
New York: Scribners, [1960].

Includes Perkins's essay on Wolfe. *On copyright page:* 'BD-4.60[H]'. Published April 1960. *Location:* NcRSM.

A 2.4.f
New York: Scribners, [1963].

De Luxe Illustrated Edition. Dust jacket. *On copyright page:* 'A-8.63 [UJ]'. Published August 1963. Price: $10.00. *Locations:* NcRSM (dj), NcU (dj).

A 2.4.g
New York: Scribners, [1968].

Includes Perkins's essay on Wolfe. *On copyright page:* 'L-8.68[Col]'. Published August 1968. *Location:* NcRSM.

A 2.6.a *Look Homeward, Angel*

A 2.4.h
Birmingham, Alabama: Southern Living Gallery, [1984].

The Southern Classics Library. Facsimile of A2.4.a including line drawings and twelve Gorseline plates. Distributed with a pamphlet containing an introduction by Louis D. Rubin. *On copyright page:* 'Special contents copyright 1984 by Oxmoor House, Inc.'. Published 13 March 1984. *Location:* Bucknell University.

A 2.5.a–b
LOOK HOMEWARD, ANGEL: | II. The Adventures of Young Gant | By THOMAS WOLFE | *With an Introduction by Edward C. Aswell* | "At *one time the earth was probably* | *a white-hot sphere like the* sun." | [tilde] Tarr and McMurry | [Signet seal] | A SIGNET BOOK | Published by THE NEW AMERICAN LIBRARY

192 pp. *Signet #697*. Published 1 December 1948. Price: 25¢. Second printing in September 1949. *Locations:* APM, DLC (JAN 10 1949), EG (2 copies), MH, NcU (3 copies; 2 copies of the first printing and 1 copy of the second printing).

Note one: This edition contains only Part II of *LHA*. Signet did not publish editions of Part I or Part III of *LHA*.

A 2.6.a
New York: Scribners, [1952].

522 pp. *Scribner Library #SL 9*. Cloth or wrappers. Includes Perkins's essay on Wolfe. Prices: $3.95, $4.95, $7.95. Reprinted at least 16 times in cloth, beginning in 1960, 25 times in wrappers. Twenty-fifth printing in wrappers is a *Scribner Library of Contemporary Classics* book. Reprints noted in cloth: on copyright page: 'F-8.62[Col]'; 'L-8.66[Col]'; 'M-12.69[C]'; '17 . . . C/C . . . 18'. Reprints noted in wrappers: on copyright page: '19 . . . C/P . . . 20', '25 . . . F/P . . . 26', 'K-10.65'. *Locations:* DLC, EG ('L-8.66'), JI, NcRSM (2 copies; 1 copy '19 . . . C/P . . . 20' and 1 copy '17 . . . C/C . . . 18'), NcU (2 copies; 1 copy 'F-8.62' and 1 copy 'K-10.65'), ScU ('M-12.69[c]'), TxL, ViU.

Note one: In "Wolfe's *Look Homeward, Angel* in the Literary Marketplace" (*The Thomas Wolfe Review*, 6 [Fall 1982], 23–26), Richard S. Kennedy indicates the following sales figures: in 1960 the Scribner Library paperback reprints sold 39,775 copies and, that same year, the *Scribner Library* cloth edition sold 4,451 copies; in 1965 the paperback reprint sold 45,531 copies and the cloth reprint sold 3,901 copies; in 1967 the paperback reprint sold 43,894 copies and the cloth reprint sold 4,363 copies. The average sale of the Scribners copies was, he adds, 43,730 copies per year in the 1960s. By 1978, sales had diminished, and the number of *Scribner Library* copies sold that year equaled 15,052 copies.

A 2.6.b
New York: Scribners, [1978].

Hudson River Editions. Dust Jacket. Price: $17.50. *On copyright page:* 27 ... F/P ... 26'. *Locations:* CJ, NcRSM.

Note one: According to Richard S. Kennedy ("Wolfe's *Look Homeward, Angel* in the Literary Marketplace," *The Thomas Wolfe Review,* 6 [Fall 1982], 23–26), the *Hudson River Edition* sold 455 copies in 1978.

A 2.6.c
New York: Scribners, [1979].

50th Anniversary Edition. Dust jacket. Price: $14.95. Also distributed by the Book-of-the-Month Club. *Locations:* APM, NcRSM (BOMC), NcU (2 copies).

Note one: BOMC copies have a blindstamped ⅛" circle or ⅛" square in the lower-right hand corner of the back cover. The NcRSM copy was further identified as a BOMC copy because of records at NcRSM.

Note two: BOMC distributed 10,175 copies of *LHA* and *OTATR* as part of its special "book dividend" arrangement. See Richard S. Kennedy, "Wolfe's *Look Homeward, Angel* in the Literary Marketplace," *The Thomas Wolfe Review,* 6 (Fall 1982), 23–26. See also A 3.1.z.

A 2.7
London: Landsborough Publications Limited, [1960].

448 pp. *A Four Square Book.* Wrappers. *On copyright page:* 'First published by William Heinemann Ltd. in 1930 | Published in a new edition in 1958 | Published as a Four Square Book in 1960'. Price: 3/6. *Locations:* BL, NcA (2 copies).

A 2.8
London: New English Library, 1968.

511 pp. *Signet Modern Classic.* Price: 7/6. *Not seen.*

A 2.9.a
Toronto, New York, and London: Bantam, 1970.

563 pp. *Bantam Books* #T5860. Wrappers. Published October 1970. Price: $1.50. *Not seen.* Latest printing noted is the third: on copyright page: 'Bantam edition published October 1970 | 2nd printing | 3rd printing'. *Locations:* JI (3rd printing), NcU (3rd printing).

A 2.9.b
New York: Scribners, [n.d.].

Scribner Classics. Wrappers. Price: $7.95. Third printing and fourth printing also noted. *Locations:* CJ (2 copies; 3rd printing and 4th printing), NcU.

A 2.14 *Look Homeward, Angel* 23

A 2.10
Franklin Center, Pennsylvania: The Franklin Library, 1977.

697 pp. *The 100 Greatest Masterpieces of American Literature*. Illustrated by Alan Reingold. Published April 1977. *Locations:* APM, InU Lilly.

Note one: Office copy noted bound in reddish orange V cloth. Front stamped in black within a double-rules frame: 'RECORD AND REFERENCE COPY'; spine stamped in black: 'LOOK | HOMEWARD, | ANGEL | THOMAS | WOLFE | RECORD | AND | REFERENCE | COPY | THE | FRANKLIN | LIBRARY'. *Location:* NcA.

Note two: The royalites paid on this edition to the estate between 1978 and 1981 amounted to $2,878.03. See Richard S. Kennedy, "Wolfe's *Look Homeward, Angel* in the Literary Marketplace," *The Thomas Wolfe Review*, 6 (Fall 1982), 23–26.

A 2.11
New York: Scribners, [1979].

520 pp. Possibly distributed as a set with a similarly bound *OTATR* (See A 3.6). Price: $17.50. Also noted in wrappers in an unnumbered *Scribner Library Edition:* on copyright page: '25 . . . Y/P . . . 24' and '17 . . . M/C . . . 18'. *Locations:* APM (2 copies in wrappers), NcRSM.

A 2.12
Franklin Center, Pennsylvania: The Franklin Library, 1981.

696 pp. *The Greatest Books of the Twentieth Century*. Illustrated by Douglas W. Gorseline. Twelve full-page illustrations from the 1947 Scribner Illustrated Edition (See A 2.4.a) are present. Published May 1981. Price: $39.00. *Locations:* APM, NcU (2 copies).

A 2.13
Cutchogue, New York: Buccaneer Books, 1981.

395 pp. Price: $14.95. *Not seen.*

A 2.14
Harmondsworth: Penguin, [1984].

550 pp. *Penguin Modern Classics*. Wrappers. Price £4.95. *Location:* CJ.

A3 OF TIME AND THE RIVER

A 3.1.a
First edition, first printing (1935)

OF TIME AND THE RIVER

A LEGEND OF MAN'S HUNGER
IN HIS YOUTH

By

Thomas Wolfe

*"Who knoweth the spirit of man that goeth upward, and
the spirit of the beast that goeth downward to the earth?"*

CHARLES SCRIBNER'S SONS
NEW YORK
1935

A 3.1.a: 8¼" × 5⅝"

> COPYRIGHT, 1935, BY
> CHARLES SCRIBNER'S SONS
>
> Printed in the United States of America
>
> *All rights reserved. No part of this book may be reproduced in any form without the permission of Charles Scribner's Sons*
>
> A

[i–xii] [1–2] 3–86 [87–88] 89–324 [325–326] 327–404 [405–406] 407–598 [599–600] 601–794 [795–796] 797–849 [850–852] 853–899 [900–902] 903–912 [913–916]

[1]¹⁰ [2]⁸ [3–29]¹⁶ [30]⁸ [31]⁶

Contents: p. i: blank; p. ii: text, headed 'PUBLISHER'S NOTE'; p. iii: half title; p. iv: blank; p. v: title; p. vi: copyright; p. vii: Dedication 'To | MAXWELL EVARTS PERKINS | A GREAT EDITOR AND A BRAVE AND HONEST MAN, WHO STUCK TO | THE WRITER OF THIS BOOK THROUGH TIMES OF BITTER HOPELESS- | NESS AND DOUBT AND WOULD NOT LET HIM GIVE IN TO HIS OWN | DESPAIR, A WORK TO BE KNOWN AS "OF TIME AND THE RIVER" IS | DEDICATED WITH THE HOPE THAT ALL OF IT MAY BE IN SOME WAY | WORTHY OF THE LOYAL DEVOTION AND THE PATIENT CARE WHICH | A DAUNTLESS AND UNSHAKEN FRIEND HAS GIVEN TO EACH PART OF | IT, AND WITHOUT WHICH NONE OF IT COULD HAVE BEEN WRITTEN | "Crito, my dear friend Crito, that, be- | lieve me, that is what I seem to hear, as | the Corybants hear flutes in the air, and | the sound of those words rings and | echoes in my ears and I can listen to | nothing else." '; p. viii: blank; p. ix: contents; p. x: blank; p. xi: half title; p. xii: twenty-one-line poem beginning ' "Kennst du das Land' (—Mignon's song at the opening of Book III of Goethe's *Wilhelm Meister's Apprenticeship*); p. 1: 'Book I | ORESTES: FLIGHT BEFORE FURY'; p. 2: epigraph, beginning '... *of wandering*'; pp. 3–86: text, headed 'I'; p. 87: 'BOOK II | YOUNG FAUSTUS'; p. 88: blank; pp. 89–324: text, headed 'VII'; p. 325: 'BOOK III | TELEMACHUS'; p. 326: blank; pp. 327–404: text, headed 'XXXIX'; p. 405: 'BOOK IV | PROTEUS: THE CITY'; p. 406: blank; pp. 407–598: text, headed 'XLVI'; p. 599: 'BOOK V | JASON'S VOYAGE'; p. 600: blank; pp. 601–794: text, headed 'LXVIII'; p. 795: 'BOOK VI | ANTÆUS: EARTH AGAIN'; p. 796: blank; pp. 797–849: text, headed 'XC'; p. 850: blank; p. 851: 'BOOK VII | KRONOS AND RHEA:

THE DREAM OF TIME'; p. 852: blank; pp. 853–899: text, headed 'XCVI'; p. 900: blank; p. 901: *BOOK VIII* | FAUST AND HELEN'; p. 902: blank; pp. 903–912: text, headed 'CII'; pp. 913–916: blank.

Typography and paper: 6⅝" (6⅞") × 4³⁄₁₆"; 39 lines per page. Running heads: rectos, book headings; versos: 'OF TIME AND THE RIVER.' Wove paper.

Binding: Black V cloth. Front: goldstamped with two medium yellowish green rectangular panels: '[two rules] | [on medium yellowish green rectangular panel] OF TIME AND THE RIVER | [two rules on black] | [on medium yellowish green rectangular panel] THOMAS WOLFE | [two rules on black]'; spine: goldstamped with four medium yellowish green rectangular panels: '[three rules] | [on medium yellowish green rectangular panel] OF TIME AND | THE RIVER | [three rules] | [medium yellowish green rectangular panel] | [three rules on black] | [on medium yellowish green rectangular panel] WOLFE | [three rules on black] | [fourteen blindstamped rules] | [two rules] | [on medium yellowish green rectangular panel] SCRIBNERS | [three rules on black]'. White wove endpapers. Top and bottom edges trimmed; fore edges rough trimmed. Green and yellow headbands and footbands.

Dust jacket: Front printed in white on a grayish green and dark green wave design with six wavy light green horizontal lines: '[ornamental lettering] of | time | and | the river | [roman] THOMAS WOLFE | AUTHOR OF "LOOK HOMEWARD ANGEL,,'. Spine printed in white on a light green wave design with six wavy black horizontal lines: 'OF | TIME | AND | THE RIVER | THOMAS | WOLFE | SCRIBNERS'. Back: photograph of Wolfe and blurb for *OTATR* quoting Sinclair Lewis's Nobel Prize acceptance speech. Front flap: biographical material. Back flap quotes from reviews of *LHA* by Margaret Wallace, John Chamberlain, Hugh Walpole, and Carl Van Doren.

Publication: 10,000 copies. Copyright #A82139. Published 8 March 1935. Date of contract: 12 July 1933. Advance: $2,050. Royalty: 15%. Price: $3.00.

Printing: Composed and printed by the Scribner Press, New York City. Bound by Scribner Press.

Locations: APM (dj), BL (5 MAR 35), BOD, CJ, EG (3 copies; 2 copies with dj), InU Lilly (dj), MH (2 copies), MJB (dj), NcA (3 copies; 1 copy with dj), NcRSM (6 copies; 4 copies with dj), NcU (4 copies; 1 copy with dj), PSt (dj), ViU (4 copies; 3 copies with dj).

Note one: OTATR was listed as an alternate selection in the April 1935 issue of the *Book-of-the-Month Club News*. Price: $3.00.

Note two: Three EG copies inscribed to "Effie," "Mabel," and "Mother" are dated 1 March 1935.

Of Time and the River

$3.00

Thomas Wolfe was born in Asheville, North Carolina, in 1900. He graduated from the University of North Carolina in 1920, at the age of 19. While there he was one of the original members of the Carolina Play-Makers. Three years later he received the degree of Master of Arts from Harvard University.

After his departure from Harvard he taught until January 1930, when he was awarded a Guggenheim Fellowship for creative writing.

In the five years that have elapsed between the publication of "Look Homeward, Angel" and "Of Time and the River," Mr. Wolfe has written almost two million words. His long short stories have appeared in Scribner's Magazine and The American Mercury, and one of them, "A Portrait of Bascom Hawke," was the co-winner with John Hermann's "The Big Short Trip" of the second Scribner Long Story Contest. Mr. Wolfe is at present (February 1935) living in Brooklyn.

---

of time and the river

THOMAS WOLFE
AUTHOR OF LOOK HOMEWARD ANGEL

OF TIME AND THE RIVER

THOMAS WOLFE

SCRIBNERS

Of Time and the River
A Legend of Man's Hunger in His Youth

by
Thomas Wolfe
author of
LOOK HOMEWARD, ANGEL

THOMAS WOLFE

In this novel Thomas Wolfe reaffirms the tribute of Sinclair Lewis in his Nobel Prize acceptance speech when Mr. Lewis said that "he may have a chance to be the greatest American writer . . . I don't see why he should not be one of the greatest world writers." And Thomas Wolfe's new novel, like "Look Homeward, Angel" is, to quote Sinclair Lewis again, "so deep and spacious that it deals with the whole of life."

It is an epic of the quest and pilgrimage of youth, specifically of an American, but essentially of the young man in all lands and ages. This pilgrimage begins in Altamont, the hero's birthplace, and takes him through a great variety of adventures and experiences—to Boston and New York, thence to Oxford and finally to Paris and the countryside of France, from which he returns to America, irresistibly drawn back to the great, sprawling continent he had fled in bitterness and disgust.

For sweep and richness, for diversity of scene and background, variety of sharply individualized characters, for drama, great gusty laughter and profoundly moving tragedy, it stands alone—a novel with the mass and movement of a great epic. In it the whole web of that America which is its underlying theme is reflected" . . . with all its clamor, naked struggle, blind and brutal strife, with all its violence, ignorance and cruelty, and with its terror, joy and mystery, its undying hope, its everlasting life."

CHARLES SCRIBNER'S SONS, NEW YORK

A few notes from the chorus of praise that greeted
LOOK HOMEWARD, ANGEL
by Thomas Wolfe
and has grown in volume ever since its publication

"As interesting and powerful a book as has ever been made out of the circumstances of provincial American life. It is at once enormously sensuous, full of the joy and gusto of life, and shriekingly sensitive, torn with revulsion and disgust."
Margaret Wallace in The New York Times

"It is a rich, positive grappling with life, a remembrance of things past untinged by the shadow of regret, of one who has found his youthful experiences full of savor. No more sensuous novel has been written in the United States."
John Chamberlain

"He has written one of the most remarkable first novels I have ever seen. It is as near perfect as a novel can be."
Hugh Walpole

"The magnificence of the manner is matched by the substance behind it . . . He has dared to lift his characters up above the average meanness of mankind, to let them live by their profounder impulses, and tell about them the things which smooth, urbane novelists insist on leaving untold about men and women."
Carl Van Doren

Dust jacket for A 3.1.a

LATER PRINTINGS WITHIN THE FIRST EDITION

A 3.1.b
Second printing

New York: Scribners, 1935.

On copyright page: 'First Printing, February, 1935 | Second Printing, March, 1935'. *Locations:* CSt, ViU (2 copies; 1 copy rebound).

Note one: An advertisement for *OTATR* in *The New York Times Book Review* for 10 March 1935 announces: "*Two Large Printings Before Publication.*"

Note two: The following textual changes were made between the first and second printings:

	FIRST PRINTING	SECOND PRINTING
29.9	moist	[most
52.14	path	[paths
89.3	elemental	[eternal
89.14	numerous	[murmurous
89.18	twisted	[twisted,
89.31	found.	[found?
92.33	board	[hoard
94.20	of most	[of the most
186.1	my	[his
187.27	*oevah-sexed*	[*ovah-sexed*
189.7	youh	[yoah
189.24	my	[his
200.37	scowly	[scowling
274.34	strange	[shining
308.9	subborn	[stubborn
317.16	Posillippo's	[Masillippo's
338.33	my	[his
400.23	promising aptly, swearing eagerly, and	[promising everything, swearing anything, and
402.36	rush	[urge
404.9	sweet	[secret
464.18	uncertitude	[incertitude
466.2	read him his	[read his
466.38	me	[Eugene
487.36	I have	[he had
519.20	ah	[so
627.25	ploddy	[plodding
678.25	character	[diameter
771.29	strong	[stormy
861.18	light, hunched	[eight hundred

A 3.1.d *Of Time and the River* 29

880.20	girl that	[girl, that
884.13	leash	[rein
885.31	the	[an
893.23	gold and	[gold nor
893.31	it,	[it;
893.32	beach,	[beach;
898.38	edict	[fierce
903.33	foundered	[founded

A 3.1.c
Third printing

New York: Scribners, 1935.

On copyright page: 'First Printing, February, 1935 | ... Third Printing, March 1935'. *Locations:* CaSRP, ScU, ViU.

Note one: An advertisement for *OTATR* in *The New York Times Book Review* for 17 March 1935 reads: "Three Large Printings Before Publication".

Note two: The following textual changes were made between the second and third printings:

	SECOND PRINTING	THIRD PRINTING
76.11	will	[with
243.34–35	gown. The boy never saw him again. [paragraph] Thirty	[gown. [paragraph] Thirty
343.32	Frankly	[F-f-f-frankly
576.13–15	you spoke with a crisp but obstinate conviction, "Joel, I know I'm right! argue	[you about the background, Madge. . . . I think you're wrong: I'd like to argue
794.18–19	her. He never saw her again. [end of Book V]	[her. [end of Book V]

A 3.1.d
Fourth printing

New York: Scribners, 1935.

March 1935. *Not seen.*

Note one: An advertisement in *The Forum and Century* dated April 1935 reads: "*Four Large Printings Before Publication*".

A 3.1.e
Fifth printing

New York: Scribners, 1935.

On copyright page: 'First Printing, February, 1935... Fourth Printing, March, 1935 | Fifth Printing, March, 1935'. *Locations:* CJ, NcA.

Note one: Advertisements for *OTATR* in *The New York Times Book Review* (24 March 1935) and in *The Saturday Review of Literature* (6 April 1935) announce, "*Fifth Large Printing on Day of Publication*".

Note two: Scribners records include a carbon copy of a TL to Wolfe dated 14 March 1935 which reads: "we have printed five editions,—30,000 copies".

Note three: The following additional textual changes were made between the third and fifth printings:

	THIRD PRINTING	FIFTH PRINTING
98.16	on a	[on, a
184.32	Louse	[Louise
193.24	dulness	[dullness
204.36	Jordan	[Sluder
205.3	Jordan	[Sluder
248.21	engines	[energies
250.39	looket	[looked
304.11	weavings	[hazards
343.32	t-t-t-trouble	[trouble
350.15	fire	[air
367.21	landing into	[ending up in
397.38	Wy-wy-wy—frankly	[Wy—f-f-f-frankly
398.1	John	[Gene
498.27	Here	[Where
499.23	transmitted	[transmuted
499.35	resins	[resinous
506.8	out of the	[out the
521.25	of that beautiful	[of this beautiful
543.8	pint	[pound
545.2	envy	[error
545.10	beings	[Kings
545.22	leonic	[leonine
545.34	the bad and almost brutal volume of	[the hard and almost brutal violence of
545.35	marked	[masked
546.35	beard	[head
549.6	dullness	[darkness
549.19	loneliness	[loveliness
588.26	ever-long	[ever-living

A 3.1.f *Of Time and the River*

591.8	that lusts and will triumph forever—the all-causing tyranny	[	that lasts and will triumph forever—the all-consuming tyranny
595.34	day	[	clay
596.32	burlesque with	[	burlesque, with
596.32	straw-blade	[	straw-pale
598.14	measure	[	menace
671.32	there	[	them
673.20	Light	[	Lift
716.6	He	[	Eugene
853.3	tune	[	time
855.4–5	on Sunday	[	in Society
870.1	loved	[	lived
910.35	Oh	[	O

A 3.1.f
Sixth printing

New York: Scribners, 1935.

On copyright page: 'First Printing, February, 1935 . . . Sixth Printing, April, 1935'. *Location:* CJ.

Note one: An advertisement for *OTATR* in *The New York Times Book Review* for 7 April 1935 reads: "SIXTH BIG PRINTING" and another for 21 April 1935 reads: "Thirtieth Thousand".

Note two: A carbon copy of a TLS from J[ohn]. H[all]. W[heelock]. to Tom Wolfe dated 18 April 1935 in the Scribners records indicates that in response to Wolfe's list of corrections, 50% were included in the last printing, and the rest would be included in the next printing.

Note three: The following additional textual changes were made between the fifth and sixth printings:

	FIFTH PRINTING		SIXTH PRINTING
54.5	him?	[	him.
102.6	Cock House	[	Cock Horse
126.28	laughted	[	laughed
243.38	three	[	two
309.20	third	[	second
361.33	two years	[	a year
509.15	craving	[	waning
510.28	mining	[	moving
517.19	gigantic	[	propitious
662.22	ate	[	et
662.24	Moray	[	Mornay
663.18	Lodge	[	Bridge
665.23	minute-whirring	[	minute-winning

669.34	*Batouale*	[	*Batouala*
672.31	lives	[	loves
673.18	mark	[	smack
678.22	list	[	listen
678.26	Vee	[	Bee
679.9	senile	[	servile
680.24	sorry	[	sorrow
863.34	Lindquist	[	Lundquist
868.13	chains	[	drains
870.1	lived, we	[	lived in solitude and in the wilderness, we

A 3.1.g
Seventh printing

New York: Scribners, 1935.

On copyright page: 'First Printing, February, 1935 ... Seventh Printing, June, 1935'. *Locations:* CJ, NcRSM.

Note one: An advertisement for *OTATR* in *The New York Times Book Review* for 12 May 1935 announces: "*Seventh Big Printing*".

Note two: No textual changes were noted in the seventh printing.

A 3.1.h
Eighth printing

New York: Scribners, 1935.

On copyright page: 'First Printing, February, 1935 ... Eighth Printing, September, 1935'. *Locations:* EG, MH, ScU (rebound).

Note one: The following additional textual change was made between the seventh and the eighth printings:

	SEVENTH PRINTING		EIGHTH PRINTING
236.20–21	and begun to	[	and began to

LATER PRINTINGS WITHIN THE FIRST EDITION

A 3.1.i
New York: Scribners, 1937.

Locations: EG, NcU.

A 3.1.j
New York: Grosset & Dunlap, [1939].

Published 19 October 1939. Price: $1.29. *Locations:* APM, EG, MH, ViU.

A 3.1.r *Of Time and the River* 33

A 3.1.k
New York: Scribners, 1942.

Location: ScU.

A 3.1.l
New York: Scribners, 1944.

Location: EG.

A 3.1.m
Garden City, New York: Sun Dial Press, [1944].

Three printings noted. Two printings with '1944 | THE SUN DIAL PRESS' on copyright page; one printed on heavy and one printed on light-weight paper. Additional type batter noted in the printing on light-weight paper. Third printing noted with 'Sun Dial Press Reprint Edition, 1944' on copyright page. *Locations:* APM, CJ, MH, NcU, ScU, ViU.

A 3.1.n
New York: Scribners, 1946.

Location: Mi.

Note one: The Scribners records include a memo from Joseph Poli dated 6 November 1947 indicating twelve printings of *OTATR*. This probably refers to the twelve Scribners printings (A 3.1.a–A 3.1.i, A 3.1.k–A 3.1.l, and A 3.1.n) and does not include the 1939 Grosset and Dunlap printing (A 3.1.j) or the 1944 Sun Dial Press printings (A 3.1.m).

A 3.1.o
New York: Scribners, 1948.

Location: NcA.

A 3.1.p
Garden City, New York: Garden City Books, [1950?].

On copyright page: 'COPYRIGHT, 1935, BY | CHARLES SCRIBNER'S SONS . . . GARDEN CITY BOOKS Reprint Edition.' Price: $1.98. *Location:* EG.

A 3.1.q
New York: Scribners, 1952.

Locations: NcA, ScU.

A 3.1.r
New York: Scribners, [1957].

On copyright page: 'I-8.57[H]'. Published August 1957. *Locations:* BOD (- 1 MAY 1975), ScU, ScCleU.

A 3.1.s
New York: Scribners, [1958].

On copyright page: 'J-12.58[H]'. Published December 1958. *Locations:* APM, DLC (MAY 22 1957).

A 3.1.t
New York: Scribners, [1960].

On copyright page: 'K-12.60[H]'. Published December 1960. *Location:* JI.

A 3.1.u
New York: Scribners, [1962].

On copyright page: 'L-3.62[H]'. Published March 1962. *Location:* DLC.

A 3.1.v
New York: Scribners, [1965].

Hudson River Editions. On copyright page: '1 . . . H/C . . . 2.' Price: $17.50. *Location:* NcRSM.

A 3.1.w
New York: Scribners, [1967].

On copyright page: 'N-12.67'. Published December 1967. *Location:* ScU.

A 3.1.x
New York: Scribners, [1969].

On copyright page: '0-12.69[H]'. Published December 1969. *Locations:* ScU, ViU.

A 3.1.y
New York: Scribners, [1971].

Scribner Library SL #284 and SL #285. Two-volume set in wrappers. Volume 1 contains books 1–3; volume 2 contains books 4–8. Price: volume 1, $2.95; volume 2, $3.95. *Not seen.* Sixth printing of volume 1 noted; third printing of volume 2 noted. *Location:* NcRSM.

A 3.1.z
New York: Scribners, [1979].

On copyright page: 'Copyright 1935 Charles Scribner's Sons'. Price: $17.50. Also distributed by the Book-of-the-Month Club. *Locations:* APM, NcRSM (BOMC), NcU.

Note one: BOMC copies have a blindstamped ⅛" diameter circle or ⅛" square in the lower right-hand corner of the back cover. The NcRSM copy was further identified as a BOMC copy because of records at NcRSM.

A 3.1.aa–dd *Of Time and the River*

Note two: BOMC distributed 10,175 copies of *LHA* and *OTATR* as part of its special "book dividend" arrangement. See Richard S. Kennedy, "Wolfe's *Look Homeward, Angel* in the Literary Marketplace," *The Thomas Wolfe Review,* 6 (Fall 1982), 23–26. See A 2.6.c.

A 3.1.aa–dd
New York: Scribners, 1980.

The Scribner Library of Contemporary Classics. Wrappers. The first one-volume edition in wrappers. Price: $9.95. Second and fourth printings noted. Price: $14.95. *Locations:* APM, CJ (2 copies; 2nd printing and 4th printing), NcRSM (2nd printing).

Note one: A check of points reveals that the text of this printing is identical to A 3.1.a. See A 3.1.f *Note two.*

A 3.2.a
First English edition, first printing (1935)

OF TIME AND THE RIVER

A LEGEND OF MAN'S HUNGER
IN HIS YOUTH

By

Thomas Wolfe

"*Who knoweth the spirit of man that goeth upward, and
the spirit of the beast that goeth downward to the earth?*"

WILLIAM HEINEMANN LTD.
LONDON
1935

A 3.2.a: 8¼″ × 5⅝″

A 3.2.a *Of Time and the River* 37

> PRINTED IN GREAT BRITAIN
> AT THE WINDMILL PRESS, KINGSWOOD, SURREY

[i–xiv] [1–2] 3–86 [87–88] 89–324 [325–326] 327–404 [405–406] 407–598 [599–600] 601–794 [795–796] 797–849 [850–852] 853–899 [900–902] 903–912 [913–914]

$[1]^{16}$ 2–29^{16}

Contents: pp. i–iii: blank; p. iv: text, headed 'PUBLISHERS' NOTE'; p. v.: half title; p. vi: blank; p. vii: title; p. viii: copyright; p. ix: dedication 'To | MAXWELL EVARTS PERKINS | A GREAT EDITOR AND A BRAVE AND HONEST MAN, WHO STUCK TO | THE WRITER OF THIS BOOK THROUGH TIMES OF BITTER HOPELESS- | NESS AND DOUBT AND WOULD NOT LET HIM GIVE IN TO HIS OWN | DESPAIR, A WORK TO BE KNOWN AS "OF TIME AND THE RIVER" IS | DEDICATED WITH THE HOPE THAT ALL OF IT MAY BE IN SOME WAY | WORTHY OF THE LOYAL DEVOTION AND THE PATIENT CARE WHICH | A DAUNTLESS AND UNSHAKEN FRIEND HAS GIVEN TO EACH PART OF | IT, AND WITHOUT WHICH NONE OF IT COULD HAVE BEEN WRITTEN | "*Crito, my dear friend Crito, that, be-* | *lieve me, that is what I seem to hear, as* | *the Corybants hear flutes in the air, and* | *the sound of those words rings and* | *echoes in my ears and I can listen to* | *nothing else.*" '; p. x: blank; p. xi: contents; p. xii: blank; p. xiii: half title; p. xiv: twenty-one-line poem beginning ' "Kennst du das Land' (—Mignon's song at the opening of Book III of Goethe's *Wilhelm Meister's Apprenticeship*); p. 1: 'BOOK I | ORESTES: FLIGHT BEFORE FURY'; p. 2: epigraph, beginning '... *of wandering*'; pp. 3–86: text, headed 'I'; p. 87: '*Book II* | YOUNG FAUSTUS'; p. 88: blank; pp. 89–324: text, headed 'VII'; p. 325: 'BOOK III | TELEMACHUS'; p. 326: blank; pp. 327–404: text, headed 'XXXIX'; p. 405: 'BOOK IV | PROTEUS: THE CITY'; p. 406: blank; pp. 407–598: text, headed 'XLVI'; p. 599: 'BOOK V | JASON'S VOYAGE'; p. 600: blank; pp. 601–794: text, headed 'LXVIII'; p. 795: 'BOOK VI | ANTÆUS: EARTH AGAIN'; p. 796: blank; pp. 797–849: text, headed 'XC'; p. 850: blank; p. 851: 'BOOK VII | KRONOS AND RHEA: THE DREAM OF TIME'; p. 852: blank; pp. 853–899: text, headed 'XCVI'; p. 900: blank; p. 901: '*BOOK VIII* | FAUST AND HELEN'; p. 902: blank; pp. 903–912: text, headed 'CII'; pp. 913–914: blank.

Typography and paper: 6½" (6¹¹⁄₁₆") × 4¼"; 39 lines per page. Running heads: rectos, book headings; versos: 'OF TIME AND THE RIVER'. Wove paper.

Binding: Black V cloth. Front: goldstamped with two medium yellowish green rectangular panels: '[two rules] | [on medium yellowish green rectangular panel] OF TIME AND THE RIVER | [two rules on black] | [on medium

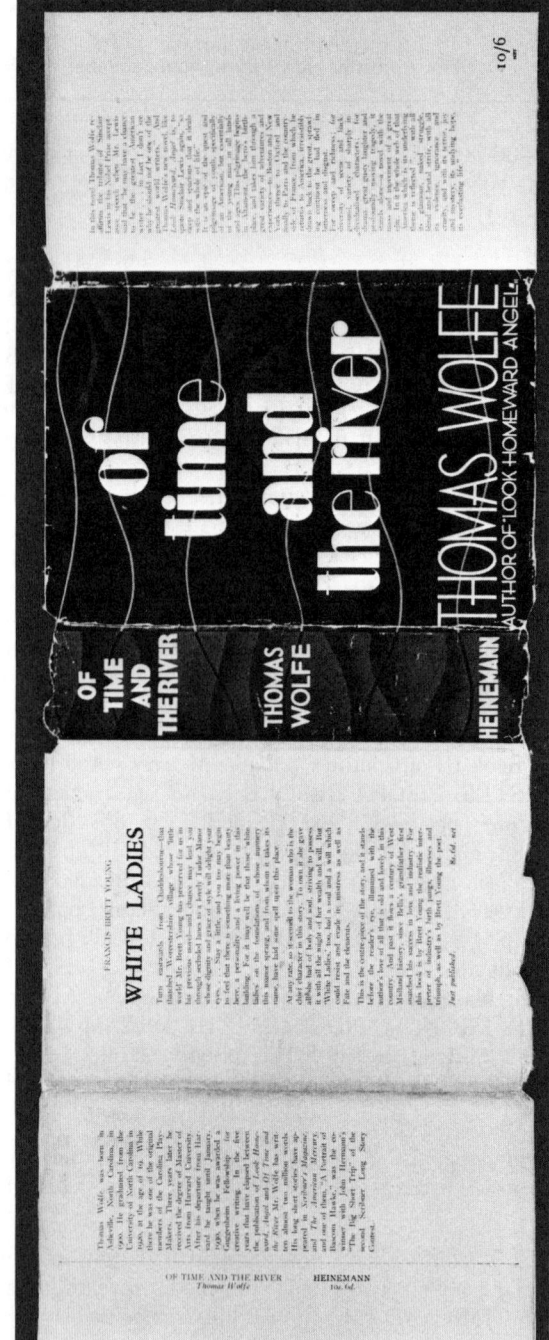

Dust jacket for A 3.2.a

A 3.2.a *Of Time and the River*

yellowish green rectangular panel] THOMAS WOLFE | [two rules on black]'; spine: goldstamped with four medium yellowish green rectangular panels: '[three rules] | [on medium yellowish green rectangular panel] OF TIME AND | THE RIVER | [three rules on black] | [medium yellowish green rectangular panel] | [three rules] | [on medium yellowish green rectangular panel] WOLFE | [three rules on black] | [fourteen blindstamped rules] | [two rules] | [on medium yellowish green rectangular panel] HEINEMANN | [three goldstamped rules on black]'; back: blindstamped Heinemann seal. White wove endpapers. All edges trimmed.

Dust jacket: Front: printed in white on a deep green and black wave design with six vivid green wavy horizontal lines: '[ornamental letters] of | time | and | the river | [roman] THOMAS WOLFE | AUTHOR OF "LOOK HOMEWARD ANGEL,, '. Spine: printed in white on a vivid green wave design with six black wavy horizontal lines: 'OF | TIME | AND | THE RIVER | THOMAS | WOLFE | HEINEMANN'. Back: blurb for Francis Brett Young's *White Ladies*. Front flap: blurb for *OTATR* quoting Sinclair Lewis's Nobel Prize acceptance speech. Back flap: biographical material.

Publication: 7,500 copies. Published 19 August 1935. Date of contract: 23 May 1934. Advance: £100. Royalty: 10% first 2,000; 15% to 5,000; 20% thereafter. Price: 10/6.

Printing: See copyright page.

Locations: BL (20AUG35), BOD (AUG 28 1935), InU Lilly (dj), MH, NcA (dj), NcU (2 copies), NcRSM (2 copies).

Note one: Heinemann's set copy from Scribners page proofs. In a carbon copy of a TLS dated 19 April 1935 to Heinemann's A. S. Frere-Reeves included in the Scribners records, Scribners' John Hall Wheelock refers to the "complete list of corrections" to *OTATR* he has already sent him. He is "sending herewith additional corrections which you may wish to make in your edition." Wheelock blames the errors on the typist's faulty transcriptions of Wolfe's handwriting: "Although they [the mistranscribed words] make sense and indeed seem quite correct, [they] were not the words which Tom had written."

Note two: In all copies observed, the page number '120' reads: '20'.

Text: The first Heinemann printing of *OTATR* varies from the first Scribners printing in 313 substantive readings:

SCRIBNERS (1935)		HEINEMANN (1935)	
27.3	lunch room	[27.3	luncheon room
31.15	vibrance	[31.15	vibrancy
35.3	on	[35.3	in
36.14	tenderness	[36.14	tendency
46.34	out the	[46.34–35	out of the

48.18	do	[	48.18	no
52.14	path	[	52.14	paths
53.25	trainman	[	53.25	railwayman
53.29	trainmen	[	53.29	railwaymen
54.5	him?	[	54.5	him.
55.7	there	[	55.7	here
73.16	bed, my balls!	[	73.16	bed!
77.10	then	[	77.11	them
89.3	elemental	[	89.3	eternal
89.14	numerous	[	89.14	murmurous
92.33	board	[	92.33	hoard
94.1	The Cock Horse Tavern	[	94.1	the 'Cock House Tavern'
94.20	of most	[	94.20	of the most
100.23	enhancement	[	100.23	enchantment
100.38	was remarkably	[	100.37	were, remarkably
103.28	pedantical	[	103.28	pedantic
107.14	pedantical	[	107.14	pedantic
109.14	winters which	[	109.14–15	winters from which
123.5	sunk	[	123.5	sank
126.28	laughted	[	126.28	laughed
138.32–34	and blind with glory, but yet carries in it a knowledge, born in such a moment	[	138.32–33	and a moment
149.7	uhearted	[	149.5	unhearted
155.38	pullman	[	155.38	Pullman
163.38	eczemic	[	163.37	eczematous
168.8	theatric	[	168.8	theatrical
171.18	theatric	[	171.18	theatrical
184.32	Louse	[	185.1	Louise
186.1	my	[	186.7	his
187.27	*oevah-sexed*	[	187.33	*ovah-sexed*
189.7	youh	[	189.12	yoah
189.24	my	[	189.29	his
195.5	dumpling-faced	[	195.12	dumpling-face
200.37	scowly	[	201.7	scowling
204.36	Jordan	[	205.5	Sluder
205.3	Jordan	[	205.11	Sluder
208.6	idiot	[	208.13	idiotic
219.20	guts	[	219.27	stomach
221.25	damn	[	221.33	damned
236.21	begun	[	236.29	began
236.36	rotten	[	237.5	goosey
242.26	make	[	242.34	catch

A 3.2.a *Of Time and the River* 41

243.34–35	gown. The boy never saw him again. [paragraph] Thirty	[	244.5–6	gown. [paragraph] Thirty
248.21	engines	[	248.29	energies
250.39	looket	[	251.9	looked
260.23	gold	[	260.33	golden
274.34	strange	[	275.8	shining
275.37	licker	[	276.10	liquor
288.33	this mad	[	289.5	his mad
299.7	Balls	[	299.17	Bosh
304.11	weavings	[	304.20	hazards
308.3	on who?	[	308.13	on whom?
308.9	suborn	[	308.19	stubborn
310.27	around	[	310.38	round
313.13	we	[	313.23	us
314.15	the genuine	[	314.25	a genuine
315.5	lovely	[	315.15	lonely
319.15	egotists	[	319.25	egoists
320.30	come	[	321.1	came
330.27	plow is	[	330.27	plough are
330.27	sunny shelf	[	330.27	sunnys helf
332.28	summer is	[	332.28	summer are
338.13	faze	[	338.13	bother
338.33	my	[	338.32	his
339.2	idiot	[	339.1	idiotic
339.3	At	[	339.2	At
339.14	idiot	[	339.13	idiotic
339.18	idiot	[	339.17	idiotic
343.32	t-t-t-trouble!	[	343.32	trouble!
345.17	conciliating	[	345.17	conciliatory
345.18	here	[	345.18	there
345.33	was	[	345.33	were
346.17	roomer	[	346.16	lodger
349.28	gas	[	349.27	p-p-p-petrol
350.15	fire	[	350.15	air
350.35	nickel	[	350.35	copper
351.5	automobiles	[	351.5	motor cars
351.14–15	an automobile	[	351.14	a car
355.8	hall-way	[	355.9	hall
355.24	shyster	[	355.25	low-down
357.36	cobbler	[	357.36	pie
360.3	philistines	[	360.3	Philistines
363.6–7	handgrip	[	363.6–7	handcase
364.18	around	[	364.18	round
365.24	guts	[	365.25	stomach
365.25	pled	[	365.27	pleaded

366.4	from	[	366.5	for
367.5	piss	[	367.5	to make water
367.21	landing into	[	367.22	ending up in
368.28	fenders	[	368.28	running-boards
373.3	wooden whore-houses	[	373.3	rickety wooden brothels
374.36	ammoniac	[	374.36	ammoniacal
382.23	easance	[	382.24	easement
387.11	tone	[	387.11	voice
390.4	earth is	[	390.2	earth are
393.9	wind-shield	[	393.10	wind-screen
395.3	our	[	395.3	their
395.11	brown cotton fields	[	395.11	brown cotton-fields
397.24	lunch room	[	397.24	luncheon room
397.38	Wy-wy-wy-frankly	[	397.38	Wy-f-f-f-frankly
398.1	John	[	398.1	Gene
400.23	promising aptly, swearing eagerly, and	[	400.23	promising everything, swearing anything, and
402.18	hallway	[	402.18	hall
402.24	hallway	[	402.24	hall
402.36	rush	[	402.36	urge
403.5	rouse	[	403.5	arouse
404.9	sweet	[	404.9	secret
408.7	out windows	[	408.7	out of windows
408.23 24	conductors	[	408.24	guards
408.27	conductor	[	408.27	guard
408.31	conductor	[	408.31	guard
408.33	conductor	[	408.33	guard
410.14	phthisic	[	410.14	phthisical
425.1	gut	[	425.1	stomach
434.29	you, too	[	434.30	you to
437.22	was	[	437.21	were
447.23–24	Then he insisted	[	447.23–24	Then insisted
449.34	department	[	449.35	brigade
451.13	balls	[	451.13	bottom dollar
452.3	bastard	[	452.3	devil
452.19	check-book	[	452.19	cheque-book
453.30	around	[	453.30	round
456.28	idiot	[	456.28	idiotic
462.17	was	[	462.16	were
464.18	uncertitude	[	464.18	incertitude
466.2	read him his	[	466.2	read his
466.38	me	[	466.38	Eugene
468.12	shysters	[	468.12	crooks
472.14	whores	[	472.16	prostitutes
473.5	lunchroom	[	473.6	luncheon-room

A 3.2.a *Of Time and the River* 43

473.7	lunchroom	[	473.8	luncheon-room
473.23	around	[	473.24	round
475.33	lunchroom	[	475.34	luncheon-room
475.37	whores	[	475.38	prostitutes
476.6	its	[	476.7	his
476.8	whores	[	476.9	prostitutes
476.19	railroad men	[	476.20	railwaymen
476.20	train conductors	[	476.21	guards
481.24	subtile	[	481.26	subtle
482.2	subtile	[	482.4	subtle
482.12	subtile-minded	[	482.14	subtle-minded
484.32	around	[	484.35	round
485.9	around	[	485.12	round
487.21–22	my guts all along!" "Your guts!" Up- shaw	[	487.24–25	me all along!" "Hated you!" Up- shaw
487.36–37	loath- | ing I have ever	[	487.39– 488.1	loathing he had ever
488.39	whore	[	489.3	prostitute
490.1	elevators	[	490.4	lifts
490.4	elevator man	[	490.7	lift-man
491.21	interne	[	491.24	doctor
493.23	around	[	493.28	round
493.38–39	streets, the	[	494.4–5	streets, nor the
494.7	sprung	[	494.12	sprang
494.23	room	[	494.28	live
495.23	around	[	495.28	round
495.24	around	[	495.29	round
498.27	Here	[	498.34	Where
499.21	idiot	[	499.28	idiotic
499.23	transmitted	[	499.30	transmuted
499.35	resins	[	500.3	resinous
500.22	would not go	[	500.28	would go
501.9	was	[	501.14	were
503.36	was	[	504.1	were
504.1	aisles	[	504.4	gangways
506.8	out of the	[	506.10	out the
506.21	his guts	[	506.23	him
507.4	gasoline	[	507.9	petrol
509.15	craving	[	509.18	waning
510.28	mining	[	510.29	moving
513.8–9	ticket-seller's	[	513.9–10	booking-office
517.19	gigantic	[	517.19	propitious
517.24	hostler	[	517.24	ostler
519.20	ah	[	519.20	so
521.25	was	[	521.25	were
521.26	that	[	521.25	this

526.36	was	[	526.37	were
540.3	telling	[	540.1	saying
542.26–27	we have done	[	542.21–22	we have have done
545.2	envy	[	544.35	error
545.10	beings	[	545.8	kings
545.22	leonic	[	545.20	leonine
561.18	adderous	[	561.19	adder-like
572.27	around	[	572.27	round
576.13–15	you spoke with a crisp but obstinate conviction, "Joel, I *know* I'm right! argue	[	576.12–13	you about the background being bad, nor that I have used too much gold on it. But I will argue
578.34	Who	[	578.33	Whom
579.2	automobiles	[	579.1	motor-cars
591.4	idle and among	[	591.2	idle among
591.8	forever	[	591.6	for ever
591.9	whores	[	591.7	prostitutes
596.33	whore's	[	596.32	prostitute's
597.10	whore	[	597.9	prostitute
597.15	aisle	[	597.14	corridor
598.2	idiot	[	598.1	idiotic
598.4–8	[paragraph] 'Yuh f——kin' Kikes!... Yuh f——kin' Jews!... I'll kick duh f——kin' s——t outa duh f——kin' lot of yuh, yuh f——kin' bastards, you.... Hey-y! You!... Yuh f——kin' dummies up deh talkin' on yer f——kin' fingers all duh time.... Hey-y! You! Inches! You f——kin' bastard, I don't give a s——t for duh whole f——kin' lot of yuh."	[	598.3–7	"Yuh———— Kikes!... Yuh———— Jews!... I'll kick duh———— s——t outa duh lot of yuh, yuh———— ————bastards, you.... Hey-y! You!... Yuh———— ————dummies up deh talkin' on yer———— fingers all duh time.... Hey-y! You! Inches! You———— bastard, I don't give a s——t for duh whole———— ————lot of yuh."
598.14	conductor	[	598.13	guard
598.16	waning	[	598.15	warning
608.19	guts	[	608.19	body

A3.2.a *Of Time and the River*

609.4	college fellows	[	609.4	undergraduates
609.17	blonde	[	609.17	blond
609.33–34	squiffed along towards ten	[	609.33–34	squiffy about ten
609.36–37	*Times* upon her w. c. just after modern plumbing was installed—Ow!	[	609.37	*Times*—Ow!
610.3	around	[	610.2	round
610.7	small lean head	[	610.7	small head
610.8	Know! Old Lambert	[	610.8	know! Lambert
617.10	blonde	[	617.12	blond
619.27	fall	[	619.28	autumn
627.1	around	[	627.1	round
627.25	ploddy	[	627.25	plodding
628.30	around	[	628.32	round
647.25	mantel	[	647.26	mantelpiece
648.26	it	[	648.26	them
648.27	it	[	648.27	them
648.29	out the	[	648.29	out of the
654.2	whores	[	654.2	ladies of easy virtue
656.25	8 h	[	656.25	8 heures
662.22	ate	[	662.22	et
662.24	moray	[	662.24	Mornay
663.1	Royale	[	663.1	Royal
663.18	Lodge	[	663.18	Bridge
669.34	*Batouale*	[	669.32	*Batouala*
672.31	lives	[	672.26	loves
672.29	whore	[	672.24	prostitute
673.1	whore's	[	672.31	prostitute's
673.3	whore's	[	672.33	prostitute's
673.18	mark	[	673.11	smack
673.31	whores	[	673.24	prostitutes
674.1–2	whore-house	[	673.31–32	strumpet-house
675.29	whore-houses	[	675.22	strumpet-houses
676.9	senile	[	676.3	servile
677.11	its	[	677.5	his
678.22	list	[	678.14	listen
678.25	character	[	678.17	diameter
678.26	Vee	[	678.18	Bee
680.6	has	[	679.34	have
680.24	sorry	[	680.15	sorrow
697.9	is	[	697.3	are
713.34	more	[	713.29	longer
717.36	stoop	[	717.33	veranda

720.14	ze—vay you	[	720.12	ze—vat you
724.10	whores	[	724.6	prostitutes
725.9	above the middle	[	725.5	above middle
726.20	Alec!	[	726.15	Alec, Alec!
728.16	around	[	728.8	round
733.5	around	[	732.34	round
737.15	around	[	737.5	round
737.26	around	[	737.16	round
742.13–14	him. He looked about the room and found everything in it good and homely. He went	[	742.5	him. He went
748.7	aisles	[	747.38	avenues
749.28	a cassis-vermouth, the	[	749.20	a vermouth–cassis, the
750.12	around	[	750.5	round
751.37	around	[	751.30	round
755.35	whores	[	755.28	prostitutes
757.34	around	[	757.26	round
759.38	around	[	759.28	round
761.6	around	[	760.34	round
768.34	expense	[	768.24	expenses
769.36	around	[	769.25	round
770.3	coldly, positively:	[	769.31	coldly:
771.11	whore	[	771.1	demi-monde
771.29	strong	[	771.19	stormy
772.20	let	[	772.11	drop
776.19	around	[	776.8	round
782.17	out the	[	782.5	out of the
787.25	around	[	787.13	round
790.32	whores	[	790.18	prostitutes
792.11	whore! You whore	[	791.36	bitch! You bitch!
792.19	whore	[	792.5	wretch
792.25	whore	[	792.11	wretch
793.34	whore	[	793.20	devil
799.34–36	eh?" "Six francs." "Ah-h! . . .	[	799.35–36	eh?" "Ah-h! . . .
801.33	package	[	801.33	packet
806.27	for	[	806.27	for
806.27	around	[	806.27	round
809.37	a maturity	[	809.37	the maturity
816.16	ascenseur	[	816.16	lift
820.8	whores	[	820.7	prostitutes
820.11	blonde	[	820.10	blond
820.11	whore	[	820.10	prostitute
823.6	carried	[	823.6	delivered

A 3.2.c *Of Time and the River*

823.15	horn	[823.14	trumpet
825.1	package	[824.39	packet
828.20	proprietor	[828.19	proprietress
829.6	for a moment she	[829.6	for an instant or two she
834.5	blonde	[834.2	blond
835.36	aisle	[835.33	avenue
842.25	around	[842.19	round
843.32	vill	[843.26	will
849.2–3	wash up and	[848.35–36	wash and
858.7	lost	[858.8	lots
858.38	guts	[858.39	body
861.18	across light, hunched miles	[861.18	across eight hundred miles
861.35	guts	[861.35	stomach
863.34	blonde	[863.34	blond
863.34	Lindquist	[863.34	Lundquist
864.20	incapable	[864.20	capable
868.13	chains	[868.10	drains
869.12	lunch-room	[869.9	luncheon-room
869.30	guts	[869.27	insides
870.1	was loved, we	[869.36–37	was lived in solitude and in the wilderness, we
872.1	out the	[871.37	out of the
873.24	four or five weeks	[873.22	four weeks
876.12	grip	[876.10	valise
885.32	idiot	[885.32	idiotic
888.37	waist	[888.37	waists
890.11	around	[890.9	round
890.15	whores	[890.13	prostitutes
893.29	or	[893.25	nor
894.33	lunchrooms	[894.31	luncheon rooms
909.19	idiot	[909.20	idiotic
910.35	moment	[910.36	moments

LATER PRINTINGS WITHIN THE FIRST ENGLISH EDITION

3.2.b
London: Heinemann, 1937.

Locations: MJB, NcU.

3.2.c
London: Heinemann, [1969].

On copyright page: 'William Heinemann Ltd | LONDON MELBOURNE TORONTO | JOHANNESBURG | AUCKLAND | First published 1935 |

Reissued 1969'. A reduced offset reprint of the 1935 printing. Price: 70/–. *Locations:* BL (23MAY69), NcU.

LATER EDITIONS

A 3.3
New York: Editions for the Armed Services, [1945?].

512 pp. #1013. Wrappers. *On copyright page:* 'Due to limitations of space, it has been necessary to greatly | reduce the material contained in the original edition of this book.' Not for sale. *Locations:* MH, MJB, NcA, NcU, NcRSM.

Note one: A TLS in the Scribners records dated 1 March 1945 from Philip Van Doren Stern to Maxwell Perkins informs Perkins that Don Wayne will condense the book.

A 3.4

Of Time and the River: | YOUNG FAUSTUS | TELEMACHUS | *by* | Thomas Wolfe | *With an Introduction by* C. HUGH HOLMAN | *"Who knoweth the spirit of man that goeth upward, and* | *the spirit of the beast that goeth downward to the earth?"* | *CHARLES SCRIBNER'S SONS* | *NEW YORK*

318 pp. *Scribner Library* #SL 106. Wrappers. *On copyright page:* 'A—1.65[MCol]'. Published January 1965. Price: $1.65. Reprintings noted: 'B-3.65[MCol]', 'D-8.67[MCol]', and 'F-2.70[MC]'. *Locations:* CJ (F), DLC (A), EG (A), NcA (B), NcRSM (D).

Note one: This edition includes only Book II, "Young Faustus," and Book III, "Telemachus".

A 3.5.a–b
[Harmondsworth]: Penguin Books, [1971].

1,035 pp. *Penguin Modern Classics.* Wrappers. *On copyright page:* 'First published in the U.S.A. 1935 | Published in Great Britain by Heinemann 1935 | Published in Penguin Books 1971'. Price: £1.25. Reprinted in 1984. Price: £5.95. *Locations:* BOD (2 DEC 1971), CJ (1984), NcU (2 copies).

A 3.6
New York: Scribners, [1979?].

886 pp. Possibly a set with a similarly bound *LHA* (see A 2.11). *Location:* NcRSM.

A4 FROM DEATH TO MORNING

Two issues have been noted.

A4.1.a₁
First edition, first printing, American Issue (1935)

FROM DEATH TO MORNING

By
Thomas Wolfe

Vigil strange I kept on the field one night.

CHARLES SCRIBNER'S SONS
NEW YORK
1935

A4.1.a₁: 7⅜" × 5⅛"

> COPYRIGHT, 1932, 1933, 1934, 1935, BY
> CHARLES SCRIBNER'S SONS
>
> Copyright, 1935, by North American Review Corporation
> Copyright, 1935, by International Magazine Company, Inc.
> Copyright, 1935, by Harper's Bazaar, Inc.
> Copyright, 1935, by F. R. Publishing Corporation
> Copyright, 1935, by the Conde Nast Publications, Inc.
> Copyright, 1935, by Virginia Quarterly Review
> Copyright, 1934, 1935, by Modern Monthly, Inc.
>
> Printed in the United States of America.
>
> *All rights reserved. No part of this book may be reproduced in any form without the permission of Charles Scribner's Sons.*
>
> A
>
>

[i–xiv] 1–304 [305–306]

[1–20]⁸

Contents: pp. i–iii: blank; p. iv: list of books by Wolfe; p. v: half title; p. vi: blank; p. vii: title; p. viii: copyright; p. ix: dedication 'TO | THE MEMORY OF HIS BROTHER | BENJAMIN HARRISON WOLFE | AND TO THE PROUD AND BITTER BRIEFNESS OF | HIS DAYS | October 27, 1892— October 20, 1918 | *Up on the mountain, down in the | valley, deep, deep, in the hill, | Ben, cold, cold, cold.*'; p. x: blank; p. xi: contents; p. xii: blank; p. xiii: half title; p. xiv: blank; pp. 1–304: text, headed 'No Door'; pp. 305–306: blank.

14 short stories: "No Door" (see C 23)#, "Death the Proud Brother," "The Face of the War," "Only the Dead Know Brooklyn," "Dark in the Forest, Strange as Time," "The Four Lost Men," "Gulliver," "The Bums at Sunset," "One of the Girls in Our Party," "The Far and the Near" (See C 44), "In the Park" #, "The Men of Old Catawba" (see C 35 and C 37), "Circus at Dawn," "The Web of Earth."

Typography and paper: 5¾" (5⅞") × 3⅝"; 34 lines per page. Running heads: rectos, story titles; versos, 'FROM DEATH TO MORNING'. Wove paper.

Binding: Dark brown V cloth. Front goldstamped: 'THOMAS WOLFE | [two rules] | FROM DEATH TO MORNING'; spine goldstamped with two blindstamped rectangular panels: 'THOMAS | WOLFE | [rule] | [blind-

Dust jacket for A 4.1.a₁

stamped rectangular panel] | [rule] | FROM DEATH | TO MORNING | [rule] | [blindstamped rectangular panel] | [rule] | SCRIBNERS'. White wove endpapers. Top edges trimmed and stained orange; bottom edges trimmed; foreedges rough trimmed.

Dust jacket: Front printed in black and vivid orange on shades of dark brown at the top brightening to shades of light orange at the bottom with two wavy horizontal vivid orange and three wavy horizontal light gray lines and, at bottom, off center to the right, a black semicircle: '[black lettering] FROM | DEATH | TO | MORNING | [vivid orange lettering] stories by | THOMAS WOLFE'. Spine printed in white, vivid orange, and light gray on shades of dark brown at the top brightening to shades of light orange at the bottom: '[white lettering] FROM | DEATH | TO | MORNING | [vivid orange lettering] THOMAS | WOLFE | [light gray lettering] SCRIBNERS'. Back: blurb for *OTATR* quoting reviews by Peter Monro Jack, Henry Seidel Canby, Harry Hansen, and Burton Rascoe, and from a review appearing in the *London Times Literary Supplement*. Front flap: blurb for *FDTM*. Back flap: author's portrait and quotation from a review by Carl Van Doren.

Publication: 7,500 copies. Copyright #A88281. Published 14 November 1935. Date of contract: 26 December 1934. Advance $1,000. Royalty: 15%. Price: $2.50.

Printing: Composed and printed by the Scribner Press, New York City. Bound by the Scribner Press.

Locations: DLC (rebound copy stamped 'NOV 16 1935'), EG (2 copies with dj), InU Lilly (dj), JI, MH, MJB (dj; review slip), NcA (3 copies; 2 copies with dj), NcRSM (3 copies; 2 copies with dj), NcU (2 copies with dj), ViU (3 copies; 2 copies with dj).

Note one: A MH copy inscribed by Wolfe to Aline Bernstein is dated 29 October 1935.

Salesman's dummy: Prints the first six pages of "The Web of Earth."

Title page: 'STORIES | By | Thomas Wolfe | AUTHOR OF "LOOK HOMEWARD, ANGEL" | AND "OF TIME AND THE RIVER" | [decoration] | CHARLES SCRIBNER'S SONS | NEW YORK LONDON | 1935'.

On copyright page: 'A'.

[i–vi] 1–6

[1]^6

Contents: printed blurb headed 'FALL PUBLICATIONS' pasted on front paste-down endpaper; p. i: half title; p. ii: blank; p. iii: title; p. iv: copyright; p. v: contents; p. vi: blank; pp. 1–6: "The Web of Earth".

Binding: Front goldstamped: 'THOMAS WOLFE | [rule]'. Back blindstamped with two vertical rules.

Location: InU Lilly.

A 4.1.a₂
English Copyright Issue of American Sheets (1935)
Identical to A 4.1.a₁ except for:

FROM DEATH TO MORNING

By

Thomas Wolfe

Vigil strange I kept on the field one night.

LONDON
WILLIAM HEINEMANN
1935

A 4.1.a₂: 7⅜" × 5⅛"

Copyright page: 'COPYRIGHT, 1932, 1933, 1934, 1935, BY | CHARLES SCRIBNER'S SONS | For the United States of America. | [rule] | Copyright, 1935, by North American Review Corporation | Copyright, 1935, by International Magazine Company, Inc. | Copyright, 1935, by Harper's Bazaar, Inc. | Copyright, 1935, by F. R. Publishing Corporation | Copyright, 1935, by Virginia Quarterly Review | Copyright, 1934, 1935, by Modern Monthly, Inc. | Printed by THE SCRIBNER PRESS, New York, U. S. A. | All rights reserved. No part of this book may be reproduced in any form without the permission of Charles Scribner's Sons. | A'.

[i–xiv] 1–304 [305–306]

$[1]^8$ ($\pm 1_4$) $[2$–$20]^8$

Binding: Black V cloth. Spine goldstamped: 'FROM | DEATH | TO | MORNING | [call numbers obscure this part of spine in the only copy located] | THOMAS WOLFE | HEINEMANN'.

Location: BL (14NOV35).

Note one: Scribners text with cancel title leaf; one of a possible dozen, issued for copyright purposes. TLS in the Wisdom Collection from A. S. Frere-Reeves to Thomas Wolfe dated 15 November 1935 reads: "In order to avoid the copyright complications which broke out over OF TIME AND THE RIVER, I have duly taken steps to secure copyright here of FROM DEATH TO MORNING on November 14th, that is to say simultaneously with Scribners' publication date. To enable me to do this Max Perkins sent over a dozen sets of sheets, which I had bound and duly dealt with. The book is setting now, and I hope to publish in the spring." See A 5.1.a$_2$.

LATER PRINTINGS WITHIN THE FIRST EDITION

A 4.1.b
New York: Scribners, 1935.

'A' omitted from copyright page. Bound in dark blue and lettered in yellow with 'SCRIBNERS' on the spine. *Locations:* CJ, NcRSM.

Note one: A memo from Joseph Poli in the Scribners records dated 6 November 1947 indicates two printings of *FDTM* prior to that date.

Note two: George R. Preston, Jr., in his *Thomas Wolfe: A Bibliography* (B12), refers to this volume as a first printing. He notes: "Approximately 1100 copies of the first edition were remaindered to the Outlet Book Company in 1940, bound in blue cloth and lettered across in yellow...." (p. 26). This information has not been verified and the two copies observed bound in blue cloth and lettered in yellow are both a later printing.

A4.1.c
New York: Scribners, [n.d.].

Locations: EG, ViU.

Note one: The EG copy was inscribed by Fred Wolfe and dated 22 July 1939.

A4.1.d
New York: Grosset and Dunlap, [after 1948].

Price: $1.49. *Locations:* CJ, MJB, NcRSM, NcU (2 copies).

Note one: A carbon copy of a TL in the Scribners records to Edward Aswell dated 21 June 1948 reads: "As regards From *Death to Morning,* there is, of course, no reprint of this. Whitney [Darrow] is looking into the possibility of such a reprint, and if there should be one we could try to get some sheets which we would bind for ourselves so as to have stock on hand."

A4.1.e
New York: Scribners, [1958].

Cloth and wrappers. *On copyright page:* 'A-1.58[H]'. Published January 1958. Price: $1.65. Reprinted at least eight times in cloth and, as *Scribner Library* #SL 117 and as *Scribner Library of Contemporary Classics* #SL 117, in wrappers. Reprints observed: on copyright page: in cloth: 'B-12.65[Col]' and 'D-3.64'; in wrappers: 'A-6.65[Col]'. 'B-12.65[Col]', '1970', and 'E-5.72'. *Locations:* APM (wrappers), EG (A-6.65 in wrappers and B-12.65 in cloth), MH (cloth), NcRSM (wrappers), NcU (4 copies; 2 copies in wrappers, 1 copy 1970 in wrappers, and 1 copy B-12.65 in wrappers), ScCleU (D-3.64 in cloth), ViU (E-5.72 in wrappers).

A4.1.f
New York: Scribners, [1963].

Cloth and wrappers. *Hudson River Editions* in cloth. *On copyright page:* 1 . . . Q/C . . . 2'. *Scribner Library of Contemporary Classics* in wrappers. On copyright page: '1 . . . Q/P . . . 2'. Ninth printing of Scribner Library of Contemporary Classics noted. *Locations:* CJ (2 copies; 1 copy *HRE* and 1 copy 9th printing *Scribner Contemporary Classics*), NcU (*Scribner Contemporary Classics*).

A 4.2.a
First English edition, only printing [1936]

FROM DEATH TO MORNING

By
Thomas Wolfe

Vigil strange I kept on the field one night.

LONDON
WILLIAM HEINEMANN LTD

A 4.2.a: 7½″ × 5″

A 4.3 *From Death to Morning* 57

> **FIRST PUBLISHED 1936**
>
> **PRINTED IN GREAT BRITAIN
> AT THE WINDMILL PRESS, KINGSWOOD, SURREY**

[i–viii] 1–280

[A]^8 B–I K–S^8

Contents: p. i: half title; p. ii: list of books by Wolfe; p. iii: title; p. iv: copyright; p. v: dedication 'TO | THE MEMORY OF HIS BROTHER | BENJAMIN HARRISON WOLFE | AND TO THE PROUD AND BITTER BRIEFNESS OF | HIS DAYS | October 27, 1892–October 20, 1918 | *Up on the mountain, down in the* | *valley, deep, deep, in the hill,* | *Ben, cold, cold, cold.*'; p. vi: blank; p. vii: contents; p. viii: blank; pp. 1–280: text, headed '*No Door*'.

Typography and paper: 5⅝" (5⅞") × 3⅝"; 34 lines per page. Running heads: rectos, story titles; versos, 'FROM DEATH TO MORNING'. Wove paper.

Binding: Black V cloth. Spine goldstamped: 'FROM | DEATH | TO | MORNING | [diamond] | THOMAS | WOLFE | HEINEMANN'; back: blindstamped Heinemann seal. White wove endpapers. All edges trimmed.

Dust jacket: Front light brown printed in blue and red within ornamental blue and red frame: '[blue lettering] FROM | DEATH | TO MORNING | [red lettering] BY | THOMAS | WOLFE | [blue lettering] author of Look Homeward, Angel'. Spine: light brown printed in blue and red: '[blue lettering] *From* | *Death to* | *Morning* | [three red stars] | [blue lettering] *Heinemann*'. Back: blurb for *OTATR* quoting articles in the *Sunday Times* and in the *Times*. Flaps: front flap missing in copy observed; back flap: lists new books.

Publication: 1,500 copies. Published 16March 1936. Price: 7/6.

Printing: See copyright page.

Locations: BL (16MAR36), BOD (MAR 21 1936), MH, NcA, NcRSM (dj), NcU.

LATER EDITIONS

A 4.3
London: World Distributors, [1965].

144 pp. *Consul Edition #1436.* Wrappers. *On copyright page: 'This Consul edition, complete and unabridged,* | *published in England, 1965, by* | WORLD DISTRIBUTORS (MANCHESTER) LTD. | 36 GREAT RUSSELL STREET, LONDON, W.C. 1'. Published October 1965. Price: 3/6. *Location:* BL.

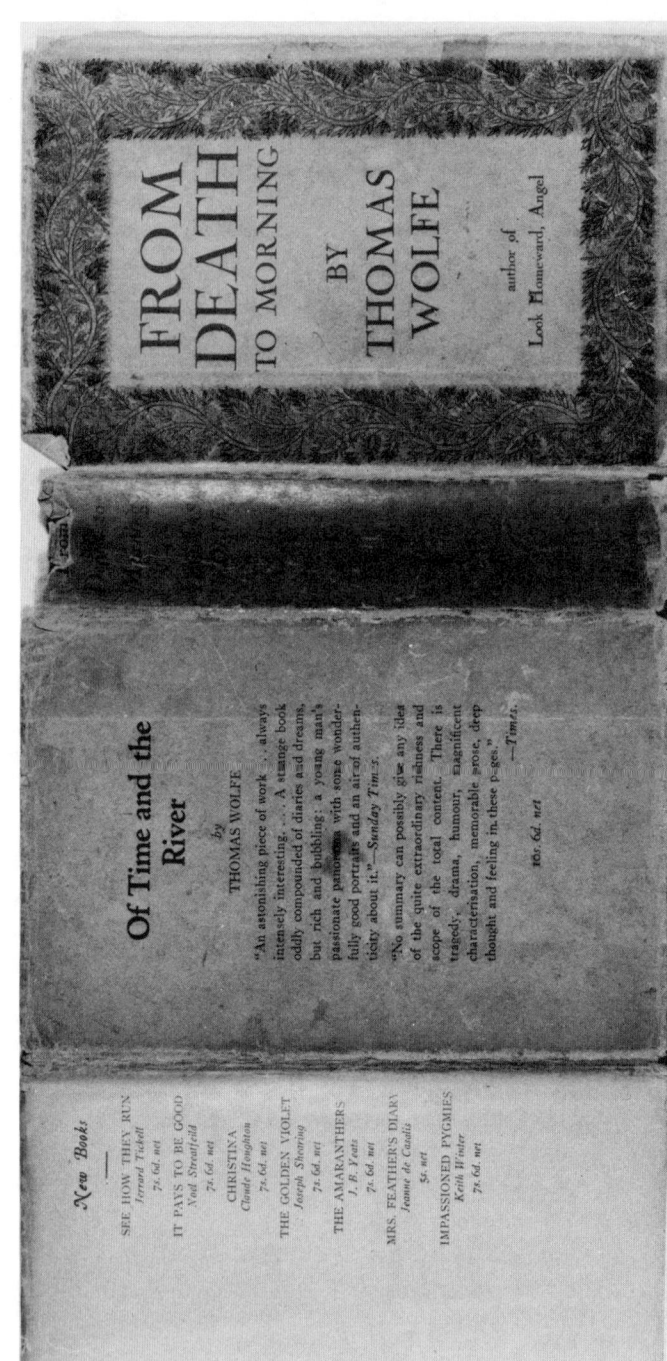

Dust jacket for A4.2.a

A 4.4 *From Death to Morning*

A 4.4
Franklin Center, Pennsylvania: The Franklin Library, 1979.

353 pp. *Franklin Library*. Illustrated by Uldis Klavins. *On copyright page:* 'Published by arrangement with Charles Scribner's Sons and William Heinemann Ltd. Special contents © 1979 Franklin Mint Corporation.' Published February 1979. *Locations:* APM, DLC (MAR 1 1979), NcA.

A 5 THE STORY OF A NOVEL

Three issues have been noted.

A 5.I.a₁
First edition, first printing, American issue (1936)

the story
of a
NOVEL

By
Thomas Wolfe

CHARLES SCRIBNER'S SONS · NEW YORK
CHARLES SCRIBNER'S SONS · LTD · LONDON
1936

A 5.I.a₁: 7½" × 4⅞"

A 5.1.a₁ *The Story of a Novel*

COPYRIGHT, 1936, BY
CHARLES SCRIBNER'S SONS

COPYRIGHT, 1935, BY THE SATURDAY REVIEW COMPANY, INC.

Printed in the United States of America

*All rights reserved. No part of this book
may be reproduced in any form without
the permission of Charles Scribner's Sons*

A

PUBLISHER'S NOTE

The text of this book, with certain modifications, first appeared in a series of three articles in *The Saturday Review of Literature* in December, 1935.

[i–viii] 1–93 [94]

[1]⁸ (+1₃) [2–5]⁸ [6]¹⁰; dedication leaf tipped in.

Contents: p. i: half title; p. ii: list of books by Wolfe; p. iii: title; p. iv: copyright; p. v: dedication 'TO | ALFRED DASHIELL | A FRIEND'; p. vi: blank; p. vii: half title; p. viii: blank; pp. 1–93: text; p. 94: blank.

Typography and paper;   5⅜" (5½") × 3³⁄₁₆"; 24 lines per page. Wove paper.

Binding: Medium reddish orange V cloth. Front goldstamped on a black rectangular panel: 'the story | of a | NOVEL | [two rules] | Thomas Wolfe'; spine goldstamped: '[vertically on a black rectangular panel] the story of a NOVEL [equal sign] Wolfe [horizontally beneath the black rectangular panel] SCRIBNERS'. White wove endpapers. Top and bottom edges trimmed; fore edges rough trimmed.

Dust jacket: Front: medium orange with black ornamental lettering on a pale yellow rectangular panel: 'The | Story Of | A Novel | Thomas Wolfe'. Spine: medium orange with vertical black lettering: 'the story of a NOVEL [equal sign] Wolfe [equal sign] Scribners'. Back: quotes from reviews by Burton Rascoe, Clifton Fadiman, Margaret Wallace. Front flap: blurb for *TSOAN*. Back flap: quotes from a review by Peter Monro Jack and from reviews appearing in the *Philadelphia Ledger* and *The Chicago Tribune*.

Publication: 3,000 copies. Copyright #A96080. Published 21 April 1936. Date of contract: 15 January 1936; revised 22 April 1936. Royalty: 15%. Price: $1.50.

Dust jacket for A 5.1.a₁

A 5.1.a₁ *The Story of a Novel* 63

Printing: Composed and printed by the Scribner Press, New York City. Bound by the Scribner Press.

Locations: APM (dj), DLC (2 copies; both stamped 'JUNE 20 1936'), EG (dj), MH (2 copies), MJB (dj), NcA (2 copies; 1 copy with dj), NcRSM.

Note one: Published in *The Saturday Review of Literature,* 13 (14 December 1935), 3–4, 12, 14, 16; (21 December 1935), 3–4, 15; (28 December 1935), 3–4, 14–16. See C 53.

A 5.1.a₂
English Copyright Issue of American Sheets (1936)
Identical to A 5.1.a₁ except for:

the story
of a
NOVEL

By

Thomas Wolfe

LONDON
WILLIAM HEINEMANN
1936

A 5.1.a₂: 7⅝" × 4⅞"

A 5.1.a₂ *The Story of a Novel*

Location: BL (30APR36).

Note one: Scribners text with Heinemann imprint printed on 3" × ¾" strip of paper pasted over Scribners imprint on the title page for copyright purposes. See A 4.1.a₂ for precedent. Only one of these has been observed and no records describing preparation of further copies have been located.

A 5.1.a₃
English issue of American sheets (1936)

Two states have been noted, priority not determined.

State A:

> # the story
> # of a
> # NOVEL
>
> By
>
> Thomas Wolfe
>
> LONDON
> WILLIAM HEINEMANN
> 1936

A 5.1.a₃: State A: 7⅝″ × 4⅞″

A 5.1.a₃ *The Story of a Novel*   67

> Copyright, 1936, by Charles Scribner's Sons, for the
> United States of America
>
> ———
>
> Copyright, 1935, by The Saturday Review Company, Inc.
>
> ———
>
> Printed by The Scribner Press, New York, U. S. A.
>
> *All rights reserved. No part of this book
> may be reproduced in any form without
> the permission of Charles Scribner's Sons*
>
> ～～～～～～～～～～～～～～～～
>
> **PUBLISHER'S NOTE**
>
> The text of this book, with certain modifications, first appeared in a series of three articles in *The Saturday Review of Literature* in December, 1935.

[i–vi] 1–93 [94]

[1]⁸ (±1₂) [2–5]⁸ [6]¹⁰

Contents: p. i: half title; p. ii: list of books by Wolfe; p. iii: title; p. iv: copyright; p. v: half title; p. vi: blank; pp. 1–93: text, beginning 'An editor'; p. 94: blank.

Typography and paper: Same as A 5.1.a₁.

Binding: Black V cloth. Spine goldstamped: 'The | Story | of a | Novel | Thomas | Wolfe | Heinemann'; back: blindstamped Heinemann seal. White wove endpapers. Top and bottom: trimmed; fore edges: rough trimmed.

Dust jacket: Front: dark reddish orange with black ornamental lettering on a white rectangular panel: 'The | Story Of | A Novel | Thomas Wolfe'. Spine: dark reddish orange with black lettering vertically: 'THE STORY OF A NOVEL [bullet] THOMAS WOLFE [bullet] HEINEMANN'. Back: blurb for *OTATR*. Front flap: blurb for *TSOAN*. Back flap: list of 'New Books'.

Publication: 500 copies. Published 9 November 1936. Price: 5/–.

Locations: BL (9NOV36), MH, MJB (dj), NcU (2 copies; 1 copy with dj), ViU.

Note one: Scribners text without dedication.

State B:

The same as State A, except for the verso of the cancel title leaf, which is blank.

Location: BOD (NOV 25 1936).

Note one: These sheets were printed in America by Scribners for Heinemann, but probably bound in England. I have been unable to determine whether the Scribners and Heinemann sheets were of the same or of separate printings.

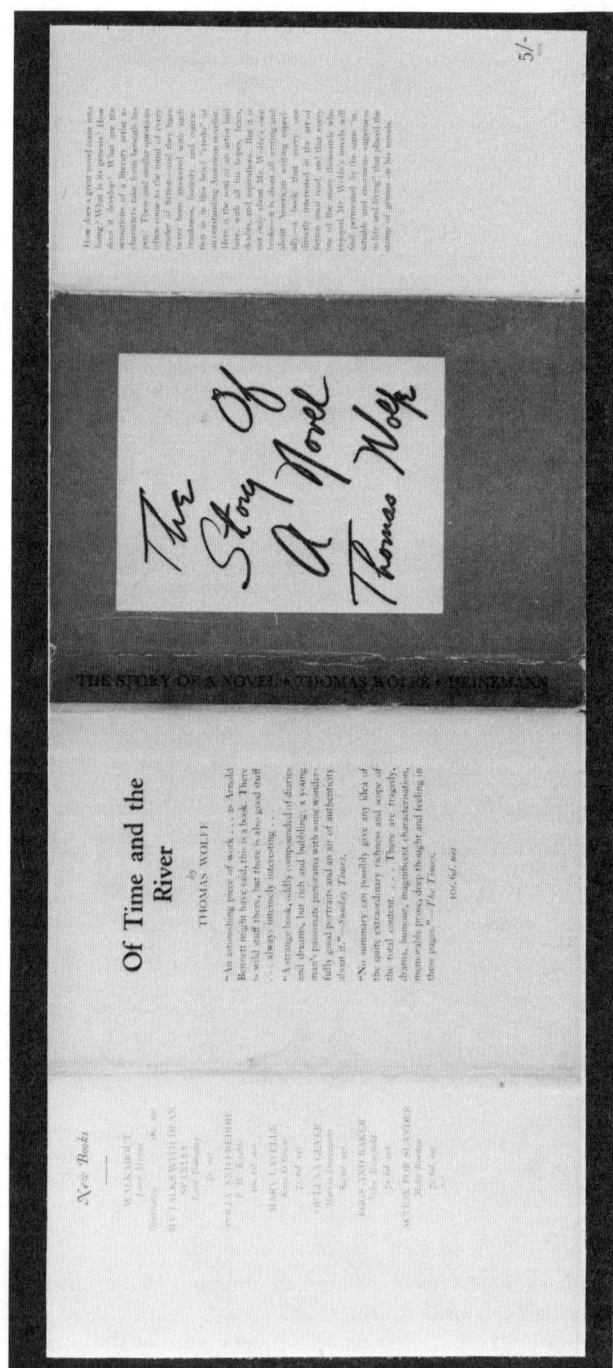

Dust jacket for A 5.1.a₃ State A

A 5.1.i *The Story of a Novel* 69

LATER PRINTINGS WITHIN THE FIRST EDITION

A 5.1.b
New York and London: Scribners, 1936.

'A' omitted from copyright page. *Locations:* EG, InU (Lilly).

A 5.1.c
New York and London: Scribners, [1941?].

Dedication to Alfred Dashiell not included. *Location:* NcA.

Note one: This copy is inscribed to Mabel Wheaton from Maxwell Perkins and dated 19 December 1941.

A 5.1.d
New York and London: Scribners, 1949.

Dedication to Alfred Dashiell is included on p. v. and is integral with the text. *Locations:* EG, NcA, NcU.

A 5.1.e
New York and London: Scribners, [1958].

On copyright page: 'D-7.58[MH]'. Published July 1958. *Locations:* APM, NcRSM.

A 5.1.f
New York: Scribners, [1962].

On copyright page: 'E-4.62[MH]'. Published April 1962. *Locations:* PSt, ScU.

A 5.1.g
New York: Scribners, [1966].

On copyright page: 'G-6.66[MH]'. Published June 1966. *Location:* NcA.

A 5.1.h
New York and London: Scribners, [1971].

On copyright page: 'K-8.71[MC]'. Published August 1971. *Location:* JI.

A 5.1.i
New York: Scribners, [n.d.].

Hudson River Editions. On copyright page: '1 . . . Q/C . . . 2. *Location:* CJ.

A 6
Only printing (1939)

A Note on Experts: Dexter Vespasian Joyner

THOMAS WOLFE

HOUSE OF BOOKS, LTD.
New York   1939

A6: 7½″ × 5″

A6 A Note on Experts: Dexter Vespasian Joyner

> Copyright, 1939, by Maxwell Perkins
> as Executor of the
> Estate of Thomas Wolfe.

[i–viii] [1–24]

[1–4]⁴

Contents: p. i–ii: blank; p. iii: 'THIS FIRST EDITION IS LIMITED TO | THREE HUNDRED COPIES. | THIS IS NO. '; p. iv: blank; p. v: title; p. vi: copyright; p. vii: text, headed 'A NOTE FROM THE EXECUTOR OF | THE ESTATE OF THOMAS WOLFE'; p. viii: blank; pp. 1–20: text, headed '[decorative rule] | [rule] | A Note on Experts: | Dexter Vespasian Joyner | [rule]'; p. 21: blank; p. 22: 'THIS IS NUMBER FIVE OF | THE CROWN OCTAVOS | PUBLISHED BY HOUSE OF BOOKS, LTD. | 19 EAST 55 STREET, NEW YORK. | PRINTED AT THE | SOUTHWORTH-ANTHOENSEN PRESS | PORTLAND, MAINE'; pp. 23–24: blank.

Typography and paper: 5¼" × 3⅜"; 27 lines per page. No running heads. Laid paper.

Binding: Medium brown V cloth. Front goldstamped: 'A NOTE ON EXPERTS: | DEXTER VESPASIAN JOYNER | THOMAS WOLFE'; spine goldstamped vertically from bottom to top: 'A NOTE ON EXPERTS [bullet] THOMAS WOLFE'. White laid endpapers. Top and bottom trimmed; fore edges rough trimmed.

Dust jacket: Glassine dust jacket.

Publication: 300 copies. Copyright #A130168/A1. Published 10 June 1939. Price: $2.50.

Printing: See contents.

Locations: APM, DLC (JUNE 17 1939), InU Lilly, MH, NcRSM (dj), NcU (3 copies with dj), ViU (2 copies).

Note one: The NcRSM copy has laid in a separate trial printing of the first leaf of the text.

A NOTE ON EXPERTS: DEXTER VESPASIAN JOYNER

THOMAS WOLFE

Binding for A 6

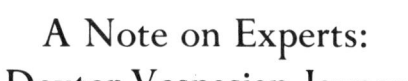

A Note on Experts: Dexter Vespasian Jayner

I HAVE often noticed that it is easier for a man to achieve distinction as an expert here in America than to attain eminence in almost any other branch of the nation's life. One must spend years, for example at hard labor on small wages, to become a first-rate carpenter. The apprenticeship of the master mechanic, the mason, the plasterer or the stone-cutter is also long, arduous and impecunious. To become a locomotive engineer, which I should say is almost the highest and the most authoritative of the mechanical positions, a man must undergo an apprenticeship that is only infrequently less than twenty years, and that requires a long and gruelling period of preparation as round-house helper, round-house mechanic, and locomotive fireman, before the candidate is deemed worthy of this highest office. Similarly, in the more professional activities, the period of preparation is also long and difficult. A young man must go through ten years of painful study and unpaid service before he is even

Trial printing for A 6

A7 THE WEB AND THE ROCK

A7.1.a
First edition, first printing (1939)

Thomas Wolfe

THE WEB
AND
THE ROCK

Harper & Brothers · Publishers
New York and London
1939

A7.1.a: 8″ × 5½″

> *By the Same Author*
>
> ✱
>
> LOOK HOMEWARD, ANGEL
>
> OF TIME AND THE RIVER
>
> FROM DEATH TO MORNING
>
> THE STORY OF A NOVEL
>
> ✱
>
> THE WEB AND THE ROCK
> *Copyright, 1937, 1938, 1939, by Maxwell Perkins as Executor
> Printed in the United States of America*
> *All rights in this book are reserved. It may not be used for dramatic, motion- or talking-picture purposes without written authorization from the holder of these rights. Nor may the book or part thereof be reproduced in any manner whatsoever without permission in writing. For information address: Harper & Brothers, 49 East 33rd Street, New York, N. Y.*
> 6/9
> FIRST EDITION
> E-O

[i–vi] vii–viii [1–2] 3–94 [95–96] 97–170 [171–172] 173–293 [294–296] 297–452 [453–454] 455–536 [537–538] 539–620 [621–622] 623–695 [696] [1–22]¹⁶

Contents: p. i: half title; p. ii: text, headed 'PUBLISHER'S NOTE'; p. iii: title; p. iv: copyright; p. v: text, headed '*AUTHOR'S NOTE*'; p. vi: epigraph, beginning '*Could I make*'; pp. vii–viii: contents; p. 1: 'Book I | THE WEB AND THE ROOT'; p. 2: blank; pp. 3–94: text, headed 'I | The Child Caliban'; p. 95: 'Book II | THE HOUND OF DARKNESS'; p. 96: epigraph, beginning '*Until his sixteenth*'; pp. 97–170: text, headed '5 | Aunt Mag and Uncle Mark'; p. 171: 'Book III | THE WEB AND THE WORLD'; p. 172: epigraph, beginning '*When George Webber's*'; pp. 173–293: text, headed '10 | Olympus in Catawba'; p. 294: blank; p. 295: 'Book IV | THE MAGIC YEAR'; p. 296: epigraph, beginning '*With the last*'; pp. 297–452: text, headed '17 | The Ship'; p. 453: 'Book V | LIFE AND LETTERS'; p. 454: epigraph, beginning '*That magic year*'; pp. 455–536: text, headed '29 | The Ring and the Book'; p. 537: 'Book VI | LOVE'S BITTER MYSTERY'; p. 538: epigraph, beginning '*The party had*'; pp. 539–620: text, headed '36 | A Vision of Death in April'; p. 621: 'Book VII | OKTOBERFEST'; p. 622: epigraph, beginning '*On the boat*'; 623–695: text, headed '44 | Time Is a Fable'; p. 696: '*Set in Linotype Granjon* | *Format by A. W. Rushmore* | *Manufactured by the Haddon Craftsmen* | *Published by* Harper & Brothers, *New York and London*'.

Typography and paper: 6½" (6¾") × 4⅛"; 39 lines per page. Running heads: rectos: chapter titles; versos: 'THE WEB AND THE ROCK'. Wove paper.

Binding: Deep blue V cloth. Front goldstamped with two deep red rectangular panels edged, top and bottom only, with gilt: '[two rules] | [on gilt-edged deep red rectangular panel] THE WEB AND THE ROCK | [two rules on deep blue] | [on gilt-edged deep red rectangular panel] THOMAS WOLFE | [two rules on deep blue]'; spine: goldstamped with three deep red rectangular panels edged, top and bottom only, with gilt: '[three rules] | [on gilt-edged deep red rectangular panel] THE WEB AND | THE ROCK | [seven rules on deep blue] | [on gilt-edged deep red rectangular panel] THOMAS WOLFE | [three rules on deep blue] | [fourteen blindstamped rules] | [two rules] | [on gilt-edged deep red rectangular panel] HARPERS | [three rules on deep blue]'. White wove endpapers. Top and bottom edges trimmed; fore edges rough trimmed.

Dust jacket: Front printed in vivid yellow and white on deep blue: '[white lettering] BY THE AUTHOR OF "LOOK HOMEWARD, ANGEL" | AND "OF TIME AND THE RIVER" | [vivid yellow ornamental lettering] Thomas Wolfe | [white roman lettering] A NEW NOVEL | ['T' not italicized] *The* WEB | AND THE | ROCK | [vivid yellow lettering] This novel, completed before Thomas | Wolfe's untimely death, ranks with | his best and truest work. | [white lettering] HARPER & BROTHERS [bullet] ESTABLISHED 1817'. Spine printed in vivid yellow and white on deep blue: '[ornamental vivid yellow lettering] Thomas Wolfe | [white roman lettering] ['T' not italicized] *The* | WEB | AND | THE | ROCK | [vivid yellow lettering] HARPERS". Back and back flap: portrait of the author and biographical material. Front flap: blurb for *TWATR*.

Publication: 31,126 copies. Copyright #A131242. Published 22 June 1939. Date of contract: 29 December 1937. Advance: $10,000. Royalty: 15%. Price: $3.00.

Printing: Composed by A. W. Rushmore. Printed and bound by the Haddon Craftsmen Inc., Camden, New Jersey.

Locations: APM, DLC (3 copies; 1 copy, rebound and stamped: 'JUL 29 1949'; 1 copy, rebound; 1 copy with dj), EG (5 copies; 4 copies with dj), MH, NcA (5 copies; 2 in dj); NcRSM (4 copies; 1 with dj), NcU (2 copies; 1 copy with dj), NjP, PSt (dj), ScCleU, ViU (4 copies; 2 copies with dj).

Note one: A ViU copy of the first printing is inscribed '*Advance Copy* | Rec'd June 6, 1939. from George Dieter of | Harper + Brothers.'

Dust jacket for A7.1.a

Promotional copies: A selection of galleys distributed to the trade in pad form.

Title page: 'Thomas Wolfe | [swelled rule] | THE WEB | AND | THE ROCK | [swelled rule] | [Harper seal] | Harper & Brothers [bullet] Publishers | *New York and London* | 1939'.

11½" × 8"

On copyright page: 'THE WEB AND THE ROCK | Copyright, *1937, 1939,* by Maxwell Perkins, as Executor | Printed in the United States of America'.

Pagination and galley numbers: [A–C] vii–viii, [galley numbers] 65–74, 101–113, 152–156, 190–194.

A pad of sheets (printed on rectos only) glued across the top edge.

Contents: p. A: title page; p. B: copyright; p. C: text, headed *'AUTHOR'S NOTE'*; pp. vii–viii: contents; galleys 65–74: text, headed: 'The Child by Tiger'; galleys, 101–106: text headed: 'The Rock'; galleys 107–113: text, headed 'The City Patriots'; galleys 190–194: text, headed 'April, Late April'.

Binding: Cover consists of one color–coated leaf depicting front and spine of the dust jacket. At bottom on white panel: 'A limited number of the following excerpts from the | galleys of *The Web and the Rock* have been specially | prepared for the trade. (Privately printed and not for sale.)'.

Locations: MH (2 copies), MJB, NcRSM, NcU, ViU.

Salesman's dummy: Includes synopsis and an excerpt from *TWATR*.

Title page: 'Thomas Wolfe | [swelled rule] | THE WEB | AND | THE ROCK | [swelled rule] | [Harper seal] | Harper & Brothers [bullet] Publishers | *New York and London* | 1939'.

8¼" × 5½"

Copyright page: '[within single-rules frame] Crown 8vo. | Price about [39 ellipses] | To be published about [29 ellipses] | HARPER & BROTHERS, NEW YORK | Established 1817'.

[i–vi] 1–10 [11–14]

[1]¹⁰

Contents: p. i: title page; p. ii: copyright; p. iii: text, headed 'THE WEB AND THE ROCK | *The Last Novel By* | THOMAS WOLFE | *SYNOPSIS*'; p. iv: blank; pp. 1–10: text, headed *Chapter 1;* pp. 11–12: blank.

Binding: Deep blue V cloth. Front goldstamped with two deep red rectangular panels edged, top and bottom only, with gilt: '[two rules] | [on gilt-edged deep red rectangular panel] THE WEB AND THE ROCK | [two rules on deep blue] | [on gilt-edged deep red rectangular panel] THOMAS

Thomas Wolfe

THE WEB
AND
THE ROCK

Harper & Brothers · Publishers
New York and London
1939

Title page for promotional copies for A 7.1.a

> THE WEB AND THE ROCK
>
> Copyright, 1937, 1939, by Maxwell Perkins, as Executor
> Printed in the United States of America
>
> All rights in this book are reserved. It may not be used for dramatic, motion- or talking-picture purposes without written authorization from the holder of these rights. Nor may the book or part thereof be reproduced in any manner whatsoever without permission in writing. For information address: Harper & Brothers, 49 East 33rd Street, New York, N. Y.

Copyright page for promotional copies for A 7.1.a

WOLFE, | [two rules on deep blue]'; back: goldstamped with three deep red rectangular panels edged, top and bottom only, with gilt: '[three rules] | [on gilt-edged deep red rectangular panel] THE WEB AND | THE ROCK | [seven rules on deep blue] | [on gilt-edged deep red rectangular panel] THOMAS WOLFE | [three rules on deep blue] | [fourteen blindstamped rules] | [two rules] | [on gilt-edged deep red rectangular panel] HARPERS | [three rules on deep blue]'. Top and bottom edges trimmed; fore edges rough trimmed.

Location: MH.

A 7.1.b
Second printing

New York and London: Harper & Brothers, 1939.

On copyright page: 'SECOND EDITION'. *Location:* BL (6 JUL 39).

A 7.1.c
Third printing

New York and London: Harper & Brothers, 1939.

On copyright page: 'E–O'. Published May 1939. *Location:* ScU (rebound).

A 7.1.d
Fourth printing

New York and London: Harper & Brothers, [1939].

On copyright page: 'F–O'. Published June 1939. *Location:* CJ.

LATER PRINTINGS WITHIN THE FIRST EDITION

A 7.1.e
Garden City, New York: Garden City, 1940.

On copyright page: 'CL'. *Locations:* JI, ViU.

A 7.1.n *The Web and the Rock* 81

A 7.1.f
Garden City, New York: Sun Dial Press, [1940].

On copyright page: '1940 | THE SUN DIAL PRESS'. *Locations:* APM, CJ, MH, NcRSM.

A 7.1.g
New York: Grosset & Dunlap, [1953].

On copyright page: 'D–C'. Published April 1953. Also observed in wrappers: *Grosset's Universal Library* #UL-12. *Locations:* EG (wrappers), MH (wrappers), NcRSM (wrappers), NcU (2 copies: cloth and wrappers), ScU (3 copies in cloth).

A 7.1.h
New York and London: Harper & Brothers, [1956].

On copyright page: 'L–F'. Published November 1956. *Location:* ScU (rebound).

A 7.1.i
New York: Harper & Brothers, [1957].

Harper Modern Classics. Includes an Introduction by William Braswell. *On copyright page:* 'M–G'. Published December 1957. *Locations:* DLC (rebound and stamped 'FEB 24 1958'), NcA.

A 7.1.j
New York: Harper & Brothers, [1958].

On copyright page: 'C–H'. Published March 1958. *Location:* ViU.

A 7.1.k
New York: Harper & Brothers, [1961].

On copyright page: 'D–L'. Published April 1961. *Location:* APM.

A 7.1.l
New York, Evanston, and London: Harper & Row, [1964].

On copyright page: 'F–O'. Published June 1964. *Locations:* DLC, PSt.

A 7.1.m
New York, Evanston, and London: Harper & Row, [n.d.].

Harper Crest Library Edition. Location: ViU.

A 7.1.n
New York, Cambridge, Philadelphia, San Francisco, London, Mexico City, São Paulo, Singapore, Sydney: Harper & Row, [1986].

Perennial Fiction Library #PL 1320. Wrappers. *On copyright page:* 'First PERENNIAL LIBRARY edition published 1973. Reissued in 1986.' Price: $10.95. *Location:* CJ.

A 7.2.a
First English edition, first printing [1947]

THE WEB
AND
THE ROCK

BY

Thomas Wolfe

WILLIAM HEINEMANN LTD
LONDON :: TORONTO

A 7.2.a: 7¾″ × 5⅛″

A 7.2.a *The Web and the Rock* 83

> FIRST PUBLISHED 1947
>
> THIS BOOK IS PRODUCED IN COMPLETE
> CONFORMITY WITH THE AUTHORISED
> ECONOMY STANDARDS
>
> ---
>
> PRINTED IN GREAT BRITAIN AT THE WINDMILL PRESS
> KINGSWOOD, SURREY

[i–vi] vii–xii 1–160 [161] 162–423 [424] 425–499 [500] 501–574 [575] 576–642 [643–644]

[A]^{18} B–I^{16} K–U^{16} W^6

Contents: p. i: half title; p. ii: list of books by Wolfe; p. iii: title; p. iv: copyright; p. v: text, headed '*AUTHOR'S NOTE*'; p. vi: epigraph, beginning '*Could I make*'; pp. vii–viii: contents; pp. ix–xii: text, headed 'Introduction'; pp. 1–89: text, headed 'BOOK I. *THE WEB AND THE ROOT*'; pp. 90–160: text, headed 'BOOK II. *THE HOUND OF DARKNESS*'; pp. 161–277: text, headed 'BOOK III. *THE WEB AND THE WORLD*'; pp. 278–423: text, headed 'BOOK IV. *THE MAGIC YEAR*'; pp. 424–499: text, headed: 'BOOK V. *LIFE AND LETTERS*'; pp. 500–574: text, headed: 'BOOK VI. *LOVE'S BITTER MYSTERY*'; pp. 575–642: text, headed 'BOOK VII. *OKTOBERFEST*'; pp. 643–644: blank.

Typography and paper: 6⅛" (6⁵⁄₁₆") × 3⅞"; 40 lines per page. Running heads: rectos, chapter headings; versos, '*THE WEB AND THE ROCK*'. Wove paper.

Binding: Black V cloth. Front goldstamped with two medium yellowish green rectangular panels: '[two rules] | [on a medium yellowish green rectangular panel] THE WEB AND THE ROCK | [two rules on black] | [on a medium yellowish green rectangular panel] THOMAS WOLFE | [two rules on black]'; spine goldstamped with four medium yellowish green rectangular panels: '[three rules] | [on a medium yellowish green rectangular panel] THE WEB AND | THE ROCK | [three rules on black] | [medium yellowish green rectangular panel] | [three rules on black] | [on a medium yellowish green rectangular panel] WOLFE | [five rules on black] | [on a medium yellowish green rectangular panel] HEINEMANN | [three rules on black]'; back: blindstamped Heinemann seal. White wove endpapers. All edges trimmed.

Dust jacket: Front and spine printed in yellow, white, and red lettering on a dark blue background. Front: '[yellow lettering] *Thomas* | *Wolfe* | [white lettering] *Author of Look Homeward, Angel* | [red lettering] THE WEB | AND | THE ROCK | [white lettering] "*HIS GREATEST NOVEL*" | *J. B. Priestley in his introduction*'. Spine: '[yellow lettering] *Thomas* | *Wolfe* | [red lettering] THE WEB | AND | THE ROCK | [yellow lettering] HEINEMANN'. Back: portrait of author with biographical material. Front and back flaps: '*From* | *J. B. Priestley's introduction*'.

Dust jacket for A7.2.a

A 7.5.a–b *The Web and the Rock* 85

Publication: Number of copies not determined. Published 27 January 1947. Date of contract: 30 September 1939. Advance: $250. Royalty: 10% on first 2000, 15% to 5000, 20% thereafter. Price: 12/6.

Printing: See copyright page.

Locations: BL (27JAN47), BOD (10 FEB 1947), CJ (dj), InU Lilly (dj), MH, MJB (dj), NcA, NcRSM (dj), NcU (2 copies), ViU (dj).

LATER PRINTINGS WITHIN THE FIRST ENGLISH EDITION

A 7.2.b
London: Heinemann, 1969.

On copyright page: 'First published 1947 | This edition 1969'. Price: 70/–.
Location: BOD (– 3 JUL 1969), NcU.

LATER EDITIONS

A 7.3
New York: Dell, [1960].

736 pp. *Laurel Edition* #LY103. Wrappers. Includes an introduction by Richard Chase. *On copyright page:* 'First Dell printing—August, 1960'. Price: 95¢. Reprint noted: 'September, 1963'. Dell publishing records identify four printings: August 1960, May 1961, September 1963, and May 1964. *Locations:* EG (August 1960), JI (September 1963), NcA (2 copies; both August 1960).

A 7.4.a
[New York]: New American Library, [1966].

640 pp. *Signet* #Q3026. Wrappers. Includes an introduction by Richard Chase. Published October 1966. Price: 95¢. Third Signet printing (*Signet Modern Classic* #CW/663) also noted. *Locations:* APM (CW/663), NcRSM (CW/663), NcU (Q3026).

A 7.4.b
New York, Evanston, San Francisco, London: Harper & Row, [1973].

Perennial Library #P313. Wrappers. Price: $1.50. Sixth *Perennial* printing in 1982 also noted. *Locations:* APM, CJ (2 copies; first and sixth printings).

A 7.5.a–b
[Harmondsworth, England, and Ringwood, Australia]: Penguin, [1972].

768 pp. *Penguin Modern Classics.* Wrappers. Price: £1.25. Reprinted in 1984. Price: £4.95. *Locations:* BOD (15 JUN 1979), CJ (1984).

A 8 YOU CAN'T GO HOME AGAIN

A 8.1.a
First edition, first printing [1940]

Thomas Wolfe

YOU CAN'T GO HOME AGAIN

Harper & Brothers · Publishers
New York and London

A 8.1.a: 8⅛" × 5½"

A8.1.a *You Can't Go Home Again*

> YOU CAN'T GO HOME AGAIN
> *Copyright, 1934, 1937, 1938, 1939, 1940,*
> *by Maxwell Perkins as Executor*
> *Printed in the United States of America*
>
> *All rights in this book are reserved. It may not be used for dramatic, motion- or talking-picture purposes without written authorization from the holder of these rights. Nor may the book or part thereof be reproduced in any manner whatsoever without permission in writing except in the case of brief quotations embodied in critical articles and reviews. For information address: Harper & Brothers, 49 East 33rd Street, New York, N. Y.*
>
> 9-0
>
> FIRST EDITION
>
> H-P

[i–vi] vii–viii [1–2] 3–146 [147–148] 149–322 [323–324] 325–396 [397–398] 399–508 [509–510] 511–618 [619–620] 621–704 [705–706] 707–743 [744]

[1–23]^{16} [24]^8

Contents: p. i: half title; p. ii: list of books by Wolfe; p. iii: title; p. iv: copyright; p. v: epigraph, beginning, 'There came to'; p. vi: blank; pp. vii–viii: contents; p. 1: 'BOOK I | THE NATIVE'S RETURN'; p. 2: blank; pp. 3–146: text, headed 'Chapter I | The Drunken Beggar on Horseback'; pp. 147–148: text, headed 'BOOK II | THE WORLD THAT JACK BUILT'; pp. 149–322: text, headed 'Chapter 10 | Jack at Morn'; pp. 323–324: text, headed 'BOOK III | AN END AND A BEGINNING'; pp: 325–396: text, headed 'Chapter 22 | A Question of Guilt'; pp. 397–398: text, headed 'BOOK IV | THE QUEST OF THE FAIR MEDUSA'; pp. 399–508: text, headed 'Chapter 27 | The Locusts Have No King'; pp. 509–510: text, headed 'BOOK V | EXILE AND DISCOVERY'; pp. 511–618: text, headed 'Chapter 32 | The Universe of Daisy Purvis'; pp. 619–620: text, headed BOOK VI | "I HAVE A THING TO TELL YOU" | [ornamental lettering] («Nun Will Ich Ihnen 'Was Sagen")'; pp. 621–704: text, headed 'Chapter 38 | The Dark Messiah'; pp. 705–706: text, headed 'BOOK VII | A WIND IS RISING, AND THE RIVERS FLOW'; pp. 707–743: 'Chapter 45 | Young Icarus'; p. 744: '*Set in Linotype Granjon | Format by A. W. Rushmore | Manufactured by the Haddon Craftsmen | Published by* HARPER & BROTHERS, *New York and London*'.

Typography and paper: 5⅞" (6⅛") × 4⅛"; 34 lines per page. Running heads: rectos, chapter titles; versos, 'YOU CAN'T GO HOME AGAIN'. Wove paper.

Binding: Deep blue V cloth. Front goldstamped with two deep red rectangular panels edged, top and bottom only, with gilt: '[two rules] | [on gilt-edged deep red rectangular panel] YOU CAN'T GO HOME AGAIN | [two rules on deep blue] | [on gilt-edged deep red rectangular panel] THOMAS WOLFE | [two rules on deep blue]'; spine goldstamped with three deep red rectangular panels edged, top and bottom only, with gilt: '[three rules] | [on gilt-edged deep red rectangular panel] YOU CAN'T GO | HOME AGAIN | [seven rules on deep blue] | [on gilt-edged deep red rectangular panel] THOMAS WOLFE | [three rules on deep blue] | [fourteen blindstamped rules] | [two rules] | [on gilt-edged deep red rectangular panel] HARPER | [three rules on blue]'. Top and bottom edges trimmed; fore edges rough trimmed.

Dust jacket: Front printed in deep brown, black, white, and deep red lettering on gold, white, and deep red rectangular panels: '[deep brown lettering on gold panel] *A Novel about a Lost Modern Who Found Himself* | BY | [black lettering] THOMAS | WOLFE | [deep red lettering on white panel] AUTHOR OF "LOOK HOMEWARD, ANGEL," "OF TIME AND THE RIVER," | AND "THE WEB AND THE ROCK" | [white lettering on deep red panel] *You Can't* | *Go Home* | *Again* | [black lettering] HARPER & BROTHERS [bullet] ESTABLISHED 1817'. Spine printed in black and white lettering on gold, white, and deep red rectangular panels: '[black lettering on gold rectangular panel] *You* | *Can't* | *Go* | *Home* | *Again* | [white rectangular panel] | [white lettering on deep red rectangular panel] THOMAS | WOLFE | [black lettering] HARPER'. Back and back flap: portrait of author, biographical material, and quotes from reviews by Clifton Fadiman, Burton Rascoe, William Allen White, George Stevens, and Harry Hansen, and from reviews appearing in *The New York Times, The New York Herald Tribune,* the *New York Post,* the *Providence Journal,* the *Atlanta Journal,* the *Buffalo Evening News,* the *Cleveland News,* and the *Cincinnati Enquirer.* Front flap: quotes from a review by Clifton Fadiman and contains blurb for YCGHA.

Publication: 23,605 copies. Copyright #A145790. Published 18 September 1940. Date of contract: 27 April 1939. Royalty: 15%. Price: $3.00.

Printing: See contents.

Locations: APM (dj), DLC (rebound and stamped 'SEP 18 1940'), EG (4 copies with dj), InU Lilly (dj), MH, NcA (4 copies; 3 with djs), NcRSM (3 copies; 1 copy with dj), NcU (dj), PSt (dj), ViU (3 copies; 2 copies with dj).

Note one: Preston (B 12) reports that a prospectus consisting of a synopsis and samples from the text was distributed prior to publication. No copies have been located.

Note two: The NcU copy the "first copy of the first Edition" is inscribed to Julia Wolfe by Edward C. Aswell and dated 30 August 1940; an NcA copy the "second copy of the first Edition" is inscribed by Edward C. Aswell to Wolfe's sister, Mabel, and dated 30 August 1940.

A 8.1.b
Second printing

New York and London: Harper & Brothers, 1940.

Not seen.

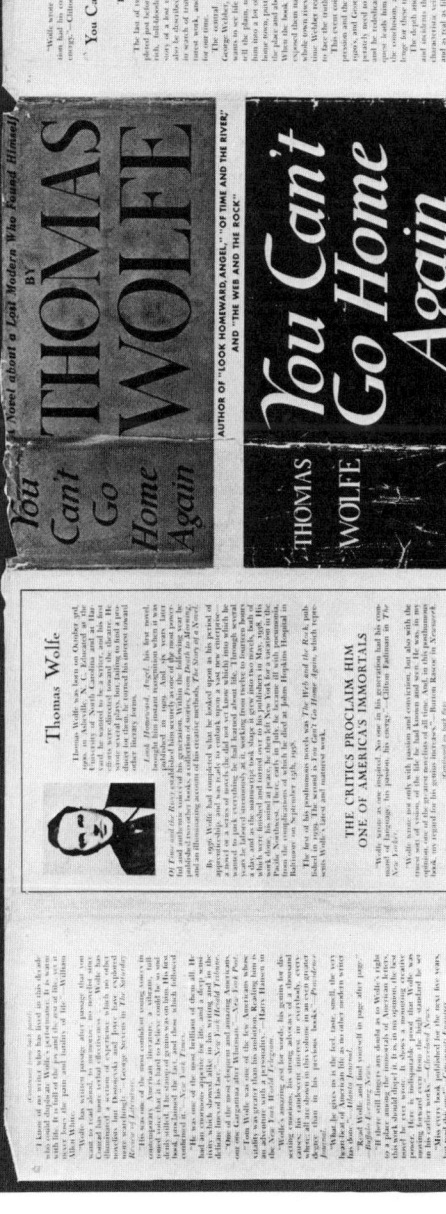

Dust jacket for A8.1.a

A8.1.c
Third printing

New York and London: Harper & Brothers, [1940].

On copyright page: '9–O | THIRD EDITION | H–P'. Published August 1940. *Location:* ScU.

A8.1.d
Fourth printing

New York and London: Harper & Brothers, [1940].

On copyright page: '9–O | FOURTH EDITION | K–P'. Published October 1940. *Location:* NcU.

A8.1.e
Fifth printing

New York and London: Harper & Brothers, 1940.

Not seen.

A8.1.f
Sixth printing

New York and London: Harper & Brothers, [1940].

On copyright page: '9–O | SIXTH EDITION | K–P'. Published October 1940. *Location:* KU, ScU.

A8.1.g
Seventh printing

New York and London: Harper & Brothers, [1940].

On copyright page: '9–O | SEVENTH EDITION | L–P'. Published November 1940. *Location:* NcU.

A8.1.h
Eighth printing

New York and London: Harper & Brothers, [n.d.].

Not seen.

LATER PRINTINGS WITHIN THE FIRST EDITION

A8.1.i–j.
Garden City, New York: Sun Dial Press, [1942].

Price: $1.49. At least two printings with variant copyright pages: '1942 | THE SUN DIAL PRESS' and 'THE SUN DIAL PRESS REPRINT EDITION, 1942'. *Locations:* EG, MH, NcRSM, NcU.

A8.1.q *You Can't Go Home Again* 91

A8.1.k
New York and London: Harper & Brothers, [1946].

On copyright page: 'NINTH EDITION | B–V'. Published February 1946. *Location:* ViU.

A8.1.l
New York and London: Harper & Brothers, [1947].

On copyright page: 'H–W'. Published August 1947. *Locations:* CJ, NcA.

A8.1.m
New York: Harper & Brothers, [1950].

Harper Modern Classics. Dust jacket. With an introduction by Edward C. Aswell. *On copyright page:* 'A–Z'. Published January 1950. Price: 95¢. Reprints observed: 'G–A' (July 1951), 'K–C' (October 1953), 'A–F (January 1956). *Locations:* EG (3 copies; 1 copy 'A–Z', 1 copy 'K–C', 1 copy 'A–F'), MH, NcA ('K–C'), NcU (2 copies; 1 copy 'G–A' and 1 copy 'K–C').

A8.1.n
Garden City, New York: Garden City Books [1952?].

On copyright page: 'GARDEN CITY BOOKS Reprint Edition'. *Location:* GU (rebound).

Note one: William H. Rose, Jr., of Harper & Brothers writes of *YCGHA* in a 17 April 1952 TLS to Edward Aswell: "Trade sales through March, 1952—47,808 | Text sales through March, 1952—6,052 | Reprint edition—127,721 (printed) | Garden City made a printing as recently as January of this year" (NcU).

A8.1.o
New York and London: Harper & Brothers, [1957].

On copyright page: 'K–G'. Published October 1957. *Location:* NcRSM.

A8.1.p
New York and London: Harper & Brothers, [1957].

On copyright page: 'L–G'. Published November 1957. *Location:* ScU.

A8.1.q
New York: Grosset & Dunlap, [1957?].

Grosset's Universal Library UL-16. Cloth and wrappers. One copy in cloth noted without Universal Library logo. *Locations:* EG (cloth without UL logo), MH (2 copies; 1 copy in cloth and 1 copy in wrappers), NcRSM (2 copies in wrappers), NcU (2 copies; 1 copy in cloth and 1 copy in wrappers).

A 8.1.r
New York and London: Harper & Brothers [1961].

On copyright page: 'A–L'. Published January 1961. *Location:* APM.

A 8.1.s
New York, Evanston, and London: Harper & Row, [1963].

On copyright page: 'D–N'. Published April 1963. *Location:* PSt.

A 8.1.t
New York: Grosset & Dunlap [1965?].

On copyright page: '© 1965'. *Location:* NcRSM.

A 8.1.u
New York, Evanston, and London: Harper & Row, [1973].

Colophon: '73 74 75 24 23 22 21 20'. *Location:* EG.

A8.2.a
First English edition, first printing [1947]

YOU CAN'T GO HOME AGAIN

BY

Thomas Wolfe

WILLIAM HEINEMANN LTD
LONDON　::　TORONTO

A8.2.a: 7¾" × 5⅛"

FIRST PUBLISHED 1947

PRINTED IN GREAT BRITAIN AT THE WINDMILL PRESS
KINGSWOOD, SURREY

[i–iv] v–vi 1–116 [117] 118 [119] 120–257 [258] 259–317 [318–319] 320–410 [411] 412 [413] 414–498 [499] 500 [501] 502–568 [569] 570–600 [601–602]

[A]^{16} B–I^{16} K–T^{16}

Contents: p. i: half title and epigraph; p. ii: list of books by Wolfe; p. iii: title; p. iv: copyright; pp. v–vi: contents; pp. 1–116: text, headed 'BOOK I. THE NATIVE'S RETURN'; pp. 117–257: text, headed 'BOOK II. *The World that Jack Built*'; p. 258: blank; pp. 259–317: text, headed 'BOOK III. *AN END AND A BEGINNING*'; p. 318: blank; pp. 319–410: text, headed 'BOOK IV. THE QUEST OF THE FAIR MEDUSA'; pp. 411–498: text, headed 'BOOK V. EXILE AND DISCOVERY'; pp. 499–600: text, headed 'BOOK VI. "I HAVE A THING TO TELL YOU" '; pp. 601–602: blank.

Typography and paper: 6⅛″ (6⁵⁄₁₆″) × 3⅞″; 40 lines per page. Running heads: rectos, chapter headings; versos, 'YOU CAN'T GO HOME AGAIN'. Wove paper.

Binding: Black V cloth. Front goldstamped with two deep yellowish green rectangular panels: '[two rules] | [on deep yellowish green rectangular panel] YOU CAN'T GO HOME AGAIN | [two rules on black] | [on deep yellowish green rectangular panel] THOMAS WOLFE | [two rules on black]'; spine: goldstamped with four deep yellowish green rectangular panels: '[three rules] | [on deep yellowish green rectangular panel] YOU CAN'T GO | HOME AGAIN | [three rules on black] | [deep yellowish green rectangular panel] | [three rules on black] | [on deep yellowish green rectangular panel] WOLFE | [five rules on black] | [on deep yellowish green rectangular panel] HEINE-MANN | [three rules on black]'; back: blindstamped Heinemann seal.

Dust jacket: Front printed in white, orange, and black lettering on white with a gray and an orange panel: '[orange lettering] *A novel by the author of "Look Homeward | Angel" and "The Web and the Rock"* | [black lettering on a gray panel] THOMAS | WOLFE | [white lettering on an orange panel] *You Can't | Go Home | Again* | [orange lettering on white] HEINEMANN'. Spine: orange with white, orange, and black lettering on a white-edged gray rectangular panel: '[black lettering] THOMAS | WOLFE | [orange lettering] *You Can't | Go Home | Again* | [Heinemann windmill] | [white lettering] Heinemann'. Back: portrait of author and biographical material. Front flap: blurb for *YCGHA;* back flap: blurb for *TWATR* quoting J. B. Priestley's introduction.

Publication: More than 7,500 copies (see *Note one*). Published 22 September 1947. Date of contract: 11 September 1946. Advance: $250. Royalty: 10% first 2,000, 15% to 5,000, 20% thereafter. Price: 12/6.

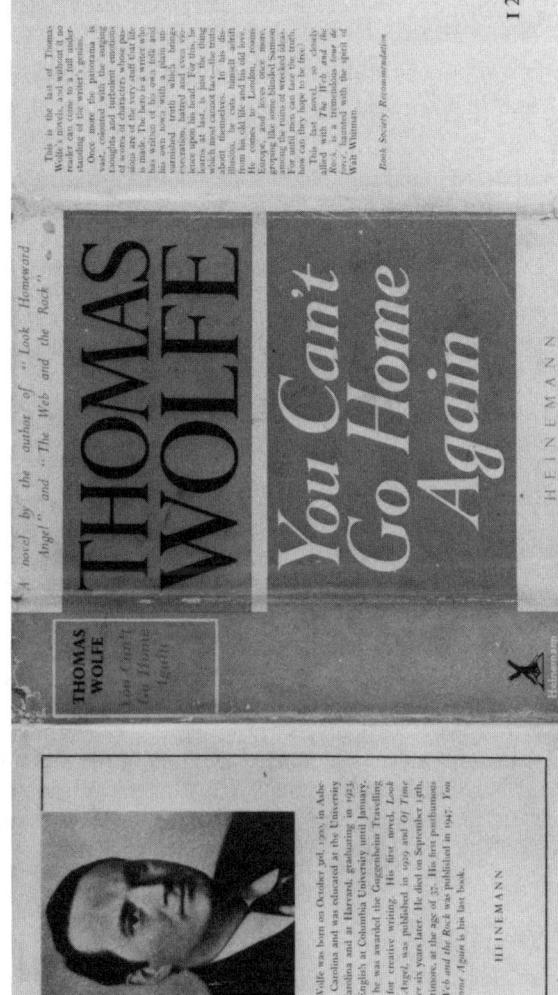

Dust jacket for A 8.2.a

Printing: See copyright page.

Locations: BL (22SEP47), BOD (10 OCT 1947), CJ, EG (3 copies with dj), InU Lilly (dj), MH, MJB (dj), NcA, NcRSM, NcU (2 copies; 1 copy with dj).

Note one: A TLS from A. S. Frere-Reeves to Edward Aswell dated 21 April 1952 reads: "I find that we sold approximately 7,500 copies of YOU CAN'T GO HOME AGAIN but only 5,500 of LOOK HOMEWARD, ANGEL" (NcU).

Note two: An undetermined number of copies of this printing, trimmed 7½" × 5", were distributed bound in medium yellowish green B cloth. Front has printed in black a circular decoration with an open book at center surrounded by the words 'EX LIBRIS'; spine stamped in black: '[two rules] | YOU CAN'T | GO HOME | AGAIN | [decorative rule] | THOMAS | WOLFE | [two rules]'. The last leaf of the final gathering has been canceled. *Location:* CJ.

LATER PRINTINGS WITHIN THE FIRST ENGLISH EDITION

A 8.2.b
London, Melbourne, Toronto, Cape Town, Auckland: Heinemann, [1968].

On copyright page: 'This edition 1968'. Price: 50/–. *Location:* BL.

LATER EDITIONS

A 8.3.a ⊕
New York: Dell, [1960].

671 pp. *Laurel Edition* #LY104. Wrappers. With an introduction by Richard Chase. Published November 1960. Price: 95¢. Dell records note four additional printings: February 1962, June 1963, October 1964, and August 1965. *Locations:* EG, JI, NcU.

A 8.4.a
New York: New American Library, [1966].

576 pp. *Signet* #Q3029. Wrappers. Published November 1966. Price: $1.50. Third printing noted. *Signet Modern Classic* #Y4136. *Locations:* APM, CJ (3rd).

A 8.4.b–f
New York, Hagerstown, San Francisco, London: Harper & Row, [1973].

Perennial Library #P314. Wrappers. Reprinted at least thirteen times. Four #P314 reprints noted: 1973, 1978, 1983, and 1985. A 1979 reprint noted with the serial number #P478. *Locations:* APM (2 copies; 1979 and 1983), CJ (2 copies; 1983 and 1985), JI (1973), MJB (1978), NcRSM (3 copies; 1 copy 1973 and 2 copies 1979), NcU (2 copies 1978).

A 8.5.a–b
Harmondsworth: Penguin Books, [1970].

680 pp. *Penguin Modern Classics*. Wrappers. Price: 12/2. *On copyright page:* 'Published in Penguin Books 1970'. Reprinted in 1984. Price: £4.95. *Locations:* BOD (– 7 May 1970), CJ (1984).

A9 THE HILLS BEYOND

A9.1.a
First edition, first printing [1941]

Thomas Wolfe

THE HILLS BEYOND

With a Note on Thomas Wolfe
by Edward C. Aswell

Harper & Brothers · Publishers
New York and London

A9.1.a: 8" × 5½"

> THE HILLS BEYOND
>
> Copyright, 1935, 1936, 1937, 1939, 1941, by Maxwell
> Perkins as Executor. Printed in the United
> States of America
>
> All rights in this book are reserved.
> No part of the book may be reproduced in any
> manner whatsoever without written permission
> except in the case of brief quotations embodied
> in critical articles and reviews. For information
> address Harper & Brothers
>
> 10-1
>
> FIRST EDITION
>
> H-Q

[i–iv] v–vi [vii–viii] 1–197 [198–200] 201–348 [349–350] 351–386 [387–392]

[1–25]^8

Contents: p. i: half title; p. ii: list of books by Wolfe; p. iii: title; p. iv: copyright; pp. v–vi: contents; p. vii: half title; p. viii: blank; pp. 1–197: text, headed 'The Lost Boy'; p. 198: blank; p. 199: 'The Hills Beyond'; p. 200: blank; pp. 201–348: text, headed '*Chapter I* | THE QUICK AND THE DEAD'; p. 349: 'A Note | on | Thomas Wolfe'; p. 350: blank; pp. 351–386: text; p. 387: '*Set in Linotype Granjon* | *Format by A. W. Rushmore* | *Manufactured by the Haddon Craftsmen, Inc.* | *Published by* HARPER & BROTHERS | *New York and London*'; pp. 388–392: blank.

7 short stories, 2 essays, 1 play, 1 long story, and 'A Note on Thomas Wolfe': "The Lost Boy," "No Cure for It",* "Gentlemen of the Press",* "A Kinsman of His Blood" (see C 41), "Chickamauga," "The Return of the Prodigal",* "On Leprechauns",* "Portrait of a Literary Critic" (see C 101), "The Lion at Morning," "God's Lonely Man" (see C 121 and D 4), "The Hills Beyond"* (see also C 56 and C 123), "A Note on Thomas Wolfe... by Edward C. Aswell".*

Typography and paper: 6¼" (6⁷⁄₁₆") × 4⅛"; 32 lines per page (pp. 1–348); 35 lines per page (pp. 351–386). Running heads: rectos, story titles; versos, 'THE HILLS BEYOND'. Wove paper.

Binding: Deep blue V cloth. Front goldstamped with two dark green rectangular panels which are edged, top and bottom only, with gilt: '[two rules] | [on gilt-edged dark green rectangular panel] | THE HILLS BEYOND | [two rules on deep blue] | [on gilt-edged deep green rectangular panel] THOMAS WOLFE | [two rules on deep blue]'; spine: goldstamped with three dark green rectangular panels which are edged, top and bottom only, with gilt: '[three rules] | [on gilt-edged dark green rectangular panel] THE HILLS | BEYOND | [seven rules on deep blue] | [on gilt-edged dark green rectangular panel] THOMAS WOLFE | [nineteen rules on deep blue] | [on gilt-edged dark green rectangular panel] HARPER | [three rules on deep blue]'. White wove endpapers. Top and bottom edges trimmed; fore edges rough trimmed.

Dust jacket: Front printed in vivid yellow and white on black: '[vivid yellow lettering] The First Appearance in Book Form of | Some of Thomas Wolfe's Best Fiction | [white lettering] Thomas Wolfe | [unevenly framed view of a small town by the side of a river] | [ornamental vivid yellow lettering] The | Hills Beyond | [white roman lettering] HARPER & BROTHERS [bullet] ES-TABLISHED 1817'. Spine printed in vivid yellow and white on black: '[ornamental vivid yellow lettering] The | Hills | Beyond | [white roman lettering] Thomas | Wolfe | HARPER'. Back: portrait of author and quotes from reviews by J. Donald Adams, Henry Seidel Canby, Stephen Vincent Benet, Clifton Fadiman, Burton Rascoe, William Allen White, and from reviews appearing in the *New York Herald Tribune Books,* the *New York Post,* the *Atlanta Journal,* and the *Cleveland News.* Front flap: blurb for *THB.* Back flap: biographical material.

Publication: 15,997 copies. Copyright #A159657. Published 15 October 1941. Date of contract: 15 July 1941. Royalty: 15%. Price: $2.50.

Printing: See contents.

Locations: BL (13NOV41), CJ, DLC (rebound and stamped 'OCT 11 19[41]'), EG (2 copies with dj), InU Lilly (dj), MH, MJB (dj), NcA (3 copies; 2 copies with dj), NcRSM (2 copies; 1 copy with dj), NcU (2 copies), PSt (dj).

Note one: Two presentation copies bound in red V cloth and stamped in gilt each with a printed leaf tipped in between pp. i and ii observed at NcA and NcU. NcU copy reads: 'This first copy | of the first edition of | THE HILLS BEYOND | has been specially bound for presentation to | MRS. JULIA E. WOLFE | with the compliments of | HARPER & BROTHERS'; NcA copy reads: 'This second copy | of the first edition of | THE HILLS BEYOND | has been specially bound | for presentation to | MABEL WOLFE WHEATON | with the compliments of | HARPER & BROTHERS'.

Note two: Both NcA and NcU presentation copies are inscribed by Edward C. Aswell and dated 29 September 1941.

Salesman's dummy: includes synopsis and table of contents for and an excerpt from *THB.*

Title page: 'Thomas Wolfe | [swelled rule] | THE HILLS | BEYOND | [swelled rule] | [Harper seal] | Harper & Brothers [bullet] Publishers | *New York and London*'.

Copyright page: '[within single-rules frame] Crown 8vo. Rough | Price about [38 ellipses] | To be published about [29 ellipses] | HARPER & BROTHERS, NEW YORK | Established 1817'.

A–B [i–iv] v–vi 1–4 [5–8]

[1]^8

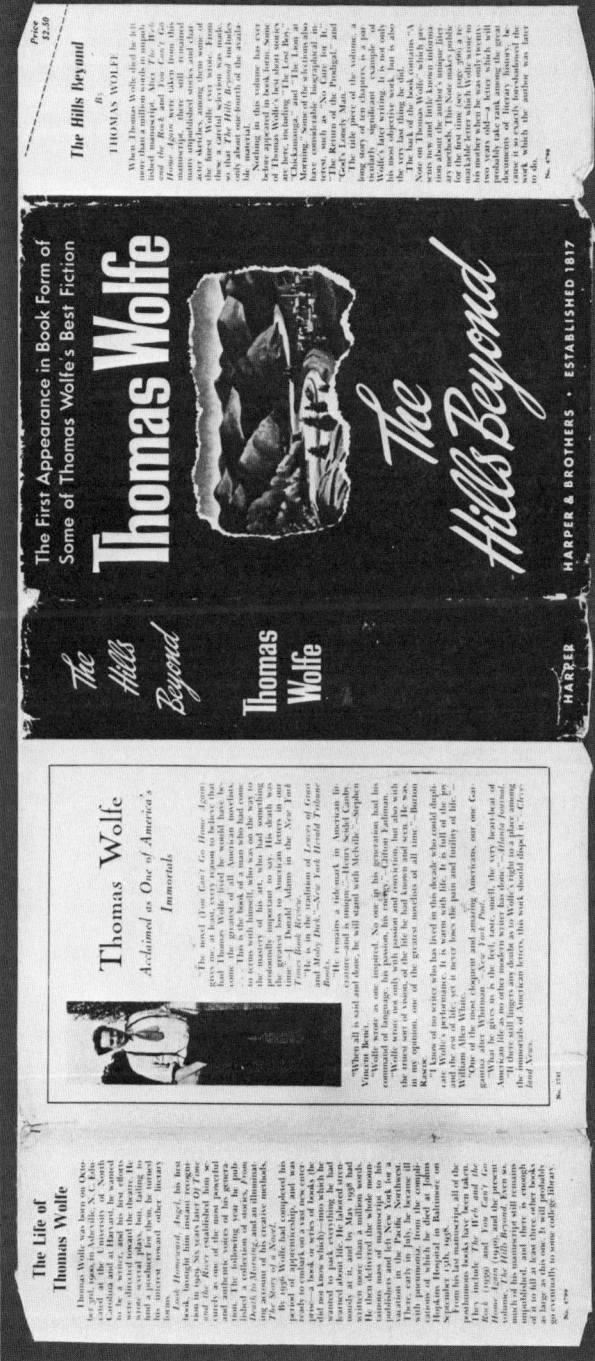

Dust jacket for A9.1.a

A9.1.b *The Hills Beyond*

Contents; pp. A–B: blank; p. i: title; p. ii: copyright; pp. iii–iv: text, headed: 'THE HILLS BEYOND | *BY* THOMAS WOLFE | *SYNOPSIS*'; pp. v–vi: contents; pp. 1–4: text, headed '*Chapter 8*'; pp. 5–8: blank.

Typography and paper: 6¼" (6½") × 4⅛"; 32 lines per page. Running heads: rectos and versos, 'THE HILLS BEYOND'. White wove paper.

Binding: Dark blue V cloth: front goldstamped with two green rectangular panels edged, top and bottom only, with gilt: '[two rules] | [on gilt-edged green rectangular panel] THE HILLS BEYOND | [two rules on blue] | [on gilt-edged green rectangular panel] THOMAS WOLFE | [two rules on blue]'; back: goldstamped with two rectangular green panels edged, top and bottom only, with gilt: '[three rules] | [on gilt-edged green rectangular panel] THE HILLS | BEYOND | [seven rules on blue] | [on gilt-edged green rectangular panel] THOMAS WOLFE | [nineteen rules on blue] | [on gilt-edged green rectangular panel] HARPER | [three rules on blue]'. All edges trimmed.

Dust jacket: Front: black with white and yellow lettering: '[yellow lettering] The First Appearance in Book Form of | Some of Thomas Wolfe's Best Fiction | [white lettering] Thomas Wolfe | [unevenly framed view of a small town] | [ornamental yellow lettering] The | Hills Beyond | [white lettering] HARPER & BROTHERS [bullet] ESTABLISHED 1817'. Back: black with white and yellow lettering: '[ornamental yellow lettering] The | HILLS | BEYOND | [white roman lettering] Thomas | Wolfe | Harper'.

Publication: Number of copies not determined. Date of publication not determined. Not for sale.

Printing: Printed by Haddon Craftsmen, Inc., Camden, New Jersey.

Locations: MH, NcU.

A9.1.b
Second printing

New York: Harper & Brothers, [1941].

On copyright page: 'SECOND EDITION | L–Q'. Published November 1941. *Location:* ScU (rebound).

LATER PRINTINGS WITHIN THE FIRST EDITION

A9.1.c
Garden City, New York: The Sun Dial Press, [1943].

At least two printings with variant copyright pages: '1943 | THE SUN DIAL PRESS' and 'SUN DIAL PRESS Reprint Edition, 1943'. Locations: CJ, MH, NcU, ScU.

A9.2 *The Hills Beyond*

A9.1.d
New York and London: Harper & Brothers, [1944].

On copyright page: 'THIRD EDITION | G–T'. Published July 1944. Price: $2.50. *Location:* ViU.

A9.1.e
New York and London: Harper & Brothers, [1950].

On copyright page: 'L–Z'. Published November 1950. *Location:* PSt.

A9.1.f
Garden City, New York: Garden City Books, [1953?]

On copyright page: 'CL'. *Location:* ViU.

A9.1.g
New York and London: Harper & Brothers, [1956].

On copyright page: 'K–F'. Published October 1956. *Location:* NcRSM.

A9.1.h
New York and London: Harper & Brothers, [1959].

On copyright page: 'D–I'. Published April 1959. *Locations:* APM, JI, ScU.

A9.1.i
New York, Evanston, and London: Harper & Row, [1964].

On copyright page: 'A-O'. Published January 1964. *Locations:* PSt, ViU.

A9.1.j
New York, Evanston, and London: Harper & Row, [1970].

On copyright page: 'D–U'. Published April 1970. *Location:* ViU.

A9.1.k
New York, Evanston, and London: Harper & Row, [1974].

Colophon: '74 75 76 77 78 20 19 18 17 16 15 14 13 12 11'. *Locations:* CJ, ScCleU.

LATER EDITIONS

A9.2
New York: Avon Books, [1944].

227 pp. *New Avon Library* #57. Wrappers. Contains only "The Hills Beyond," "On Leprechauns," "Portrait of A Literary Critic," "God's Lonely Man," and "A Note on Thomas Wolfe . . . by Edward C. Aswell." Price: 25¢.

Locations: APM, DLC (MAR 15 1945), EG, MH, NcA (2 copies), NcRSM, NcU.

A 9.3.a
New York: Lion Books, [1955].

288 pp. *Lion Library Edition* #LL 19. Wrappers. *On copyright page:* 'published March 1955'. Price: 35¢. *Locations:* EG, MH, MJB, NcU.

A 9.3.b–c
New York: Pyramid Books, [1958].

Pyramid Books Edition #R321. Published 1958. Reprinted in December 1961 as Pyramid #X-676. *Locations:* JI (1961), MH, NcA (1958), NcU (1958 and 1961).

A 9.4
New York, Evanston, and London: Harper & Row, [1964].

181 pp. *Perennial Library Edition* #P20. Wrappers. Contains only "The Hills Beyond." *On copyright page:* 'M–O'. Published December 1964. Price: 60¢. *Locations:* NcA, NcRSM, NcU.

A 9.5
THOMAS WOLFE / [decoration] The Lost Boy / With a Note on Thomas Wolfe / by EDWARD C. ASWELL / [Perennial seal] / PERENNIAL LIBRARY / Harper & Row, Publishers / NEW YORK AND EVANSTON

247 pp. *Perennial Library Edition* #P32. Wrappers. Contains only "The Lost Boy," "No Cure for It," "Gentlemen of the Press," "A Kinsman of His Blood," "Chickamauga," "The Return of the Prodigal," "On Leprechauns," "Portrait of a Literary Critic," "The Lion at Morning," "God's Lonely Man," and "A Note on Thomas Wolfe." *On copyright page:* 'C–P'. Published March 1965. Price: 75¢. *Locations:* JI, MJB, NcU (2 copies).

A 9.6.a
New York and Toronto: New American Library, [1968].

304 pp. *Signet Classic* #CQ435. Wrappers. *On copyright page:* 'First Signet Printing, November, 1968'. Price: 95¢; $1.50. Third printing labeled #CW925 also noted. *Locations:* APM, JI, NcA, NcRSM (third printing #CW925), NcU.

A 9.6.b
New York and Scarborough, Ontario: New American Library, [1982].

A PLUME BOOK #Z5697. Wrappers. With a note on Thomas Wolfe by Edward C. Aswell. *On copyright page:* 'First Plume Printing, June, 1982'. Price: $6.95. Second printing noted. *Locations:* APM, CJ (2 copies: 1st printing and 2d printing).

A 10 GENTLEMEN OF THE PRESS

A 10
Only printing [1942]

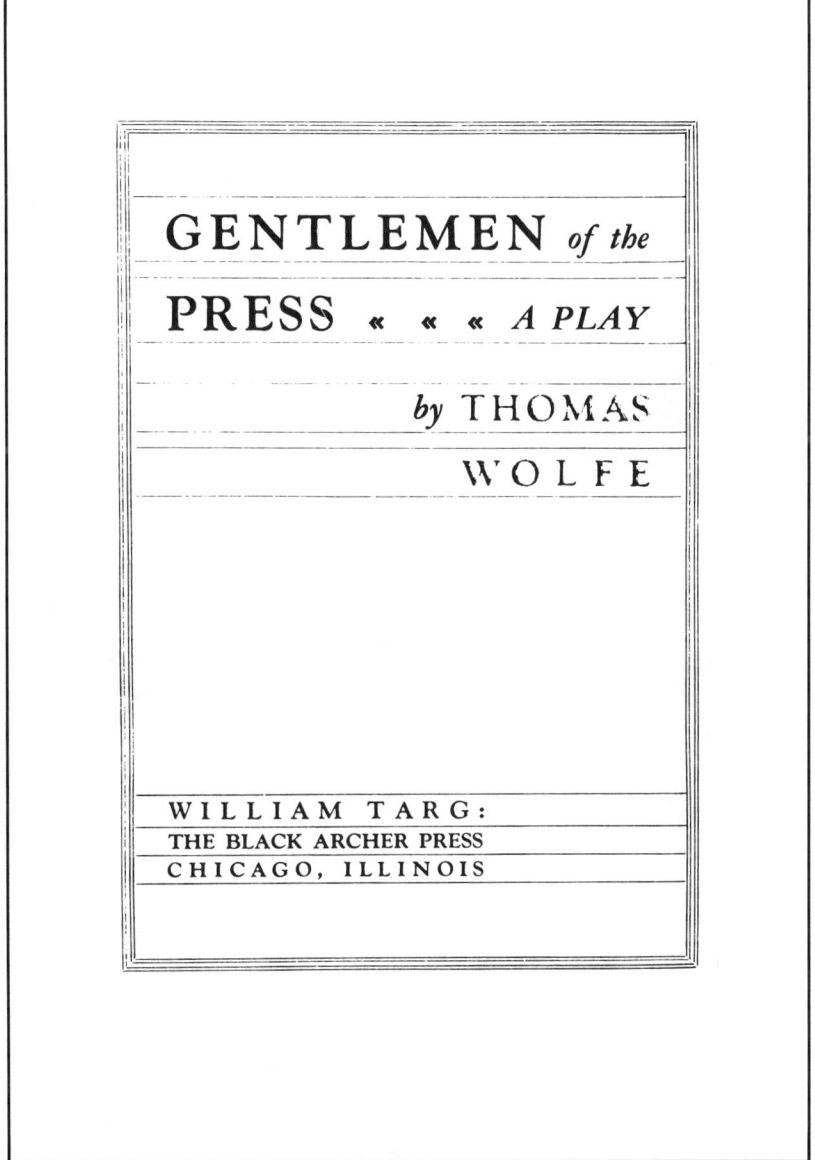

A 10: 7¾" × 5¼": 'THOMAS WOLFE' printed in orange.

> GENTLEMEN OF THE PRESS is the first separate printing of this play and is issued in a limited edition of 350 copies for subscribers
>
> *
>
> Copyright 1942 by Maxwell Perkins as executor. Printed in the United States of America by William Targ: The Black Archer Press, Chicago
>
> *
>
> 483

[1–7] 8–27 [28–32]

[1]¹⁶

Contents: p. 1: half title; p. 2: list of books by Wolfe; p. 3: title; p. 4: copyright; p. 5: half title; p. 6: blank; pp. 7–27: text, headed 'GENTLEMEN OF THE PRESS'; pp. 28–32: blank.

Typography: 5⅞″ (6¼″)×4″; 30 lines per page. Laid paper.

Binding: Deep yellowish green V cloth with 2⅝″×7¼″ rectangular deep yellow paper pasted over cloth 3⅜″ onto front over spine and 3⅜″ onto back. Front printed in black on paste-down paper: '[rule] / GENTLEMEN / [two rules] / OF THE PRESS / [two rules] / *by* / THOMAS WOLFE / [two rules] / THE BLACK ARCHER PRESS / [rule]'; spine printed in black vertically from bottom to top on paste-down paper: 'THOMAS WOLFE'; back: printed on paste-down paper same as front. Light green wove endpapers. All edges trimmed.

Publication: 350 copies. Published 19 January 1942. Date of contract: 26 November 1941. Payment: $50.00 paid by William Targ to Maxwell Perkins as Wolfe's literary executor 'for the right to make this limited edition' (ViU). Price: $1.00.

Printing: Possibly bound by Stewart's Bindery, Chicago, Illinois.

Locations: APM, BL (30JUN62), DLC, InU Lilly, NcA (2 copies), NcRSM, NcU, ViU.

Note one: First published in *THB*. See A 9, A 29, and AA 2.

Note two: Corrected page proofs dated 12 December 1941 and folded sheets dated 29 December 1941 noted (ViU).

Note three: The inscription in the ViU copy reads: "This is copy *number One* to be issued from the Black Archer Press."

Binding for A 10

A II.1.a
Only edition, first printing (1943)

Thomas Wolfe's
LETTERS TO HIS MOTHER
Julia Elizabeth Wolfe

―――

EDITED WITH AN INTRODUCTION
BY
JOHN SKALLY TERRY

Department of English
Washington Square College
New York University

NEW YORK
CHARLES SCRIBNER'S SONS
1943

A II.1.a: 8¼" × 5⅝"

> COPYRIGHT, 1943, BY
> CHARLES SCRIBNER'S SONS
>
> Printed in the United States of America
>
> *All rights reserved. No part of this book may be reproduced in any form without the permission of Charles Scribner's Sons*
>
> A

[i–vi] vii–xxxv [xxxvi] 1–358 [359–360] 361–368; coated leaf with portrait of Julia Elizabeth Wolfe on verso tipped in after p. ii.

$[1-12]^{16} [13]^{10}$

Contents: p. i: blank; p. ii: list of books by Wolfe; p. iii: half title; p. iv: blank; p. v: title; p. vi: copyright; pp. vii–xxxv: text, headed '[ornamental lettering] Introduction: / [roman] BY JOHN SKALLY TERRY'; p. xxvi: blank; pp. 1–358: text, headed '[ornamental lettering] Thomas Wolfe's Letters / to His Mother'; p. 359: '[ornamental lettering] Index'; p. 360: blank; pp. 361–368: index.

Typography and paper: 6¼" (6½")×4"; 32 lines per page. Running heads: rectos and versos, 'THOMAS WOLFE'S LETTERS TO HIS MOTHER'. Wove paper.

Binding: Black V cloth. Front goldstamped: [two rules] / THOMAS WOLFE'S LETTERS / [two rules] / TO HIS MOTHER / [two rules]'; spine: goldstamped: '[three rules] THOMAS / WOLFE'S / LETTERS / TO HIS / MOTHER / [six rules] / [thirteen blindstamped rules] / [two rules] / SCRIBNERS / [three rules]'. Endpapers are coated with facsimile of a manuscript letter. Top and bottom edges trimmed; fore edges rough trimmed.

Dust jacket: Front printed in white ornamental lettering on soft blue with a 2½"-wide rectangular black panel extending along the length of the spine and, in the upper right hand corner, a white-edged portrait of Wolfe decorated at the sides with vertical white ornamental rules: 'Thomas Wolfe's | LETTERS | to his | MOTHER'. Spine printed in white ornamental and black roman lettering on soft blue: '[white ornamental lettering] Thomas | Wolfe's | Letters | to his | Mother | [black decoration] | [black roman lettering] Scribners'. Back: blurb for *FOAN* quoting from reviews appearing in the *Saturday Review of Literature* and the *Chicago Tribune* and from a review

Dust jacket for A11.1.a

A 11.1.g *Thomas Wolfe's Letters to His Mother* 111

by Benjamin De Casseres. Front flap: blurb for *TWLTHM;* back flap: blurb for *SOAN* quoting reviews appearing in the *New York Herald Tribune* and the *New York Times.*

Publication: 5,015 copies. Copyright #AA174379. Published 3 May 1943. Date of contract: 3 April 1943. Royalty: 15% (3% to Estate, 6¾% to Julia E. Wolfe, 5¼% to John Terry). Price: $3.00.

Printing: Composed, printed, and bound by Scribner Press, New York City.

Locations: DLC (2 copies; both stamped 'APR 28 1943'), EG (dj), MH (3 copies), MJB (dj), NcA, NcRSM (2 copies with dj), NcU (2 copies), PSt (dj), RPB (2 copies), ScCleU, ViU (2 copies; 1 copy with dj).

Note one: The inscription to Effie Gambrell in the EG copy is dated 1 May 1943.

LATER PRINTINGS

A 11.1.b
New York: Scribners, 1943.

'A' omitted on copyright page. *Locations:* NcRSM, ScCleU, ViU (dj).

A 11.1.c
New York: Scribners, 1944.

Location: ViU.

A 11.1.d
New York: Scribners, 1945.

Location: NcU.

A 11.1.e
New York: Scribners, 1946.

Locations: AU, ViU.

A 11.1.f
New York: Scribners, 1948.

Location: NcD.

A 11.1.g
New York: Scribners, 1951.

Locations: EG, NjMD.

A 11.1.h
New York: Scribners, [1958].

On copyright page: 'H-3.58[MH]'. Published March 1958. *Locations:* APM, BL, NcRSM.

A 11.1.i
New York: Scribners, [1962].

On copyright page: 'I–11.62[MH]'. Published November 1962. *Locations:* JI, NcU (2 copies), ScCleU.

A 12
Only printing [1968]

> *THE LETTERS OF*
> *THOMAS WOLFE*
> *TO HIS MOTHER*
>
>
> *Newly edited from the original manuscripts*
>
>
> *by* C. HUGH HOLMAN
> *and* SUE FIELDS ROSS

A 12: 9" × 6"

> Copyright 1943 by Charles Scribner's Sons
> New edition by arrangement with Charles Scribner's Sons
> Copyright © 1968 by
> The University of North Carolina Press
> Manufactured in the United States of America
> Library of Congress Catalog Card Number: 68–14361
> Printed by Kingsport Press, Inc., Kingsport, Tennessee

[i–ix] x–xiv [xv] xvi–xxii [xxiii] xxiv–xxviii [xxix] xxx–xxxi [xxxii] [1–3] 4–296 [297–300] 301–306 [307] 308–309 [310–311] 312–320; wove leaf with portrait of Wolfe and his mother on verso inserted as frontispiece after p. ii.

[1–11]^{16}

Contents: p. i: half title; p. ii: 'The University of | North Carolina Press | Chapel Hill, 1968'; p. iii: title; p. iv: copyright; p. v: dedication 'To MRS. C. REID ROSS | Mother to Sue and | tireless worker on this book'; p. vi: blank; p. vii: contents; p. viii: blank; pp. ix–xiv: introduction; pp. xv–xxii: text, headed '[decoration] CALENDAR OF WOLFE'S | LETTERS TO HIS MOTHER'; pp. xxiii–xxviii: text, headed '[decoration] CHRONOLOGY OF THOMAS | WOLFE'S LIFE'; pp. xxix–xxxi: text, headed '[decoration] MEMBERS OF THOMAS | WOLFE'S FAMILY'; p. xxxii: blank; p. 1: half title; p. 2: blank; pp. 3–296: text, beginning '*1. 19 June 1909, Letter*'; p. 297: '[decoration] APPENDICES'; p. 298: blank; p. 299: text, headed '*APPENDIX A*'; pp. 300–309: text, headed '*APPENDIX B*'; p. 310: blank; pp. 311–320: text, headed 'INDEX'.

Typography and paper: 7″ (7¼″) × 4⅛″; 42 lines per page. Running heads: rectos: '*The Letters of Thomas Wolfe to His Mother* [followed by the italicized year of the last letter on the page]'; versos: '*The Letters of Thomas Wolfe to His Mother* [followed by the italicized year of the first letter on the page]'. Wove paper.

Binding: Light grayish blue V cloth. Spine goldstamped vertically in two lines: '[in two lines] *Wolfe* | *Holman-Ross* [in two lines] [decoration] *The Letters of* THOMAS WOLFE | *to His Mother* [in two lines] *Chapel Hill* | [decoration]'. Medium grayish blue endpapers. All edges trimmed. Blue and white headbands and footbands.

Dust jacket: Front printed on soft grayish blue: '[white lettering on a photograph of a stack of envelopes being opened] THE LETTERS OF | THOMAS WOLFE | TO HIS MOTHER | [black lettering on soft grayish blue] *Newly Edited from the Original Manuscripts* | [white lettering] *by* C. Hugh Holman and Sue Fields Ross'. Spine printed horizontally and vertically on soft grayish blue: '[horizontal black lettering] *Wolfe* | [rule] | *Holman-Ross* | [vertically in white lettering] *The Letters of* THOMAS WOLFE *to His Mother* [horizontally in black lettering] *Chapel Hill*'. Back: blurb for *The Window of Memory*. Front and back flaps: blurb for *TLOTWTHM*.

Dust jacket for A 12

Publication: 2,544 copies. Published c. June 1968. Price $14.95.
Printing: Printed by Kingsport Press, Inc., Kingsport, Tennessee.
Locations: CJ(dj), MH.

A 13.1.a *Mannerhouse: A Play in a Prologue and Three Acts* 117

A 13 MANNERHOUSE: A PLAY IN A PROLOGUE AND THREE ACTS

Two printings published simultaneously (1948)

A 13.1.a
Trade printing

MANNERHOUSE

A Play

in a Prologue and Three Acts

by

Thomas Wolfe

NEW YORK
HARPER & BROTHERS PUBLISHERS
1948

A 13.1.a: Trade printing: 8″ × 5½″; ornamental decoration, Harper seal, and date printed in medium orange.

A 13.1.a *Mannerhouse: A Play in a Prologue and Three Acts*

> 11-8
>
> COPYRIGHT, 1946, BY MAXWELL E. PERKINS AS EXECUTOR (OF THE ESTATE OF THOMAS WOLFE). COPYRIGHT, 1948, BY EDWARD C. ASWELL, ADMINISTRATOR C.T.A. (OF THE ESTATE OF THOMAS WOLFE) PRINTED IN THE UNITED STATES OF AMERICA. ALL RIGHTS IN THIS BOOK ARE RESERVED.
>
> CAUTION! Professionals and Amateurs are hereby warned that all rights, including professional, amateur, motion picture, recitation, lecturing, public reading, radio broadcasting and the right of translation into foreign languages, are strictly reserved. Particular emphasis is laid on the question of readings, permission for which must be secured from the Administrator in writing. All inquiries should be addressed to Edward C. Aswell, Administrator C.T.A. (of the Estate of Thomas Wolfe), 330 West 42 Street, New York 17, New York.
>
> FIRST EDITION
>
> K-X

[i–vi] 1–17 [18] 19–83 [84] 85 [86] 87–139 [140] 141–165 [166] 167–183 [184–186]

[1–6]^{16}

Contents: p. i: half title; p. ii: list of books by Wolfe; p. iii: title; p. iv: copyright; p. v: half title; p. vi: list of persons in the prologue and persons in the play; pp. 1–17: text, headed 'Prologue'; p. 18: blank; pp. 19–83: text, headed 'Act One'; p. 84: blank; p. 85: text, headed 'Interlude'; p. 86: blank; pp. 87–139: text, headed 'Act Two | Part One'; p. 140: blank; pp. 141–165: text, headed 'Act Two | Part Two'; p. 166: blank; pp. 167–183: text, headed 'Act Three'; p. 184: blank; p. 185: 'Set in Linotype Janson | Format by A. W. Rushmore | Manufactured by The Haddon Craftsmen | Published by HARPER & BROTHERS, *New York*'; p. 186: blank.

Typography and paper: 5⅜″ (6″) × 3⅝″; 26 lines per page. Running heads: rectos, act numbers; versos, 'MANNERHOUSE'. Wove paper.

Binding: Dark blue V cloth. Front has blindstamped Harper & Brothers seal; spine goldstamped: '[three rules] | Manner- | house | *by* | Thomas Wolfe | [three rules] | HARPER'. White wove endpapers. Top and bottom edges trimmed; fore edges rough trimmed.

Dust jacket: Front: white and dark grayish green lettering on deep orange, dark grayish green, and white rectangular panels: '[white ornamental lettering on a deep orange rectangular panel] Thomas Wolfe | [white ornamental rule on dark grayish green rectangular panel] | [dark grayish green ornamen-

A 13.1.b *Mannerhouse: A Play in a Prologue and Three Acts* 119

tal lettering on a white rectangular panel] Mannerhouse | [dark grayish green ornamental lettering on a deep orange rectangular panel] A Play in a Prologue and Three Acts | [white ornamental rule on a dark grayish green rectangular panel] | [white lettering on a deep orange rectangular panel] "Wolfe wrote as one inspired. No one in his | generation had his command of language, his pas- | sion, his energy." — *Clifton Fadiman* | "He remains a tidemark in American literature | —and is unique." —*Henry Seidel Canby* | [dark grayish green lettering] HARPER & BROTHERS ESTABLISHED 1817 | [dark grayish green rectangular panel]'. Spine: dark grayish green with white ornamental lettering arranged vertically with a deep orange rectangular panel edged at top and bottom with white ornamental rules: 'Thomas Wolfe [on deep orange rectangular panel edged top and bottom with white ornamental rules] MANNERHOUSE [on dark grayish green] HARPER'. Back: portrait of the author. Front flap: blurb for *Mannerhouse*. Back flap: biographical material.

Publication: Approximately 3,000 copies. Copyright #DP17701. Published c. 24 November 1948. Price: $3.00.

Printing: See contents.

Locations: DLC (penciled: 'November 28 1948'), MH, MJB, NcA (dj), NcRSM (2 copies with dj), NcU (2 copies).

Note one: A memo in the Wisdom collection from JF to Miss Elizabeth Lawrence dated 29 July 1948 indicates that Harpers intended the first printing to be "approximately 3,000."

Note two: Copy-text for this edition is the 1948 prompt copy prepared by Franklin Heller. See A 14 *Note one*.

Note three: See B 30.

A 13.1.b
Limited printing

Title page and copyright page are identical to A 13.1.a, except for size: 8⅝" × 5⅝".

[i–iv] [A–P] [v–vi] 1–17 [18] 19–83 [84] 85 [86] 87–139 [140] 141–165 [166] 167–183 [184–186]; coated leaf with portrait of Wolfe on verso inserted after p. iv as frontispiece; [A–P] inserted.

[1]⁴ [2]⁴ [3–13]⁸; 8-leaf facsimile inserted between 1₂ and 1₃.

Contents: p. i: 'Of the first edition of *Mannerhouse* 500 numbered copies, | with a portrait of Thomas Wolfe and a twelve page fac- | simile of a holograph letter by him, have been specially | printed and bound. | This copy is number'; p. ii: list of books by Wolfe; p. iii: title; p. iv: copyright; p. A: 'THE LETTER which follows, reproduced in facsimile, | is Thomas Wolfe's comment on his play, *Mannerhouse*, | addressed to Miss Lewisohn of the Neighborhood | Playhouse in New York. Both letter and play were | probably written in 1926, or three years before the | publication of *Look Homeward, Angel*. The

Dust jacket for trade printing for A 13.1.a

A13.1.b *Mannerhouse: A Play in a Prologue and Three Acts*   121

letter, | never before published, is here reproduced through | the courtesy of the Harvard College Library, which | has the original in its Thomas Wolfe Collection. | Permission for its use was also granted by the Ad- | ministrator of the Estate of Thomas Wolfe.'; p. B: blank; pp. C–N: twelve-page facsimile of holograph letter from Wolfe to Miss Lewisohn; pp. O–P: two-page transcription of that letter; p. v: half title; p. vi: list of persons in the prologue and persons in the play; pp. 1–17: text, headed 'Prologue'; p. 18: blank; pp. 19–83: text, headed 'Act One'; p. 84: blank; p. 85: text, headed 'Interlude'; p. 86: blank; pp. 87–139: text, headed 'Act Two | Part One'; p. 140: blank; pp. 141–165: text, headed 'Act Two | Part Two'; p. 166: blank; pp. 167–183: text, headed 'Act Three'; p. 184: blank; p. 185: '*Set in Linotype Janson | Format by A. W. Rushmore | Manufactured by The Haddon Craftsmen | Published by* HARPER & BROTHERS, *New York*'; p. 186: blank.

Typography and paper: Printed on a heavier paper stock than the trade edition.

Binding: Black V cloth. Spine printed in dark blue on 2½" × 1" rectangular light grayish blue paste-down paper: '[three rules] | Manner- | house | by | Thomas | Wolfe | [rule] | HARPER | [three rules]'. White wove endpapers. Top and bottom trimmed; fore edges rough trimmed.

Dust jacket: Light grayish blue. Front printed in dark blue: '[three rules] | Mannerhouse | A Play in a | Prologue and Three Acts | by | Thomas Wolfe | [three rules] | Thomas Wolfe said of Mannerhouse: "*It became the mold for an | expression of my secret life, of my own dark faith. . . . If you would | know what that faith is, distilled, my play tries to express my passion- | ate belief in all myth, in the necessity of defending and living not for | truth— but for divine falsehood.*" | It is believed that Mannerhouse *was written in 1926, or three years | before the publication of* Look Homeward Angel. *One of three plays | Thomas Wolfe wrote, it is significant to his development as an artist | because—unlike his novels—it is not autobiographical. This edition, | limited to 500 copies, contains a rare portrait of Thomas Wolfe and a | twelve-page facsimile of a holograph letter by him, never before published, | in which he discusses the play's purpose and meaning.*' Spine printed in dark blue: '[three rules] | Manner | house | by | Thomas | Wolfe | [rule] | HARPER | [four rules] | *Limited Edition | Copy No.* | [rule]'. Front flap: price.

Slipcase: Black coated paper-covered boards with light grayish blue paper pasted over covering all but top and bottom and ¼" at the top and bottom of front, back, and spine. Front printed in black on light grayish blue paste-down paper within an ornamental frame: 'Mannerhouse | A Play in a | Prologue and Three Acts | by | Thomas Wolfe | [rule] | *LIMITED EDITION* | [rule] | HARPER & BROTHERS, *Publishers* | Established 1817'.

Publication: Simultaneous publication. 500 copies. Copyright #DP17701. Published c. 24 November 1948. Price: $5.00.

Locations: APM (dj and slipcase), DLC (NOV 26 1948), EG (dj and slipcase), InU Lilly (dj and slipcase), MH, NcA, NcU, ViU (dj and slipcase).

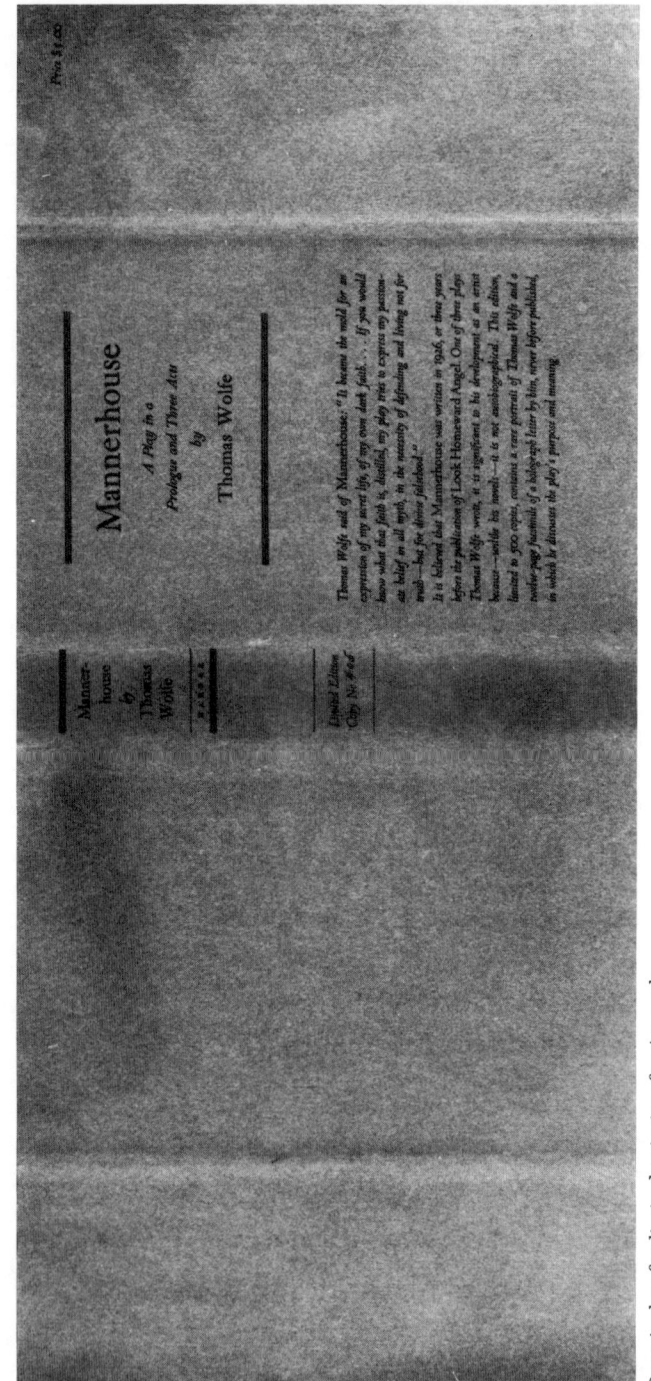

Dust jacket for limited printing for A 13.1.b

Slipcase for limited printing for A 13.1.b

A 13.1.c
Third printing

New York: Harper & Brothers, 1948.

On copyright page: 'M–X | The original manuscript of *Mannerhouse* is | part of the William B. Wisdom Collection of | Thomas Wolfe at Harvard College Library'. Published December 1948. *Locations:* APM (dj), EG, MH, MJB, NcRSM, NcU.

A 13.2.a
First English edition, only printing [1950]

MANNERHOUSE

*A Play
in a Prologue and Three Acts*

by

THOMAS WOLFE

WILLIAM HEINEMANN LTD
MELBOURNE :: LONDON :: TORONTO

A 13.2.a: 7¼" × 4¾"

> This play is fully protected by copyright. Application for performance, professional or amateur, should be addressed to Edward C. Aswell, Administrator C.T.A. (of the Estate of Thomas Wolfe), 330 West 42 Street, New York, and no performance must be given until permission is secured in writing from the Administrator.
>
> FIRST PUBLISHED 1950
>
> PRINTED IN GREAT BRITAIN
> AT THE WINDMILL PRESS
> KINGSWOOD, SURREY

[i–xx] 1–39 [40] 41 [42] 43–77 [78] 79–86 [87–88]

[A]^8 B^6 C–G^8

Contents: p. i: half title; p. ii: list of books by Wolfe; p. iii: title; p. iv: copyright; p. v: text; p. vi: blank; pp. vii–xvi: facsimile of holograph letter from Wolfe to Miss Lewisohn; pp. xvii–xviii: transcription of that letter; p. xix: half title; p. xx: lists of Persons in the Prologue and Persons in the Play; pp. 1–39: text, headed 'PROLOGUE'; p. 40: blank; p. 41: text, headed 'INTERLUDE'; p. 42: blank; pp. 43–77: text, headed 'ACT TWO | PART ONE'; p. 78: blank; pp. 79–86: text, headed 'ACT THREE'; pp. 87–88: blank.

Typography and paper: 5⅝" (6") × 3⅝"; 37 lines per page. Running heads: rectos and versos, 'MANNERHOUSE' and act number. Wove paper.

Binding: Black V cloth. Spine: silverstamped vertically '*Thomas Wolfe* [bullet] MANNERHOUSE [bullet] *Heinemann*'; back: blindstamped Heinemann seal. White wove endpapers. All edges trimmed.

Dust jacket: Medium reddish orange decorations and black lettering on a yellowish white background decorated with three medium reddish orange vertical rules: '[within ornamental medium reddish orange frame] MANNERHOUSE | *a play by* | THOMAS WOLFE | [beneath frame] WILLIAM HEINEMANN'. Spine: '[lettered vertically in black within two medium reddish orange vertical rules] MANNERHOUSE [medium reddish orange decoration] *THOMAS WOLFE* [medium reddish orange decoration] HEINEMANN'. Back: blurbs for *LHA* and *OTATR*. Front and back flaps: blurb for *Mannerhouse*.

Publication: Number of copies not determined. Published 8 August 1950. Price: 7/6.

Printing: See copyright.

Locations: BL (18JUL50), BOD (15 AUG 1950), EG (dj), MH, NcA (dj), NcU.

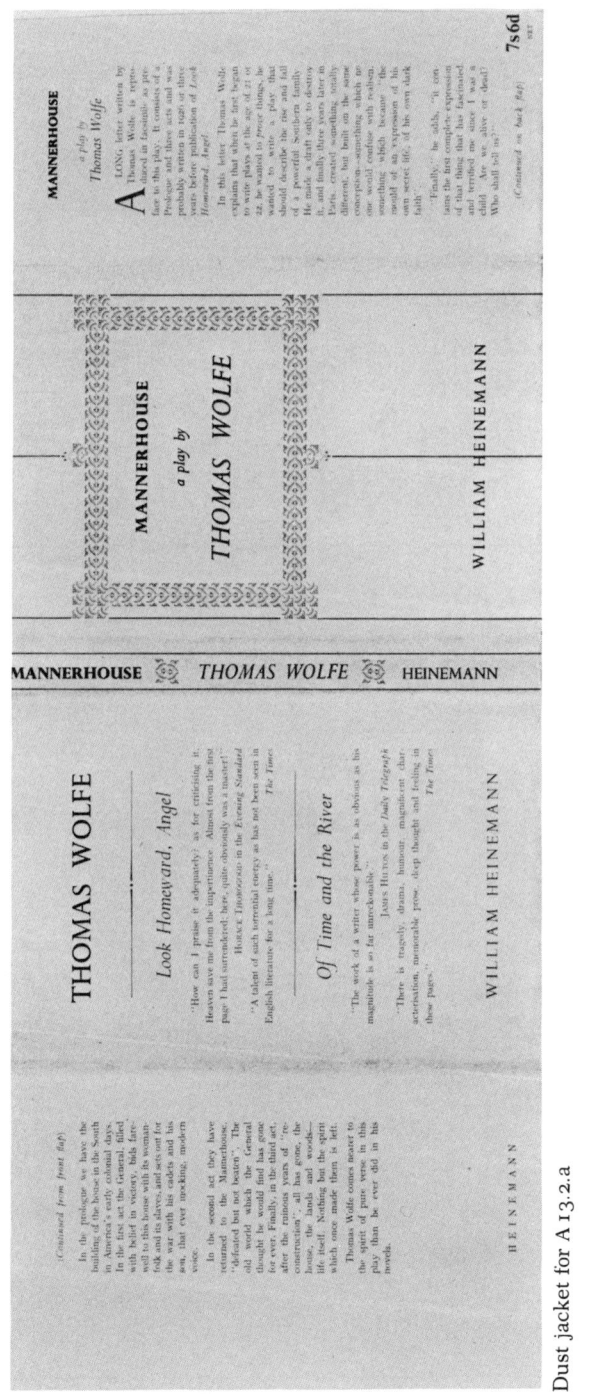

Dust jacket for A 13.2.a

A 14 MANNERHOUSE A PLAY IN A PROLOGUE AND FOUR ACTS

A 14
Only printing [1985]

MANNERHOUSE

A Play in a Prologue and Four Acts by

THOMAS WOLFE

Edited by Louis D. Rubin, Jr.

and John L. Idol, Jr.

LOUISIANA STATE UNIVERSITY PRESS

BATON ROUGE AND LONDON

A 14: 9″ × 5¾″

> Copyright © 1985 by Paul Gitlin, Administrator,
> C.T.A. of the Estate of Thomas Wolfe
> Introduction copyright © 1985 by Louis D. Rubin, Jr.
> The Text and the Background of the Play copyright © 1985
> by John L. Idol, Jr.
> All rights reserved
> Manufactured in the United States of America
> Designer: Joanna V. Hill
> Typeface: Linotron Garamond #3
> Typesetter: G & S Typesetters
> Printer: Thomson-Shore
> Binder: John Dekker
>
> LIBRARY OF CONGRESS CATALOGING IN PUBLICATION DATA
>
> Wolfe, Thomas, 1900–1938
> Mannerhouse: a play in a prologue and four acts.
> (Southern literary studies)
> 1. United States—History—Civil War, 1861–1865—
> Drama.   I. Rubin, Louis Decimus, 1923–   .   II. Idol,
> John L.   III. Title.   IV. Series.
> PS3545.O337M3   1985   812'.54   85-6814
> ISBN 0-8071-1242-9

[i–xii] [1] 2–9 [10] 11–26 [27–29] 30–39 [40–43] 44–80 [81–85] 86–115 [116–119] 120–134 [135–137] 138–147 [148]

[1–5]^{16}

Contents: p. i: '*Southern Literary, Studies* | Louis D. Rubin, Jr., Editor'; p. ii: blank; p. iii: half title; p. iv: blank; p. v: title; p. vi: copyright; p. vii: contents; p. viii: blank; p. ix: acknowledgments; p. x: blank; p. xi: half title; p. xii: blank; pp. 1–9: text, headed '[decoration] | Introduction'; pp. 10–26: text, headed '[decoration] | The Text and the Background of the Play'; p. 27: '[decoration] | [ornamental lettering] | MANNERHOUSE | [rule] | A Play in a Prologue and | Four Acts by | [rule] | THOMAS WOLFE'; p. 28 blank; pp. 29–39: text, headed '[decoration] | Prologue'; p. 40: blank; p. 41: '[decoration] | [ornamental lettering] ACT ONE | [rule]'; p. 42: blank; pp. 43–80: text, beginning '*When the curtain rises, all*'; p. 81: text, headed '[decoration] | Interlude'; p. 82: blank; p. 83: '[decoration] | [ornamental lettering] ACT TWO | [rule]'; p. 84: blank; pp. 85–115: text, beginning '*When the curtain rises the stage*'; p. 116: blank; p. 117: '[decoration] | [ornamental lettering] ACT THREE | [rule]'; p. 117: blank; pp. 118–134: text, headed '*Towards sundown of a day*'; p. 135: '[decoration] | [ornamental lettering] ACT FOUR |

[rule]'; p. 136: blank; pp. 137–147: text, beginning '*Late on a night*'; p. 148: blank.

Typography: 6¼" (6¾") × 4"; 35 lines per page. Running heads: rectos, section titles; versos, 'Mannerhouse'. Wove paper.

Binding: Medium green V cloth. Spine goldstamped vertically: 'WOLFE [decoration] MANNERHOUSE [decoration] LOUISIANA'. Blue-flecked white wove end papers. All edges trimmed. Purple and white headbands and footbands.

Dust jacket: Front printed in medium yellow, black, and white on medium green: '[medium yellow decoration, outlined in black] | [medium yellow lettering outlined in black] MANNERHOUSE | [black rule] | [black lettering] A Play in a Prologue and Four Acts by | [white lettering] THOMAS WOLFE | [black rule] | [black lettering] *Edited by Louis D. Rubin, Jr.* | *and John L. Idol, Jr.* | [medium yellow decoration outlined in black]'. Spine printed vertically and horizontally in black and medium yellow: '[vertical black lettering] *Rubin and Idol* | [medium yellow lettering outlined in black] MANNERHOUSE | [black lettering] A Play by Thomas Wolfe | [at bottom horizontally] 1935 | [LSU seal] | 1985'. Back: blurbs for *WTOC* and *TWI*. Front and back flaps: blurb for *Mannerhouse* and biographical material for Rubin and Idol.

Publication: Number of copies not determined. Copyright #R567375. Published November 1985. Price: $17.50.

Locations: CJ (dj), DLC (2 copies; 1 stamped 'JAN 27 1986' and 1 stamped 'JUN 19 1986'); JI (dj).

Note one: Copy-text for this edition is the 1925 typescript of *Mannerhouse* located in the William B. Wisdom Collection at Harvard University with revisions in Wolfe's hand. See A 13.1.a *Note two* and B 30.

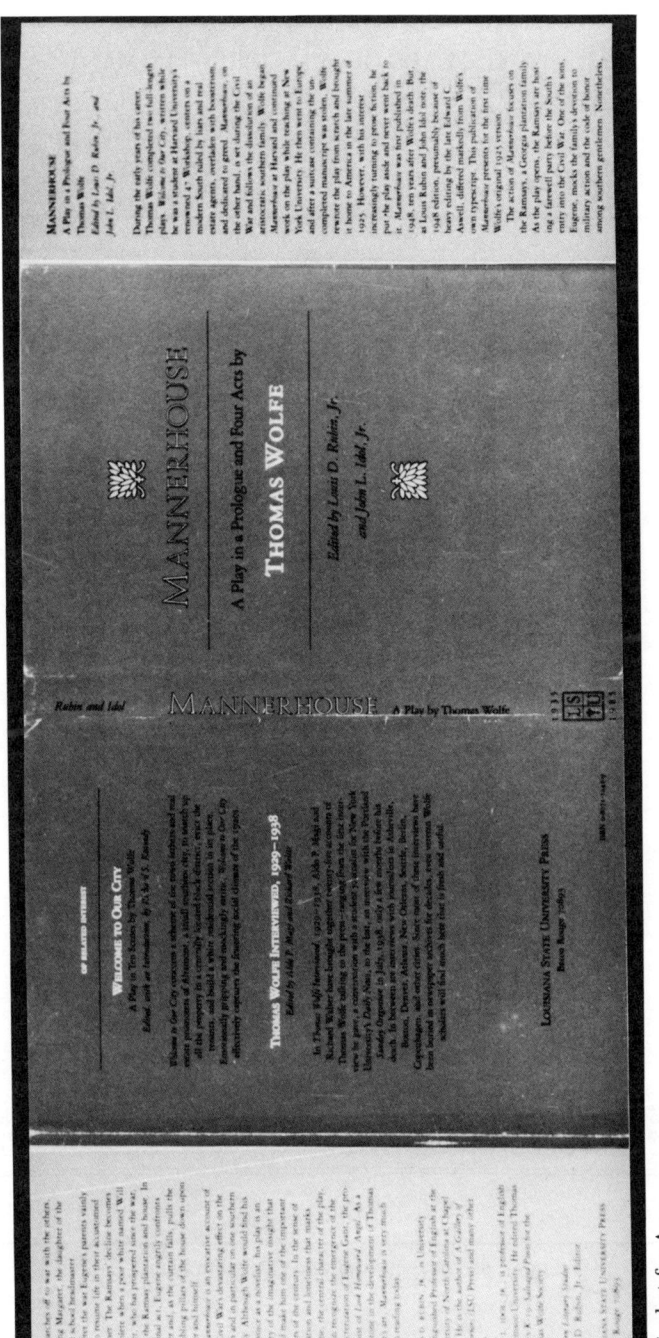

Dust jacket for A 14

A 15 . . . "THE YEARS OF WANDERING IN MANY LANDS AND CITIES"

A 15
Only printing [1949]

A 15: 12″ × 9¾″; frames, decorations, and title printed in blue.

A 15 ... *"The Years of Wandering in Many Lands and Cities"*

> Copyright, 1949, by Edward C. Aswell as Administrator, C. T. A. of the Estate of Thomas Wolfe. All rights in this book are reserved. All inquiries should be addressed to Edward C. Aswell, Administrator, C. T. A. of the Estate of Thomas Wolfe, 330 West 42nd Street, New York 18, N. Y.
>
> Quotations from *Look Homeward, Angel* and *Of Time and the River* are printed with the kind permission of Charles Scribner's Sons.
>
> THIS EDITION IS LIMITED
> TO 600 COPIES

[1–24]

[1–3]⁴

Contents: p. 1: title; p. 2: copyright; pp. 3–8: text, headed 'FOREWORD'; p. 9: '[ornamental lettering] "The Last Journey, The Longest, The Best." '; p. 10: blank; 19 manuscript facsimiles mounted on pages 11–21; pp. 22–24: blank.

Typography: 6¾" (9½") × 5"; 27 lines per page. No running heads. Wove paper.

Binding: Light gray paper printed in red and blue pasted over front and back boards with imitation dark blue leather covering the spine and extending along the spine ½" onto front and back. Front printed in blue ornamental lettering on white within a central red-edged outline of the United States superimposed on a red-edged white 'W' with, in the background, twelve rows of assorted blue trains, motorcars, ships, boats, and horse-drawn carriages alternating with thirteen sets of five red rules: '. . . "The Years of Wandering | in many lands and cities" | Thomas Wolfe'. White wove endpapers. Top and fore edges trimmed; bottom rough-trimmed.

Slipcase: Imitation dark blue leather. Front printed in blue ornamental lettering on white within a central red-edged outline of the United States superimposed on a red 'W': '. . . "The Years of Wandering | in many lands and cities" | Thomas Wolfe'.

Publication: 600 copies. Copyright #A40134. Published 15 November 1949. Price not determined.

Printing: Printed and bound by North River Press, New York City.

Locations: APM (with slipcase), BL (15 MAY 70), EG (2 copies with slipcase), InU Lilly (with slipcase), MH (with slipcase), MJB (with slipcase), NcA, NcRSM (with slipcase), NcU, ViU (with slipcase).

Binding for A 15

A 16 A WESTERN JOURNAL

A 16.1.a
First edition, first printing (1951)

A Western Journal

A Daily Log
of
The Great Parks Trip

June 20—July 2, 1938

by
THOMAS WOLFE

1951
UNIVERSITY OF PITTSBURGH PRESS

A 16.1.a: 9" × 6"

Copyright, 1951, by Edward C. Aswell,
Administrator, C.T.A. of the Estate of Thomas Wolfe

[i–iv] v–x [xi–xii] [One] Two–Forty-two [A–B] Forty-three–Seventy 71–72 [73–74]

[1–4]⁸ [5]⁴ [6]⁸

Contents: p. i: half title; p. ii: blank; p. iii: title; p. iv: copyright; pp. v–vi: text, headed 'Note on | "*A Western Journey*" | BY EDWARD C. ASWELL | (*From the Virginia Quarterly Review, Summer, 1939*)'; pp. vii–ix: text, headed 'Notes on | "*A Western Journal*" | BY THE UNIVERSITY OF PITTSBURGH PRESS'; p. x: quotations from *SOAN* and *AWJ;* p. xi: half title; p. xii: text numbered '2' in upper left-hand corner followed by facsimile of p. 3 of 'A Daily Log'; pp. One–Forty-two: text, headed '*A Daily Log* | *of* | *The Great Parks Trip*'; p. A: blank; p. B: facsimile of manuscript page 218; Forty-three–Seventy: text, headed '216'; pp. 71–72: text, headed 'Editorial Notes'; p. 73: 'Printed in U.S.A. by | The Eddy Press Corporation for | The University of Pittsburgh Press'; p. 74: blank.

Typography and paper: 6¼" (7") × 3⅜"; 27 lines per page. Running heads: rectos, 'THOMAS WOLFE'; versos, 'A WESTERN JOURNAL'. Wove paper.

Binding: Vivid red B cloth. Front goldstamped: 'A WESTERN JOURNAL | BY | [ornamental lettering] Thomas Wolfe | [decoration]'; spine goldstamped vertically 'UNIVERSITY OF PITTSBURGH PRESS [bullet] PITTSBURGH, PENNSYLVANIA'. White wove endpapers. Top and bottom trimmed; fore edges rough trimmed.

Dust jacket: Light purple and medium purple front contains drawing of a cactus tree in strong purple and drawing of the rear view of an automobile at center: '[white ornamental lettering] A | Western | Journal | [strong purple lettering] BY THOMAS WOLFE | UNIVERSITY OF PITTSBURGH PRESS'. Back: portrait of Wolfe and blurb for *AWJ*. Front and back flaps: blurbs for 'RECENT BOOKS | OF THE | UNIVERSITY OF PITTSBURGH PRESS'.

Publication: 2,500 copies. Copyright #A57276. Published July 1951. Price: $3.00.

Printing: See contents.

Locations: EG (dj), InU Lilly (dj), MH, MJB (dj), NcA, NcRSM (dj), NcU, PSt (dj).

Note one: See C 101 and C 147.

A 16.1.b
Second printing

On copyright page: 'Second Printing, August, 1951'. 2,241 copies. *Locations:* APM, MJB, NcRSM, ScCleU.

Dust jacket for A 16.1.a

A 16.1.c
Third printing

Wrappers. *On copyright page:* 'Third printing 1967'. Front matter and notes have been reset. Trim size reduced to 8" × 5½"; running heads and folios removed from tops of the pages; pages have been newly paginated. 2,988 copies published October 1967. *Locations:* APM, NcRSM.

A 16.1.d
Fourth Printing

Wrappers. *On copyright page:* 'Fourth Printing 1980'. 2,500 copies published November 1980. Same as A 16.1.c. *Location:* CJ.

A 17 THE CORRESPONDENCE OF THOMAS WOLFE AND
HOMER ANDREW WATT

Two printings published simultaneously (1954)

A 17.1.a
Limited printing

> THE CORRESPONDENCE OF
>
> THOMAS WOLFE
>
> AND
>
> HOMER ANDREW WATT
>
> EDITED BY OSCAR CARGILL
>
> AND
>
> THOMAS CLARK POLLOCK
>
> **New York University Press**
>
> WASHINGTON SQUARE · NEW YORK
>
> London: Geoffrey Cumberlege Oxford University Press
> 1954

A 17.1.a: New York University Press / Oxford University Press printing: 9¼" × 6⅛"; arch printed in grayish yellow.

All of the letters from Thomas Wolfe in this volume copyright 1954 by Edward C. Aswell, Administrator C.T.A. of the Estate of Thomas Wolfe.

All of the letters from Homer Andrew Watt and the letter from Chancellor Harry Woodburn Chase and all other materials in this volume except the aforesaid letters from Thomas Wolfe copyright 1954 by New York University.

COPYRIGHT 1954 BY NEW YORK UNIVERSITY

ALL RIGHTS RESERVED

Library of Congress catalogue card: NUMBER 54-5274

MANUFACTURED IN THE UNITED STATES OF AMERICA

THE SPIRAL PRESS · NEW YORK

[i–vi] vii–xi [xii] [1–2] 3–45 [46–48] 49–53 [54–56]; portrait of Watt inserted as frontispiece after p. ii; facsimile manuscript, "THE LAND ALWAYS WINS," inserted after p. 16.

[1]^8 [2]^{10} [3–4]^8

Contents: p. i: half title; p. ii: blank; p. iii: title; p. iv: copyright; p. v: dedication 'TO THE GOOD MEMORY OF | HOMER ANDREW WATT'; p. vi: blank; pp. vii–viii: contents; pp. ix–xi: text, headed 'INTRODUCTORY | NOTE'; p. xii: blank; p. 1: half title; p. 2: blank; pp. 3–45: text, headed: '[bullet] I [bullet]'; p. 46: blank; p. 47: 'THE WOLFE [tilde] WATT CORRESPONDENCE [bullet] SUPPLEMENT'; p. 48: blank; pp. 49–53: text, headed: '[bullet] I [bullet]'; pp. 54–56: blank.

Typography and paper: 6¾" (7") × 4¼"; 32 lines per page. No running heads. Wove paper.

Binding: Grayish reddish orange V cloth. Front stamped in black: 'THE WOLFE [tilde] WATT [on a redstamped Washington Square Monument seal] CORRESPONDENCE'; spine stamped vertically: '[black lettering] The Correspondence of Thomas Wolfe and Homer Andrew Watt [red lettering] NEW YORK UNIVERSITY PRESS'. White wove endpapers. All edges trimmed.

Slipcase: Boards covered with unprinted coated black paper. See *Note one.*

A 17.1.a *The Correspondence* 141

Dust jacket: Front light grayish yellowish brown with a very pale violet Washington Square Monument drawn in the lower right hand corner and, at bottom a 1" very pale violet rectangular panel extending on to the spine: 'The Correspondence | OF | Thomas Wolfe | AND | Homer Andrew Watt | EDITED BY | OSCAR CARGILL | AND | THOMAS CLARK POLLOCK | [on very pale violet rectangular panel] NEW YORK UNIVERSITY PRESS'. Spine is printed vertically in black on light grayish yellowish brown: 'The Correspondence of Thomas Wolfe and Homer Andrew Watt *New York University Press* [very pale violet rectangular panel]'. Back: blurbs for *Melville's Early Life and "Redburn"* and *A Bibliography of Oliver Wendell Holmes.* Flaps: biographical material for Wolfe and Watt.

Publication: Possibly 1,200 to 2,000 copies. Copyright #A124250. Published 29 January 1954. Price: see *Note one.*

Printing: Printed by the Spiral Press, New York City.

Locations: APM (dj), BL (16MAR54), CJ (dj and slipcase), DLC (Jan 11 1954), MH, MJB (dj), NcU (dj), NcWsW, ViU (3 copies; 1 copy with dj).

Note one: The copies bearing the New York University Press Geoffrey Cumberlege/Oxford University Press imprint and those bearing the New York University Press (A 17.1.b) imprint only are separate printings. Although the texts of both printings have been printed from the same setting of type, the roman numbers and tapered rules at the heads of the letters have been reset; moreover, the half title and the section title (p. 47) were also reset between printings. The fact that only the NYUP/OUP printing bears the Spiral Press imprint suggests that the two printings were produced by different printers. Joseph Blumenthal, owner of the Spiral Press, in a note to Carol Johnston dated 21 April 1985, recalls the Spiral Press printing (NYUP/OUP) to be the first printing. The NYUP printing, he suggests, may have been "offset from the first printed pages, blanking out the data not pertinent to its second printing."

This, plus the irregularity of the gatherings in the NYUP printing and the fact that the NYUP/OUP printing leaves measure 9¼" × 6⅛" while the NYUP leaves measure 8⅞" × 5¹⁵⁄₁₆" strongly indicates that the NYUP/OUP printing preceded the NYUP printing. The weekly list of publications in *Publishers' Weekly,* in addition to the copyright records and deposit copy stamping at the library of Congress, however, suggests simultaneous publication.

The *PW* list of publications (30 January 1954) notes that *The Correspondence of Thomas Wolfe and Homer Andrew Watt* (see B 22) was published by NYUP the previous week "separately and in a boxed set with 'Thomas Wolfe at Washington Square'." The book sold for $2.50 and the boxed set sold for $10.00. An NYUP advertisement appearing in the 22 May 1954 issue of *PW* (p. 2122) referred to this boxed set as a "Limited Edition."

Thomas Wolfe at Washington Square bears the NYUP/OUP imprint and is the same size as the NYUP/OUP printing of *The Correspondence of Thomas Wolfe and Homer Andrew Watt.* The NYUP/OUP printing was included in the only boxed set located.

The Correspondence of Thomas Wolfe and Homer Andrew Watt

EDITED BY

OSCAR CARGILL
*Chairman of the Department of English
Washington Square College of Arts and Science
New York University*

&

THOMAS CLARK POLLOCK
*Dean of
Washington Square College of Arts and Science
New York University*

In January of 1924, Thomas Wolfe, A.M., twenty-three years old and a promising member of George Pierce Baker's 47 Workshop at Harvard, wrote to Homer Andrew Watt to apply for a post as Instructor in English. Professor Watt, chairman of the Department of English in what was then simply called the Washington Square College of New York University, found himself liking the letter and feeling that he might come to like the writer. It was a feeling corroborated by the event, and very early in Wolfe's tenure the fledgling instructor and the mature professor

(Continued on back flap)

The Correspondence
OF
Thomas Wolfe
AND
Homer Andrew Watt

EDITED BY
OSCAR CARGILL
AND
THOMAS CLARK POLLOCK

NEW YORK UNIVERSITY PRESS

The Correspondence of Thomas Wolfe and Homer Andrew Watt *New York University Press*

MELVILLE'S EARLY LIFE AND "REDBURN"
BY WILLIAM H. GILMAN. 378 PAGES. $5.00

This study of Melville's life from 1819 to 1841 shows the relation between his early years and *Redburn*, the book which seems to picture Melville's boyhood and youth. Using both old and unexplored sources, Dr. Gilman discusses *Redburn* both as a reflection of Melville's life and as a work of art in itself. No such study has been made before, and this book gives a new understanding of Melville's life and work.

A BIBLIOGRAPHY OF OLIVER WENDELL HOLMES
BY THOMAS FRANKLIN CURRIER, EDITED BY ELEANOR M. TILTON. 708 PAGES. ILLUSTRATED. $20.00

"A prime source of a vast amount of hitherto unknown or uncollected information concerning the literary and medical writings of Dr. Holmes as well as of works about him; it is a superb example of bibliographical technique adapted to the requirements of a specific author which remains at the same time a model of universal excellence; it is a handsomely printed and well made volume which will be a credit to the shelves of any library." *The Library Journal.*

NEW YORK UNIVERSITY PRESS
WASHINGTON SQUARE · NEW YORK 3, N.Y.

(Continued from front flap)

formed a relationship filled with genuine sincerity on the one side, with generous consideration and discernment on the other, and with mutual affection on both.

The letters incorporating this relationship as it developed over the six-year period of Wolfe's association with New York University, 1924-1930, edited with an Introduction by Dean Pollock, make up *The Correspondence of Thomas Wolfe and Homer Andrew Watt*. A correspondence of no ordinary kind, it reflects a great deal more than just official connection. Wolfe, whose pen was forever irrepressible, filled his letters with such flashes as "The most reckless people, I believe, are those who never gamble," and his department head reveals the astute understanding in twinkling perceptions like "Your ability to land on your feet . . . makes me think that you are more like a Thomas cat than a Thomas Wolfe."

Professor Watt, almost on the eve of his death in 1948, stated that his relation with the author of *Look Homeward, Angel* was the most important part of his career as a departmental administrator and expressed his hope that the surviving correspondence might be published under its present editorship for the benefit of a Thomas Wolfe Scholarship Fund for the Study of American Literature. Of that hope this volume is the fulfillment.

Dust jacket for New York University Press / Oxford University Press printing for A17.1.a

It is possible that the NYUP/OUP printing of *The Correspondence of Thomas Wolfe and Homer Andrew Watt* was sold in the set and separately. This would make the NYUP printing a second rather than a simultaneous publication.

A 17.1.b
Trade printing

THE CORRESPONDENCE OF

THOMAS WOLFE

AND

HOMER ANDREW WATT

EDITED BY OSCAR CARGILL

AND

THOMAS CLARK POLLOCK

New York University Press

WASHINGTON SQUARE · NEW YORK

1954

A 17.1.b: New York University Press printing: 8⅞" × 5⁹⁄₁₆"; arch printed in orangish red.

A17.1.b *The Correspondence*

All of the letters from Thomas Wolfe in this volume copyright 1954 by Edward C. Aswell, Administrator C.T.A. of the Estate of Thomas Wolfe.

All of the letters from Homer Andrew Watt and the letter from Chancellor Harry Woodburn Chase and all other materials in this volume except the aforesaid letters from Thomas Wolfe copyright 1954 by New York University.

COPYRIGHT 1954 BY NEW YORK UNIVERSITY
ALL RIGHTS RESERVED
Library of Congress catalogue card: NUMBER 54-5274
MANUFACTURED IN THE UNITED STATES OF AMERICA

[i–vi] vii–xi [xii] [1–2] 3–45 [46–48] 49–53 [54–56]; portrait of Watt inserted as frontispiece after p. ii; facsimile manuscript, "THE LAND ALWAYS WINS," inserted after p. 16.

[1–3]^8 [4]^2 [5]^8; 5$_8$ beneath rear paste-down endpaper.

Contents: p. i: half title; p. ii: blank; p. iii: title; p. iv: copyright; p. v: dedication 'TO THE GOOD MEMORY OF | HOMER ANDREW WATT'; p. vi: blank; pp. vii–viii: contents; pp. ix–xi: text, headed 'INTRODUCTORY | NOTE'; p. xii: blank; p. 1: half title; p. 2: blank; pp. 3–16: text, headed '[bullet] I [bullet]'; pp. 17–45: text; p. 46: blank; p. 47: 'THE WOLFE—WATT CORRESPONDENCE [bullet] SUPPLEMENT'; p. 48: blank; pp. 49–53: text, headed '[bullet] I [bullet]'; pp. 54–56: blank.

Typography and paper: 6½" × 4¼"; 32 lines per page. Wove paper.

Locations: MJB (dj), NcRSM (dj), NcU (dj), NcWsW (3 copies).

A 18 THE LETTERS OF THOMAS WOLFE

A 18.1.a
First edition, first printing [1956]

THE LETTERS OF
THOMAS
WOLFE

Collected and Edited,
with an Introduction and
Explanatory Text, by
ELIZABETH NOWELL

New York
CHARLES SCRIBNER'S SONS

A 18.1.a: 8⅞" × 5½"

A 18.1.a *The Letters of Thomas Wolfe* 147

> © COPYRIGHT 1956 BY EDWARD C. ASWELL, ADMINISTRATOR C.T.A.
> OF THE ESTATE OF THOMAS WOLFE
>
> COPYRIGHT 1946, 1947, 1950 BY EDWARD C. ASWELL, ADMINISTRATOR C.T.A.
> OF THE ESTATE OF THOMAS WOLFE.
>
> A-7.56[V]
> ALL RIGHTS RESERVED. NO PART OF THIS BOOK
> MAY BE REPRODUCED IN ANY FORM WITHOUT
> THE PERMISSION OF CHARLES SCRIBNER'S SONS.
>
> PRINTED IN THE UNITED STATES OF AMERICA
> LIBRARY OF CONGRESS CATALOG CARD NUMBER 56-9880

[i–vi] vii–xviii [xix–xx] 1–797 [798]; coated leaf with portrait of Wolfe on verso inserted as frontispiece after p. ii, but numbered continuously with the text.

$[1-13]^{16}$ $[14]^{8}$ $[15-26]^{16}$

Contents: p. i: half title; p. ii: list of books by Wolfe; p. iii: blank; p. iv: portrait of Wolfe, p. v: title; p. vi: copyright; pp. vii–x: text, headed 'ACKNOWLEDGMENTS'; pp. xi–xii: contents; pp. xiii–xviii: text, headed 'INTRODUCTION'; p. xix: half title; p. xx: blank; pp. 1–778: text, headed 'I | CHILDHOOD AND CHAPEL HILL | 1908–1920'; pp. 779–797: text, headed 'INDEX'; p. 798: blank. Section titles: pp. 1, 9, 56, 111, 160, 214, 267, 295, 350, 400, 451, 495, 537, 555, 607, 657, 701, 742, 779.

Typography and paper: 7" (7⅜") × 4½"; 42 lines per page. Running heads: rectos, section titles; versos, 'THE LETTERS OF THOMAS WOLFE'. Wove paper.

Binding: Two formats have been noted; priority not determined.

> *Format A:* Black V cloth with 2½"-wide strips of black-flecked blue pastedown paper extending along the fore edges of the front and back. Front goldstamped within a goldstamped single-rules frame 'THE LETTERS | OF | [ornamental lettering] THOMAS | WOLFE'; spine goldstamped with two goldstamped single-rules frames: '[within first frame] THE | LETTERS | OF | [ornamental lettering] THOMAS | WOLFE | [within second frame in roman lettering] EDITED BY | ELIZABETH | NOWELL | [beneath second frame] *Scribners*'; back: blindstamped Scribners seal. White wove endpapers. All edges trimmed. Blue and yellow headbands and footbands.
>
> *Format B.* Identical to format A, except for the absence of the 2½"-wide strip of black-flecked blue paste-down paper.

Dust jacket: Front printed in black and white ornamental lettering on brilliant yellow with a central panel composed of three superimposed squares ranging from gray to black arranged at angles so that all twelve corners are exposed: '[black ornamental lettering] The Letters | of | [white ornamental lettering on the central panel] Thomas | Wolfe | [black ornamental lettering on brilliant yellow] Edited, with an Introduction, by | ELIZABETH NOW-ELL'. Spine printed in black ornamental lettering on brilliant yellow: 'The | Letters | of | Thomas | Wolfe | Edited by | ELIZABETH | NOWELL | SCRIBNERS'. Back: portrait of Wolfe and list of books by him. Front and back flaps: blurb for *TLOTW*; back flap: biographical material for Elizabeth Nowell.

Publication: Number of copies not determined. Copyright #A249244. Published prior to 22 August 1956. Price: $10.00.

Printing: Printed by Vail-Ballou Press, Inc., Binghamton, New York.

Locations: Binding A: APM (dj), EG (2 copies; 1 copy with dj), MH (2 copies), NcRSM (dj), ViU (2 copies); Binding B: DLC (rebound copy, stamped 'AUG 24 1956'); NcA (dj), ViU.

A 18.1.b
Second printing

New York: Scribners, [1956].

On copyright page: 'B-10.56[V]'. Published October 1956. *Location:* CJ.

A 18.1.c
Third printing

New York: Scribners, [1957].

On copyright page: 'C-1.57[V]'. Published January 1957. *Locations:* NcRSM, ViU.

A 18.1.d
Fourth printing

New York: Scribners, [1961].

On copyright page: 'D-2.61[V]'. Published February 1961. *Location:* NcA.

A 18.1.e
Fifth printing

New York: Scribners, [1966].

On copyright page: 'E-4.66[V]'. Published April 1966. *Location:* ScCleU.

Dust jacket for A 18.1.a

A 18.2.a₁
First English edition, first printing, first issue [1958]

SELECTED LETTERS OF

Thomas Wolfe

*

*Edited, with an Introduction
and explanatory text by*
ELIZABETH NOWELL
and selected by
DANIEL GEORGE

HEINEMANN

LONDON   MELBOURNE   TORONTO

A 18.2.a₁: 8¼" × 5½"

> William Heinemann Ltd
>
> LONDON MELBOURNE TORONTO
>
> CAPE TOWN   AUCKLAND
>
> THE HAGUE
>
> ★
>
> *The Letters of Thomas Wolfe*
>
> from which this selection has been made
>
> was first published in America in 1956.
>
> This selection first published 1958
>
> ★
>
> © by Edward C. Aswell 1958
>
> Administrator C.T.A.
>
> of the Estate of Thomas Wolfe
>
> *All rights reserved*
>
> ~~~~~~
>
> Printed in Great Britain
>
> at The Windmill Press
>
> Kingswood, Surrey

[i–vi] vii [viii] ix–xiii [xiv] xv–xxii [xxiii–xxiv] 1–313 [314] 315–326 [327–328]; portrait of Wolfe inserted as frontispiece after p. ii.

[A]^{16} B–I^{16} K–L^{16}

Contents: p. i: half title; p. ii: list of books by Wolfe, p. iii: title; p. iv: copyright; p. v: contents; p. vi: blank; p. vii: text, headed 'Publishers' Note'; p. viii: blank; pp. ix–xiii: text, headed 'Acknowledgments'; p. xiv: blank; pp. xv–xxii: text, headed 'Introduction'; p. xxiii: half title; p. xxiv: blank; pp. 1–313: text, headed 'CHAPTER ONE | Home Life and Harvard | 1908–1923'; p. 314: blank; pp. 315–326: text, headed 'Index'; pp. 327–328: blank. Section titles: pp. 1, 20, 51, 112, 174, 208, 243, 287, 298.

Typography and paper: 6" (6⅝") × 3¹³⁄₁₆"; 34 lines per page. Running heads: rectos, section titles; versos, 'SELECTED LETTERS OF THOMAS WOLFE'. Wove paper.

Binding: Dark grayish blue V cloth. Spine goldstamped: 'SELECTED | LETTERS OF | Thomas | Wolfe | [star] | *Edited by* | ELIZABETH NOWELL |

HEINEMANN'; back: blindstamped Heinemann seal. White wove endpapers. All edges trimmed.

Dust jacket: Front printed in white on a deep yellowish green background: 'SELECTED LETTERS | OF | [ornamental lettering] Thomas Wolfe | [orange, brown, green, and white 'W' in foreground superimposed on green 'T' and green 'W' in background] | *Edited, with an introduction, by* | ELIZABETH NOWELL'. Spine printed in white lettering on a deep yellowish green background: 'SELECTED | LETTERS | OF | [ornamental lettering] Thomas | Wolfe | [unevenly shaded green panels] | [light blue lettering] HEINEMANN'. Back: blurb for *LHA*. Front flap: blurb for *SLOTW;* back flap: quotes from an article by Robert Coughlan.

Publication: Number of copies not determined. Published 15 September 1958. Price: 25s.

Printing: See copyright page.

Locations: APM (dj), BL (25 AUG 58), BOD (6OCT1958), MH, MJB (dj), NcA (dj), NcRSM (dj), NcU, ScU, ViU (dj).

Note one: A selection of eighty-three letters printed in A 18.1.a.

Note two: A piece of black tape has been pasted over the four lines below the second star on the copyright of the APM copy; a rectangular patch of purple residue partially obscures these four lines in the ScU copy. See A 18.2.a$_2$.

Advance copies: Uncorrected proof copy.

Identical to A 18.2.a$_1$, except for:

Wrappers: Light gray. Front printed in black: '*UNCORRECTED PROOF COPY* | (NOT FOR SALE) | [wavy rule] | SELECTED LETTERS OF | THOMAS WOLFE | *Edited with an Introduction by* | *Elizabeth Nowell* | *Selected by Daniel George* | [wavy rule]'. Spine printed vertically in black: '[Heinemann seal] Selected Letters of Thomas Wolfe [in two lines] *Edited with an Introduction by Elizabeth Nowell* | *Selected by Daniel George* [in a single line the Heinemann seal]'.

Dust jacket: Identical, except for back which contains blurb for 'THE LETTERS | OF | D. H. LAWRENCE' by Aldous Huxley and the front flap which is stamped vertically from bottom to top: '[in blue ink] [T]O BE PUBLISHED JUN [1958] [in black ink] PRICE [in blue ink] ABOUT £1 —5–0'.

Location: NcWsW.

Dust jacket for A 18.2.a₁

A 18.2.a₂
First English edition, first printing, second issue [1969]

SELECTED LETTERS OF
Thomas Wolfe
★

*Edited, with an Introduction
and explanatory text, by*
ELIZABETH NOWELL
and selected by
DANIEL GEORGE

HEINEMANN : LONDON

A 18.2.a₂: 8⅛″ × 5½″

A 18.2.b *The Letters of Thomas Wolfe*

> William Heinemann Ltd
>
> LONDON MELBOURNE TORONTO
>
> JOHANNESBURG AUCKLAND
>
> ★
>
> *The Letters of Thomas Wolfe*
> from which this selection has been made
> was first published in America in 1956.
> This selection first published 1958
> Reissued 1969
>
> ★
>
> © by Edward C. Aswell 1958
> Administrator C.T.A.
> of the Estate of Thomas Wolfe
>
> ★
>
> 434 52400 x
>
> Printed in Great Britain
> at The Windmill Press
> Kingswood, Surrey

Identical to A 18.2.a$_1$ except for:

[A] I^{16} (±A$_2$) B–I^{16} K–L^{16}

Location: BOD (2 8 Aug 1969)

Note one: Cancel title leaf.

A 18.2.b
Second printing

London: Heinemann, [1969].

Title page and copyright page identical to A 18.2.a$_2$, but integral to text.
Locations: BL (25 JUL 69), NcA.

A 19
Only printing (1964)

Thomas Wolfe's Purdue Speech "Writing and Living"

edited from the dictated and revised
typescript with an introduction and notes by

WILLIAM BRASWELL
and
LESLIE A. FIELD

1964
Purdue University Studies

A 19: 8¹⁵⁄₁₆″ × 15¹⁵⁄₁₆″

©1964 by Purdue Research Foundation
Library of Congress Catalog No. 64-63462

[1–4] 5 [6] 7 [8] 9–17 [18–20] 21–23 [24] 25–83 [84] 85–129 [130] 131–133 [134–136]

[1–6]⁸ [7]⁴ [8–9]⁸

Contents: p. 1: half title; p. 2: 'Frontispiece: A page of Wolfe's original typescript of the | Purdue Speech, showing his own handwrit- | ten corrections'; p. 3: title; p. 4: copyright; p. 5: text, headed 'ACKNOWLEDGMENTS'; p. 6: blank; p. 7: contents; p. 8: blank; pp. 9–17: text, headed 'INTRODUCTION'; p. 18: blank; p. 19: half title; p. 20: blank; pp. 21–23: text, headed 'Editor's Note on the Reading Text'; p. 24: blank; pp. 25–78: text, headed 'Writing and Living*'; pp. 79–83: text, headed 'TEXTUAL NOTES ON READING TEXT'; p. 84: blank; pp. 85–129: text, headed 'APPENDIX I | *PASSAGES OF THE DICTATED SPEECH | REVISED FOR USE IN | "YOU CAN'T GO HOME AGAIN"* '; p. 130: blank; pp. 131–133: index; p. 134: 'This book was set in Linotype Baskerville, a face known as a | traditional design bridging the gap between "old-style" and "mod- | ern-style" faces. The book was printed by C. E. Pauley and Co., | Indianapolis, on 60 lb. Glatex Antique Offset stock and bound by | Heckman Bindery, North Manchester, Ind. Frontispiece engraving | by Rheitone, Inc., Indianapolis. The jacket was designed by | Moroni St. John and printed by offset lithography by Krieger, Rags- | dale and Co., Evansville, Ind.'; pp. 135–136: blank.

Typography and Paper: 7 9/16" (7 5/8") × 4 1/8"; 39 lines per page. Running heads: versos, 'Thomas Wolfe's'; rectos, 'Purdue Speech' and section headings. Wove paper.

Binding: Vivid green V cloth. Spine goldstamped vertically from top to bottom: 'BRASWELL and FIELD [bullet] THOMAS WOLFE'S PURDUE SPEECH [bullet] PURDUE'. Back: plain. All edges trimmed. White wove endpapers. Green and yellow headbands and footbands.

Dust jacket: Front printed in white, black, and medium yellowish green lettering on medium yellowish green, white, and black rectangular panels with a green and white fountain pen traced on the medium yellowish green and white panels: '[white lettering on medium yellowish green rectangular panel] Thomas Wolfe's | [black lettering on medium yellowish green rectangular panel] Purdue Speech | [medium yellowish green lettering on white rectangular panel] *"Writing and Living"* | [white lettering on black rectangular panel] William Braswell | and | Leslie A. Field'. Spine printed vertically in black lettering on white: 'BRASWELL and FIELD [green bullet] THOMAS WOLFE'S PURDUE SPEECH [green bullet] PURDUE'. Back: blurbs for 'THREE PURDUE PAPERBACKS'. Front flap: blurb for 'THOMAS WOLFE'S PURDUE SPEECH' continuing on to back flap. Back flap: biographical material for Braswell and Field.

THOMAS WOLFE'S PURDUE SPEECH
"Writing and Living"

Thomas Wolfe wrote "Writing and Living" for delivery at the annual Purdue University Literary Awards Banquet in 1938—a few months before his death. It was his last public appearance. Some of the speech appears in the last section of *You Can't Go Home Again*. Elizabeth Nowell frequently refers to it and quotes from it in her biography of Wolfe. Now for the first time the entire "Purdue Speech" appears in print.

The speech itself is a significant document—a famous American writer's candid discussion of his craft. Wolfe stresses that, earlier, he had been too much the sensitive artist aloof from his environment, the artist scornful of the Philistines and the Babbitts. He now realized the necessity of living in the world and trying to understand it—politically, economically, socially. In the Purdue Speech he was trying to describe the new direction his writing was taking and why, in the era of the Great Depression, the rise of the Nazis, and the Spanish Civil War, it had to be so. This volume includes the complete speech, textual notes, an appendix giving passages of the Purdue Speech revised for use in *You Can't Go Home Again*, and William Braswell's first-

(continued on back flap)

$2.95

BRASWELL and FIELD • THOMAS WOLFE'S PURDUE SPEECH • PURDUE

Thomas Wolfe's Purdue Speech

"Writing and Living"

William Braswell and Leslie A. Field

(continued from front flap)

hand account of the Purdue affair, "Thomas Wolfe Lectures and Takes a Holiday," which appeared in 1959.

"A painstakingly careful, thorough, and commendable job of editing a very significant unpublished Thomas Wolfe document . . . I strongly recommend it."

—C. Hugh Holman, University of North Carolina professor and noted Wolfe scholar

WILLIAM BRASWELL is professor of English at Purdue, where he has taught since 1955. He was Fulbright Professor of American Literature at the University of Athens in 1954-55. The author of *Melville's Religious Thought*, he now received the B.A. and M.A. from Duke University and the Ph.D. from the University of Chicago.

LESLIE A. FIELD, instructor in English at Purdue since 1956, received the B.A. and M.A. from Wayne State University and completed his Ph.D. coursework at Indiana University. His articles have appeared in *Bucknell Review*, *New York Folklore Quarterly*, and other journals.

PURDUE UNIVERSITY STUDIES
WEST LAFAYETTE, INDIANA

THREE PURDUE PAPERBACKS

MARK TWAIN AND LITTLE SATAN
The Writing of "The Mysterious Stranger"
by John S. Tuckey

This book solves the longstanding literary mystery about the times of composition of the several versions of Mark Twain's most important later work. "Indispensable to anyone seriously interested in Mark Twain's work during the last ten or fifteen years."
—Henry Nash Smith

101 pages $1.75

THE PARADOX OF GEORGE ORWELL
by Richard J. Voorhees

The first American study of the author of *1984*, *Homage to Catalonia*, and *Animal Farm*, a crusader and independent thinker who dealt with the major issues of our time. "The perfect book on Orwell . . . ideal for layman and literateur."—*The Dubliner*

128 pages $1.95

HAMLET: A TRAGEDY OF ERRORS
by Weston Babcock

Shakespeare's play through Elizabethan eyes and ears. A fresh approach to *Hamlet* as a play. "Persuasive, illuminating, and ingenious."—*Educational Theatre Journal*

136 pages $1.75

PURDUE UNIVERSITY STUDIES
308 State Street
West Lafayette, Ind. 47906

Dust Jacket for A 19

A 19 *Thomas Wolfe's Purdue Speech "Writing and Living"*

Publication: 1,000 copies. Copyright #A712944. Published 20 September 1964. Price: $2.95.

Printing: See contents.

Locations: APM, DLC (2 copies; both stamped 'Aug- 3 1964'), InU Lilly, JI (dj), MH, NcU.

Note one: See AA 8 and C 87.

A 20 THE MOUNTAINS

A 20.1.a
First edition, first printing [1970]

THE MOUNTAINS
A PLAY IN ONE ACT

THE MOUNTAINS
A DRAMA IN THREE ACTS
AND A PROLOGUE

by THOMAS WOLFE

EDITED WITH AN INTRODUCTION *by Pat M. Ryan*

THE UNIVERSITY OF NORTH CAROLINA PRESS
CHAPEL HILL

A 20.1.a: 8½" × 5½"

A 20.1.a *The Mountains*

> Copyright © 1970 by The University of North Carolina Press
> All rights reserved
> Manufactured in the United States of America
> Printed by Heritage Printers, Inc.
> ISBN 0-8078-1138-6
> Library of Congress Catalog Card Number 70-109458
>
> For production rights, contact the Estate of Thomas Wolfe,
> Paul Gitlin, Administrator, C.T.A., 5 West 45th Street,
> New York, N.Y. 10036.

[i–xii] [1–3] 4–45 [46–47] 48–50 [51–53] 54–84 [85–87] 88–177 [178–180]
[1–6]^{16}

Contents: p. i: half title; p. ii: quotes five-line verse from Doris Halman's *The 47 Varieties* (1922); p. iii: title; p. iv: copyright; p. v: dedication 'To NORMAN HOLMES PEARSON, | mentor and friend.'; p. vi: blank; p. vii: 'ACKNOWLEDGMENTS'; p. viii: blank; p. ix: contents; p. x: blank; p. xi: text, headed 'THE TEXTS'; p. xii: blank; p. 1: 'INTRODUCTION'; p. 2: blank; pp. 3–45: text, headed 'INTRODUCTION'; p. 46: blank; pp. 47–50: text, headed 'BIBLIOGRAPHY'; p. 51: half title; p. 52: blank; pp. 53–84: text; p. 85: half title; p. 86: blank; pp. 87–177: text; pp. 178–180: blank.

Typography and paper: 6¼" (6¹³⁄₁₆") × 4"; 37 lines per page. Running heads: rectos, section headings; versos, '[virgule] *The Mountains*'. Wove paper.

Binding: Deep grayish green V cloth. Spine silverstamped vertically: '[in two lines] WOLFE | RYAN [followed by in one line] THE MOUNTAINS CHAPEL HILL'. Light gray endpapers. All edges trimmed. Black and white headbands and footbands.

Dust Jacket: Front is printed in vivid yellow on black-flecked strong grayish blue with a portrait of a young man extending over onto the spine: '[vertically] THE MOUNTAINS | [horizontally] by THOMAS WOLFE | Edited with an Introduction | by Pat M. Ryan'; spine printed vertically in vivid yellow on black-flecked strong grayish blue: '[in two lines] WOLFE | RYAN [followed by in one line] THE MOUNTAINS CHAPEL HILL'; back: blurb for *The Window of Memory* and *The Letters of Thomas Wolfe To His Mother*. Front flap and back flap: blurb for *The Mountains;* back flap: portrait of Ryan.

Publication: 1,366 copies. Copyright #A191031. Published in August 1970. Price: $8.00.

Printing: Printed by Heritage Printers in Charlotte, North Carolina.

Locations: APM (dj), DLC (NOV 17 1970), InU Lilly (dj), MH, NcA (dj), NcRSM (dj), NcU (4 copies with dj), ViU.

Dust jacket for A 20.1.a

A 20.1.b
Second printing

On copyright page: 'Second printing, October 1972'. 500 copies published October 1972. Printed by Litho Crafters. *Location:* NcRSM.

A21 THE NOTEBOOKS OF THOMAS WOLFE (VOLUMES 1 AND 2)

A21
Only printing [1970]

THE NOTEBOOKS OF
Thomas Wolfe

Edited by
RICHARD S. KENNEDY
and
PASCHAL REEVES

Volume I

THE UNIVERSITY OF
NORTH CAROLINA PRESS
Chapel Hill

A21: 9" × 6"

A 21 The Notebooks of Thomas Wolfe (Volumes 1 and 2)

> Copyright © 1970 by
> The University of North Carolina Press
> All rights reserved
> Manufactured in the United States of America
> Printed by Kingsport Press, Inc.
> Library of Congress Catalog Card Number 70-80917

I: [i–vi] vii–xi [xii] xiii–xxxviii [1–2] 3–175 [176–178] 179–290 [291–292] 293–410

II: [i–vi] vii–viii [411–412] 413–570 [571–572] 573–638 [639–640] 641–670 [671–672] 673–751 [752–754] 755–818 [819–820] 821–959 [960–962] 963–992 [993–994] 995–1024 [1025–1026]

I: [1–14]^{16}

II: [1–18]^{16} [19]^8 [20]^{16}

Contents: p. i: half title; p. ii: quotes fourteen lines from *OTATR;* p. iii: title; p. iv: copyright; p. v: dedication *'For* | ELLA KENNEDY | *and* SUZANNE REEVES'; p. vi: blank; pp. vii–xiv: text, headed 'Preface'; p. xii: text, headed 'Abbreviations'; pp. xiii–xiv: contents; pp. xv–xxviii: text, headed '*Introduction*'; pp. xxix–xxxviii: text, headed '*A Chronology*'; p. 1: 'PART ONE [tilde] | *THE LONG* | *APPRENTICESHIP*'; p. 2: blank; pp. 3–175: text, headed '*Notes from the Harvard Years* | *1920–1923*'; p. 176: blank; p. 177: 'PART TWO [tilde] | *EUROPEAN* | *WANDERING*'; p. 178: blank; pp. 179–290: text, headed '*Pocket Notebook 4* | *September 4, 1928, to October 24, 1928*'; p. 291: 'PART THREE [tilde] | *PUBLICATION* | *AND FAME*'; p. 292: blank; pp. 293–410: text, headed '*Pocket Notebook 8* | *December 20, 1928 to January 26, 1929;* vol. II: p. i: half title; p. ii: blank; p. iii: title; p. iv: copyright; p. v: text, headed '*Abbreviations*'; p. vi: blank; pp. vii–viii: contents; p. 411 'PART FOUR [tilde] | *THE SEARCH* | *FOR A SECOND NOVEL*'; p. 412: blank; pp. 413–570: text, headed '*Pocket Notebook 13* | *February, 1930, to May, 1930*'; p. 571: 'PART FIVE [tilde] | *DROWNING* | *IN BROOKLYN*'; p. 572: blank; pp. 573–638: text, headed *Pocket Notebook 18* | *January, 1932, to August, 1932*'; p. 639: 'PART SIX [tilde] | *RESCUE OPERATION*'; p. 640: blank; pp. 641–670: text, headed '*Pocket Notebook 21* | *ca. January, 1934, to April, 1934*'; p. 671: 'PART SEVEN [tilde] | *ANOTHER LOOK* | *AT EUROPE*'; p. 672: blank; pp. 673–751: text, headed '*Pocket Notebook 25* | *March, 1935*'; p. 752: blank; p. 753: 'PART EIGHT [tilde] | *A SENSE OF* | *THE AMERICAN CONTINENT*'; p. 754: blank; pp. 755–818: text, headed '*Pocket Notebook 28* | *June, 1935, to September, 1935*'; p. 819: 'PART NINE [tilde] | *CITIZEN OF* | *A DARKENING WORLD*'; p. 820: blank; pp. 821–959: text, headed '*Pocket Notebook 31* | *August 20, 1936, to Late September, 1936*'; p. 960: blank; p. 961: 'PART TEN [tilde] | *THE RETURN TO THE WEST*'; p. 962: blank; pp. 963–992: text, headed *A Western Jour-*

nal | *June 20, 1938, to July 2, 1938*'; p. 993: '*Index*'; p. 994: blank; pp. 995–1024: index; pp. 1025–1026: blank.

Typography and paper: 7⅛″ (7⅜″) × 4¼″; 42 lines per page. Running heads: rectos, chapter headings; versos, section headings. Wove paper.

Binding: Medium gray V cloth with light gray PM cloth pasted over all but the spine and ⅞″ of the front and back cover. Front has facsimile of a charcoal drawing of Wolfe; spine stamped vertically and horizontally in blue: '[vertically in two lines] The Notebooks of [over] THOMAS WOLFE | [roman number appropriate to that volume stamped horizontally] | *Kennedy* | *Reeves* | [vertically] *Chapel Hill*'. Endpapers coated with facsimile manuscripts from Notebooks. All edges trimmed; top edges stained strong blue. Different facsimile manuscript pages coat the endpapers in Volume I and Volume II. Blue and white headbands and footbands.

Slipcase: Boards covered with strong blue PM cloth. Front: printed in black and strong blue on 9¼″ × 5⅝″ rectangular paste-down white paper: '[black lettering] *THE NOTEBOOKS OF* | *[strong blue lettering] THOMAS WOLFE* | [black lettering] *Edited by* | RICHARD S. KENNEDY | *and* | PASCHAL REEVES | [sketch of Wolfe] | [strong blue lettering] *THE UNIVERSITY OF* | *NORTH CAROLINA PRESS* | *Chapel Hill* | [black lettering] *Sketch by Olin Dows, 1923, courtesy of the Harvard Library* $30.00'.

Publication: 3,433 copies. Copyright #A132957. Published 21 February 1970. Price: $30.00.

Printing: See copyright.

Locations: APM (with slipcase), DLC (MAR- 9 1970), JI, NcA, NcRSM (2 sets; 1 set with slipcase), NcU, ScCleU.

Note one: See B 37.

Binding for A 21

A 22 A PROLOGUE TO AMERICA

A 22
Only printing [1978]

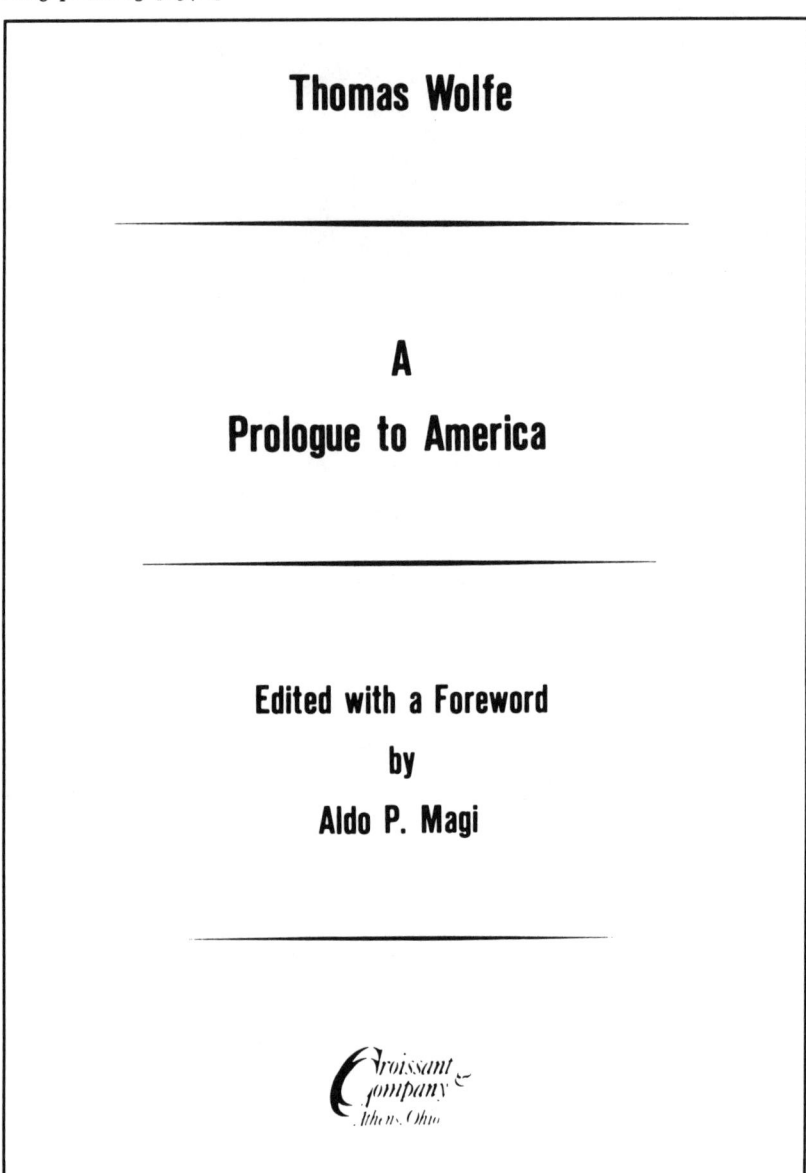

A 22: 8½" × 5½": printed in blue.

A 22 *A Prologue to America* 169

> Copyright © 1938, 1966 by The Condé Nast Publications, Inc.
>
> Copyright 1938 by Maxwell Perkins, Executor, Estate of Thomas Wolfe; Copyright renewed 1966 by Paul Gitlin, Administrator, C.T.A., Estate of Thomas Wolfe.
>
> Copyright © 1978 by Croissant & Company
>
> ~~~~~~~~~~~~~~~~~~~~~~~~~~~~~~~~~~~
>
> The present edition published by
> Croissant & Company
> Route 1, Box 51
> Athens, Ohio 45701
>
> Book design by Charles T. Mayer

[A–B] [i–iv] v–vi [vii–viii] 1–12 [13–14]

$[1]^{12}$

Contents: pp. A–B: blank; p. i: title; p. ii: copyright; p. iii: blank; p. iv: dedication; pp. v–vi: text, headed 'FORWARD'; p. vii: above a drawing of a train 'A PROLOGUE TO AMERICA'; p. viii: drawing of a train station; pp. 1–11: text, beginning 'SCENE'; p. 12: 'COLOPHON | This edition of Thomas Wolfe's lyrical piece, *A Prologue to America*, has | been set and printed for Croissant & Company at the press of Lettershop | Plus, Athens, Ohio. The text is 80 lb. Pyreness White Strathmore Grandee | Text and the covers are 75 lb. White Howard Felt cover. | This edition of *A Prologue to America* is limited to 100 numbered copies. | This copy is no. '.

Typography and paper: 6¾" × 4⅜"; 42 lines per page. Wove paper.

Binding: Wrappers, saddlebound. White paper coated on inside front and back with vivid reddish orange and with a 2⅝" overlap front and back folded inward to create front and back flaps. Front printed in dark blue within a dark blue and a vivid reddish orange double-rules frame: 'A | Prologue to America | Thomas Wolfe'.

Publication: 100 copies. Copyright #TX-421-067. Published 21 September 1978. Price $12.50.

Printing: Printed by Lettershop Plus, Athens, Ohio.

Locations: APM (with review slip), DLC (SEP 1 9 1979), MH (with review slip), NcRSM (2 copies), NcU.

Note one: First complete reprinting of the original. See A 29, B 11, and C 85.

Wrappers for A 22

A 23 WELCOME TO OUR CITY

A 23
Only printing [*1983*]

WELCOME TO OUR CITY

A PLAY IN TEN SCENES BY

THOMAS WOLFE

EDITED, WITH AN INTRODUCTION,

BY RICHARD S. KENNEDY

LOUISIANA STATE UNIVERSITY PRESS
BATON ROUGE AND LONDON

A 23: 8½″ × 5½″

> Copyright © 1983 by Paul Gitlin, Administrator,
> C.T.A. of the Estate of Thomas Wolfe
> Introduction, and a Note on the Text, copyright © 1983
> by Richard S. Kennedy
> All rights reserved
> Manufactured in the United States of America
>
> This version of the play is the Harvard 47 Workshop
> production script of 1923, published by permission
> of the Houghton Library, Harvard University.
>
> Also, acknowledgment is made to the University of
> North Carolina Library for permission to print the
> two critiques from the Wolfe Papers in the North
> Carolina Collection.
>
> Designer: Albert Crochet
> Typeface: Linotron Palatino
> Typesetter: G&S Typesetters, Inc.
> Printer: Thomson-Shore, Inc.
> Binder: John H. Dekker & Sons, Inc.
>
> LIBRARY OF CONGRESS CATALOGING IN PUBLICATION DATA
> Wolfe, Thomas, 1900–1938.
>   Welcome to our city.
>
>   (Southern literary studies)
>   I. Kennedy, Richard S.   II. Title.   III. Series.
>   PS3545.O337W49   1983   813'.52   82-20838
>   ISBN 0-8071-1085-X

[i–xi] xii [xiii–xvi] [1] 2–8 [9–11] 12–14 [15] 16–31 [32] 33–53 [54] 55–72 [73] 74–76 [77] 78–85 [86] 87–93 [94] 95–110 [111] 112–120 [121] 122–128 [129] 130–132 [133–136]

$[1-2]^{16}$ $[3]^4$ $[4]^8$ $[5-6]^{16}$

Contents: p. i: 'SOUTHERN LITERARY STUDIES | Louis D. Rubin, Jr., Editor'; p. ii: blank; p. iii: half title; p. iv: blank; p. v: title; p. vi: copyright; p. vii: 'In memory of Paschal Reeves— | Wolfe scholar, critic, and editor'; p. viii: blank; p. ix: contents; p. x: blank; pp. xi–xiii: text, headed 'A NOTE ON THE TEXT'; p. xiii: half title; pp. xiv–xv: facsimile captioned 'Playbill for the original performance at Harvard'; p. xvi: blank; pp. 1–8: text, headed 'IN-TRODUCTION | by Richard S. Kennedy'; p. 9: text, headed 'WELCOME TO OUR CITY | A Play in Ten Scenes'; p. 10: blank; pp. 11–128: text, headed

'SCENE 1'; pp. 128–132: text, headed 'APPENDIX | Two Contemporary Critiques'; pp. 133–136: blank. Scene divisions: pp. 11, 15, 32, 54, 73, 77, 86, 94, 111, 121.

Typography and paper: 6" (6½") × 3¾"; 33 lines per page. Running heads: rectos, scene numbers, versos 'WELCOME TO OUR CITY'. Wove paper.

Binding: Dark blue V cloth. Spine silver-stamped vertically and horizontally: '[horizontally] Wolfe | [vertically] WELCOME TO OUR CITY Louisiana'. Deep reddish orange wove endpapers. All edges trimmed. Red and white headbands and footbands.

Dust jacket: Front printed in red, white, and black on deep blue: within a black frame rounded at the top: '[red lettering] WELCOME | TO OUR CITY | [white lettering] A PLAY IN TEN SCENES | BY | THOMAS WOLFE | [within a second black frame rounded at top a drawing of stage setting for *WTOC*] | [beneath second frame in red lettering] EDITED, WITH AN INTRODUCTION, | BY RICHARD S. KENNEDY'. Spine printed vertically: '[red lettering] WELCOME TO OUR CITY [white lettering] A PLAY IN TEN SCENES BY THOMAS WOLFE [LSU seal] [red lettering] KENNEDY'. Back: '[LSU seal in red] | [white lettering] LOUISIANA STATE | UNIVERSITY PRESS | Baton Rouge 70803 | ISBN 0-8071-1085-X'. Front and back flaps: blurb for *WTOC*.

Publication: 2,500 copies. Copyright #TX-1-775-607–TX-1-775-608. Published 24 April 1983. Price: $12.95.

Printing: Printed by Thomson-Shore, Dexter, Michigan.

Locations: APM, CJ (dj), DLC (2 copies; 1 copy stamped 'APR 1 8 1983' and 1 copy stamped 'APR17 1985'), MH, NcA (2 copies with dj), NcRSM (dj), ScCleU.

Note one: First published in *Esquire* in 1957 (see C 151) by Edward C. Aswell who abridged the copy-text, a later version of *WTOC* (expanded by Wolfe for presentation to the Theatre Guild), in preparing it for publication. Kennedy's edition uses an earlier working script prepared by Wolfe and George Pierce Baker for presentation at the 47 Workshop production presented at the Agassiz House Theater on 11 and 12 May 1923 as copy-text.

Note two: See B 30.

Note three: Date of publication on copyright registration (1 May 1983) differs from that provided by the publisher (24 April 1983).

Dust jacket for A 23

A 24 K-19: SALVAGED PIECES

A 24
Only printing (1983)

> # THOMAS WOLFE
> # K-19: Salvaged Pieces
>
> Edited, with an introduction, by
> John L. Idol, Jr.
>
> THE THOMAS WOLFE SOCIETY
> 1983

A 24: 7½" × 5"

The facsimile of the dummy of "K-19" is the fourth in a series of annual publications for members of The Thomas Wolfe Society.

Approved by Mr. Paul Gitlin, Administrator, C. T. A., Estate of Thomas Wolfe.

Permissions:
From the William B. Wisdom Collection, the essay entitled "K19" (b MS AM 1883 [314] is printed for the first time by permission of Paul Gitlin and the Houghton Library, Harvard University.

The dummy of "K-19" is reproduced by permission of Charles Scribner's Sons and Robert H. Pettit.

The words from *You Can't Go Home Again,* copyright 1940 by Maxwell Perkins as executor and renewed 1968 by Paul Gitlin, Administrator, C. T. A., are reprinted by permission of Harper & Row, Publishers, Inc.

Acknowledgments:
I extend grateful acknowledgment to Mrs. Leo Linder, A. S. Eggerton, Jr., Frank Clodfelter, Aldo P. Magi, Richard S. Kennedy, Selwyn King, Warren R. Howell, and to Myra Champion, to whom this publication is dedicated. I especially thank Robert H. Pettit, whose cooperation made this publication possible.

This is copy number _____ in an edition of 400 copies.

Copyright 1983 by Paul Gitlin,
Administrator, C. T. A., Estate
of Thomas Wolfe

Printed by The R. L. Bryan Company,
Columbia, S. C.

2

[1] 2–7 [8] [A–H] 1–10 [27] 28–35 [36]

[1]^{18}

Contents: p. 1: title; p. 2: copyright; pp. 3–7: text, headed 'FOREWARD'; p. 8: blank; p. A: title for dummy of 'K-19'; p. B: text, headed 'FALL PUBLICATIONS'; pp. C–D: blank; p. E: half title; p. F: copyright for dummy of 'K-19'; p. G: text, headed 'WO'; p. H: blank; p. 1: text, headed 'PROLOGUE'; pp. 2–10: text, headed 'CHAPTER I | THE STATION'; pp. 27–33: text, begin-

A24 *K-19: Salvaged Pieces* 177

ning 'Printed below is a heretofore unpublished piece entitled "K 19," in the Wisdom Collection numbered b MS AM 1883 [bracket] 314 [bracket]'; pp. 34–35: five captioned photographs of trains; p. 36: blank.

Typography and paper: 6" (6¼") × 4"; 38 lines per page. Running heads (facsimile of 'K-19' only): rectos: 'THE STATION'; versos: 'K-19'. Wove paper.

Binding: Wrappers, saddlebound. A facsimile of the front and spine of the dust jacket prepared for *K-19*. Front: facsimiles the front of the original dust jacket: '[medium violet ornamental letters] K–19 [on a drawing of a light grayish blue and light yellow circular saw-blade–like disc representing a train wheel partially obscuring a light grayish blue and light yellow train track drawn in perspective on a medium violet background decorated with light grayish blue drawings and eight light grayish blue and light yellow stripes] | [light yellow ornamental letters] THOMAS WOLFE [holograph] Author, of | [ornamental letters] LOOK HOMEWARD ANGEL'. Back: a vertical white panel 3½" in width and the spine of the original dust jacket 1¾" in width: '[in yellow ornamental letters on medium violet] K–19 | THOMAS | WOLFE | [light grayish blue drawing of mountain tops] | [medium violet roman letters on a light grayish blue and light yellow train track] SCRIBNERS'. All edges trimmed.

Publication: 400 numbered copies. Copyright #TX-1-239-479. Published 2 February 1983. Not for sale. Distributed to members of the Thomas Wolfe Society.

Printing: See copyright.

Locations: APM, CJ, JI, NcRSM (3 copies).

Note one: This edition is a reduced facsimile of a Scribners dummy prepared during the summer or fall of 1932 (complete with dust jacket, title page, a quotation from Heine, and a prologue). The dummy was discarded by a Scribners book clerk when the novel was canceled, and retrieved from the trash basket by Leo H. Linder. The original of the dummy is now at NcU.

Note two: Over half of the text of *K-19* was incorporated by Edward Aswell into chapter 5 of *YCGHA*.

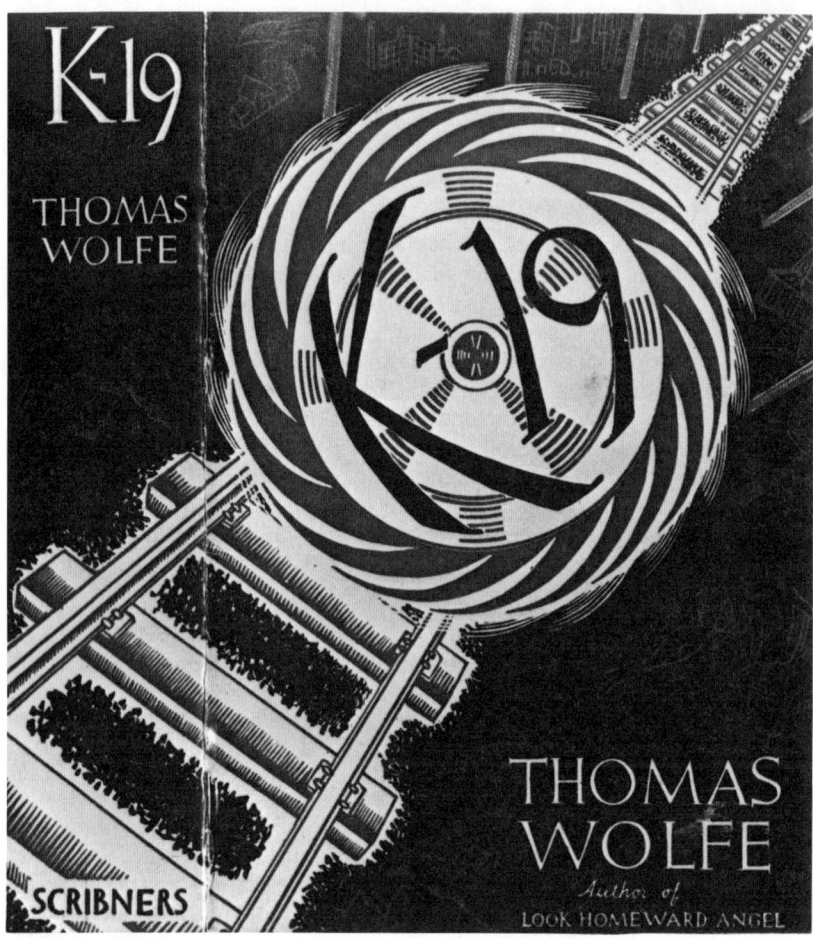

Wrappers for A 24

A 25 BEYOND LOVE AND LOYALTY

A 25.1.a
First edition, first printing [1983]

Beyond Love and Loyalty

The Letters of Thomas Wolfe

and Elizabeth Nowell

Together with "No More Rivers"

A Story by Thomas Wolfe

Edited by Richard S. Kennedy

The University of North Carolina Press

Chapel Hill and London

A 25.1.a: 9" × 5⅜"

> © 1983 Richard S. Kennedy
>
> All rights reserved
>
> Manufactured in the United States of America
>
> Letters of Thomas Wolfe © 1983 Paul Gitlin,
> Administrator, C.T.A.,
> Estate of Thomas Wolfe
>
> Letters of Elizabeth Nowell © 1983
> Clara Perkins Stites
>
> Library of Congress Cataloging in Publication Data
>
> Wolfe, Thomas, 1900–1938.
>   Beyond love and loyalty.
>   Includes index.
>   1. Wolfe, Thomas, 1900–1938—Correspondence.
> 2. Nowell, Elizabeth—Correspondence. 3. Novelists,
> American—20th century—Correspondence. 4. Literary
> agents—United States—Correspondence. I. Nowell,
> Elizabeth. II. Wolfe, Thomas, 1900–1938. No more
> rivers. 1983. III. Kennedy, Richard S. IV. Title.
> PS3545.O337Z49 1983   813'.52 [B]   82-15939
> ISBN 0-8078-1545-4

[i–xi] xii–xxii [xxiii–xxvi] [1] 2–13 [14–15] 16–26 [27] 28–40 [41] 42–50 [51] 52–81 [82–83] 84–98 [99] 100–108 [109] 110–136 [137] 138–139 [140] 141–158 [159] 160–164 [165–166]

[1–6]^{16}

Contents: p. i: half title; p. ii: portrait of Elizabeth Nowell; p. iii: title; p. iv: copyright; p. v: dedication '*For | My Own Liddy*'; p. v: blank; p. vi: contents; p. vii: blank; p. viii: acknowledgments; p. ix: blank; pp. x–xxii: text, headed 'Introduction: A Unique Relationship'; p. xxiii: text, headed 'A Note on the Text'; p. xxiv: blank; p. xxv: half title; p. xxvi: blank; pp. 1–136: text, headed 'PART I [decoration] 1934 | Wolfe and the Maxim Lieber Agency'; pp. 137–158: text, headed ' "No More Rivers" '; pp. 159–164: index; pp. 165–166: blank. Section titles: pp. 1, 15, 27, 41, 51, 83, 99, and 109.

Typography and paper: 6⅞" (7⁹⁄₁₆") × 4¹⁄₁₆"; 42 lines per page. Running heads: (pp. 2–136) rectos, section titles; versos: letter dates; (pp. 138–158): rectos and versos: '*No More Rivers*'. Wove paper.

A 25.1.b *Beyond Love and Loyalty*

Binding: Light blue V cloth. Spine stamped in black, vertically in two lines: '[vertically in two lines] Beyond Love | and Loyalty [followed by vertically in two lines] The Letters of Thomas Wolfe | and Elizabeth Nowell [followed by vertically in two lines] Edited by | Richard S. Kennedy [horizontally] Chapel | Hill'. White wove endpapers imprinted on front and back paste downs and on front free and back free with blue geometric designs. All edges trimmed. White headbands and footbands.

Dust jacket: Front medium gray with soft blue geometric designs printed in white, medium gray, and black on a soft blue rectangular panel within triple-rules frame (black, medium gray, black): '[white lettering] [rule] | [ornamental lettering] BEYOND | [rule] | LOVE AND | [rule] | LOYALTY | [rule] | [medium gray roman lettering] THE LETTERS OF | THOMAS WOLFE AND | ELIZABETH NOWELL | [white rule] | [black lettering] TOGETHER WITH "NO MORE RIVERS" | A STORY BY THOMAS WOLFE | [white rule] [medium gray lettering] EDITED BY RICHARD S. KENNEDY'. Spine printed on medium gray in blue and black letters, horizontally and, in two lines, vertically: '[horizontally in blue lettering] Kennedy [vertically in two lines in black lettering] BEYOND LOVE AND LOYALTY | THE LETTERS OF THOMAS WOLFE AND ELIZABETH NOWELL [horizontally in blue lettering] Chapel | Hill'. Back: blurbs for *MOL* and *TLOTWTHM*. Front flap: quotes blurb by David Donald; front and back flaps; blurb for *BLAL* and biographical material for Kennedy.

Publication: 1,521 copies. Copyright numbers #TX-1-255-685–TX-1-255-687. Published 29 September 1983. Price: $18.95.

Printing: Printed by Thomson-Shore, Dexter, Michigan.

Locations: APM (dj), CJ (dj), DLC (2 copies; 1 stamped 'JUL 1 9 1983' and 1 stamped 'SEP 30 1983'), JI (dj), MH, NcRSM, NcU (2 copies), ScCleU.

A 25.1.b
Chapel Hill and London: University of North Carolina Press, 1984.

On copyright page: 'Second printing, May 1984'.

822 copies. Published June 1984. Printed by Thomson-Shore, Dexter, Michigan. *Location:* CJ (dj).

Dust jacket for A25.1.a

A 26 MY OTHER LONELINESS

A 26
Only printing [1983]

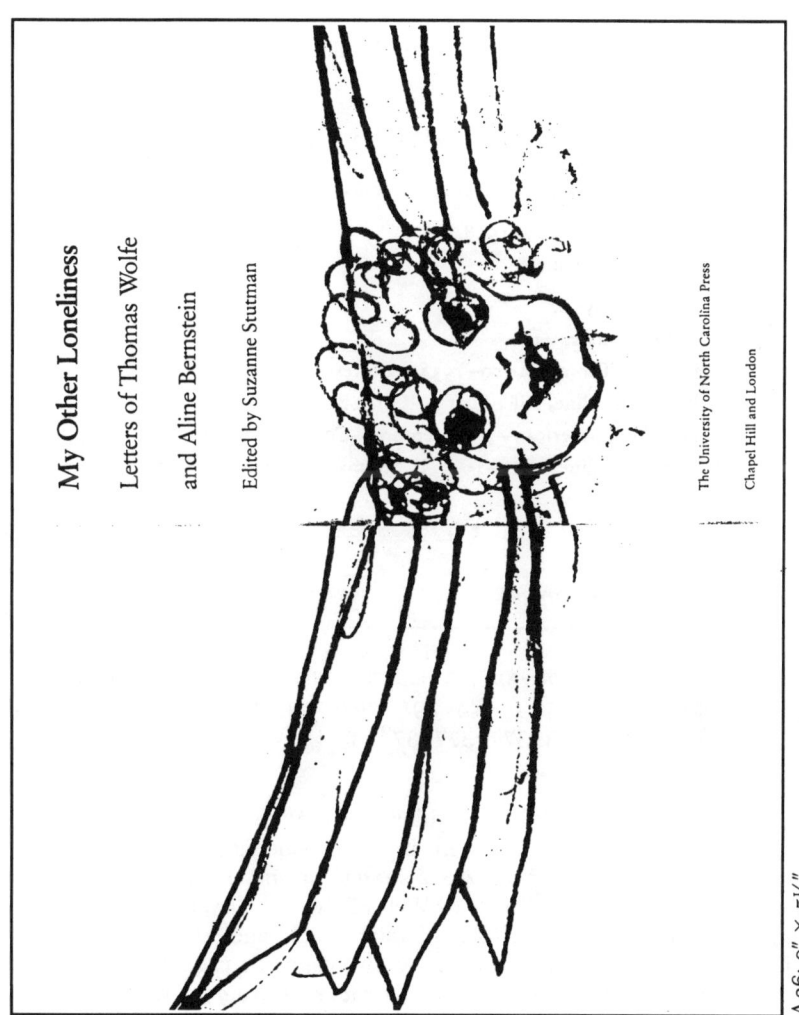

A 26: 9" × 5½"

© 1983 The University of North Carolina Press

All rights reserved

Manufactured in the United States of America

Letters of Thomas Wolfe © 1983 Paul Gitlin, Administrator, C.T.A. Estate of Thomas Wolfe

Letters of Aline Bernstein © 1983 Edla Cusick

Library of Congress Cataloging in Publication Data

Wolfe, Thomas, 1900–1938.
  My other loneliness.

  Bibliography: p.
  Includes index.
  1. Wolfe, Thomas, 1900–1938—Correspondence.
  2. Bernstein, Aline, 1881–1955—Correspondence.
  3. Novelists, American—20th century—Correspondence.
  I. Bernstein, Aline, 1881–1955. II. Stutman, Suzanne.
  III. Title.
  PS3545.O337Z483 1983   813'.52   82-20102
  ISBN 0-8078-1543-8
  ISBN 0-8078-4117-X pbk.

[i–xiii] xiv–xvi [xvii] xviii–xix [xx–xxi] xxii [xxiii] xxiv–xxv [xxvi] [1–3] 4–40 [41] 42–141 [142–143] 144–291 [292–293] 294–320 [321] 322–349 [350–351] 352–372 [373] 374–377 [378–379] 380 [381] 382–390 [1–13]¹⁶

Contents: p. i: half title; p. ii: drawing by Aline Bernstein; p. iii: ' "My tender and golden love, | you were my other loneliness, | the only clasp of hand and heart that I had. | I was a stranger, alone and lost | in the wilderness, and I found you" | THOMAS WOLFE, 1928 | "If you will listen, to me some day, you will hear the voice of your friend | and your angel" | ALINE BERNSTEIN, October 1931'; pp. iv–v: two-page title page; p. vi: copyright; p. vii: dedication, *'To Fred, | Robert, Rhonda, and Craig*'; p. viii: blank; p. ix: contents; p. x: blank; p. xi: list of illustrations; p. xii: blank; pp. xiii–xvi: text, headed 'Chronological List of Letters'; pp. xvii–xix: text, headed 'Forward | by Richard S. Kennedy'; p. xx: blank; pp. xxi–xxii: text, headed 'Acknowledgments'; pp. xxiii–xxv: text, headed 'Editorial Policy'; p. xxvi: blank; p. 1: half title; p. 2: blank; pp. 3–40: text, headed 'Introduction'; pp. 41–141: text, headed '1925–1926: Idyllic Years'; p. 142: blank; pp. 143–291: text, headed '1927–1928: The Grand Renunciation'; p. 292: blank; pp. 293–320:

A26 *My Other Loneliness*

text, headed '1929–1930: The Long, Bitter | War of Separation'; pp. 321–349: text, headed '1931–1932: The Final Break'; p. 350: blank; pp. 351–372: text, headed '1933–1934: One-Sided Love'; pp. 373–376: text, headed '1935–1936: Friendship'; p. 377: portrait of Aline Bernstein; p. 378: blank; pp. 379–380: bibliography; pp. 381–390: index.

Typography and paper: $7\frac{3}{16}''$ ($7\frac{11}{16}''$) × $4\frac{1}{4}''$; 44 lines per page. Running heads: rectos, section titles; versos, years.

Binding: Two formats have been noted.

Format 1: Light grayish brown V cloth. Spine silver-stamped: '[horizontally] Stutman | [vertically along two lines separated by a rule] My Other Loneliness | Letters to Thomas Wolfe and Aline Bernstein | [horizontally] Chapel Hill'. White wove endpapers. All edges trimmed. Brown and yellow headbands and footbands.

Format 2: White unprinted wrappers.

Dust jacket: Accompanying binding formats 1 and 2. Front printed on brownish pink: '[orange lettering] My Other Loneliness | [black lettering] Letters of Thomas Wolfe and Aline Bernstein | Edited by Suzanne Stutman | Foreward by Richard S. Kennedy | [rule] | [overlapping arrangement of a photograph of Wolfe, a photograph of Bernstein, a page from a manuscript letter by Wolfe, and a page of a manuscript letter by Bernstein] | [rule]'. Spine printed on brownish pink horizontally and vertically: '[horizontally in black lettering] Stutman | [vertically in three lines] [orange lettering] My Other Loneliness | [yellow rule] | [white lettering] Letters of Thomas Wolfe and Aline Bernstein [horizontally in black lettering] Chapel Hill'. Back: blurbs for *Beyond Love and Loyalty* and *The Letters of Thomas Wolfe to His Mother*. Flaps: blurb for *MOL* and biographical material.

Publication: 3,031 copies in cloth; 1,479 copies in wrappers. Published 29 September 1983. Copyright numbers #TX-1-211-331–TX-1-211-333. Price: $30.00, cloth; $14.95, wrappers.

Printing: Printed by Thomson-Shore, Dexter, Michigan.

Locations: CJ (wrappers with dj), MH (cloth), NcRSM (cloth with dj), NcU (2 copies in cloth), ScCleU (cloth).

Dust jacket for A 26

A 27 HOLDING ON FOR HEAVEN

A 27
Only printing (1985)

HOLDING ON FOR HEAVEN

The Cables and Postcards of Thomas Wolfe and Aline Bernstein

Edited by Suzanne Stutman

The Thomas Wolfe Society
1985

A 27: 9⅞" × 6½"

© 1985 The Thomas Wolfe Society
All rights reserved
Manufactured in the United States of America

Postcards and Cablegrams of Thomas Wolfe © 1985
Paul Gitlin, Administrator, C.T.A. Estate of Thomas Wolfe

Postcards and Cablegrams of Aline Bernstein © 1985
Missy Cusick

Introduction and Commentary © 1985
Suzanne Stutman

All illustrations by permission of The Houghton Library,
Harvard University

Design and production
Thomas Mair and Duane Schneider

This edition of *Holding on for Heaven: Cables and Postcards of
Thomas Wolfe and Aline Bernstein* is the sixth
annual publication for the members of the Thomas Wolfe Society.

This is copy number ___345___
in an edition of 500 copies.

[i–vi] vii–viii [ix–x] 11–21 [22–24] 25–42 [43–44] 45–52 [53–54] 55–60 [61–62] 63–66 [67–68] 69–70 [71–72]

[1]³⁶

Contents: p. i: half title; p. ii: blank; p. iii: title; p. iv: copyright; p. v: dedication 'To Richard S. Kennedy'; p. vi: blank; pp. vii–viii: text, headed '*Introduction*'; p. ix: '1925–1926 | *Idyllic Years*'; p. x: blank; pp. 11–21: text, headed '1925–1926 | *Idyllic Years*'; p. 22: blank; p. 23: '1927–1928 | *The Grand Renunciation*'; p. 24: blank; pp. 25–42: text headed '1927–1928 | *The Grand Renunciation*'; p. 43: '1929–1930 | *The Long Bitter War of Separation*'; p. 44: blank; pp. 45–52: '1929–1930 | *The Long Bitter War of Separation*'; p. 53: '1931–1932 | *The Final Break*'; p. 54: blank; pp. 55–60: text, headed '1931–1932 | *The Final Break*'; p. 61: '1933–1934 | *One-Sided Love*'; p. 62: blank; pp. 63–66: text, headed '1933–1934 | *One-Sided Love*'; p. 67: '1935–1936 | *Friendship*'; p. 68: blank; pp. 69–70: text, headed '1935–1936 | *Friendship*'; pp. 71–72: blank.

Typography and paper: 7¼" (8½") × 4¾"; 35 lines per page. Running heads: rectos, 'Thomas Wolfe and Aline Bernstein | [rule]'; versos, '*Holding On For Heaven* | [rule]'.

Binding: Light gray wrappers, saddlebound. Front printed in black on background of facsimile of three holograph postcards: 'HOLDING | ON | FOR | HEAVEN | The Cables and Postcards | of Thomas Wolfe | and Aline Bernstein | [facsimile of typescript] scribner interested book dearest aline +'. All edges trimmed.

Wrappers for A 27

Publication: 500 copies. Published 1985. Not for sale. Distributed to members of the Thomas Wolfe Society.

Printing: See copyright.

Locations: CJ, CW.

A 28 THOMAS WOLFE INTERVIEWED, 1929–1938

A 28
Only printing [*1985*]

Thomas Wolfe Interviewed
1929–1938

Edited by
Aldo P. Magi and Richard Walser

Louisiana State University Press
Baton Rouge and London

A 28: 8½" × 5½"

> Copyright © 1985 by Louisiana State University Press
> All rights reserved
> Manufactured in the United States of America
> *Designer:* Joanna Hill
> *Typeface:* Century
> *Typesetter:* G & S Typesetters, Inc.
>
> Grateful appreciation is extended to Paul Gitlin for permission to print excerpts from an unpublished letter by Thomas Wolfe to Marion L. Starkey (in the Special Collections of the Mugar Library, Boston University) and to reprint a passage from Thomas Wolfe's *A Note on Experts: Dexter Vespasian Joyner* (New York, 1939). Copyright © 1983 by Paul Gitlin, Administrator C.T.A., Estate of Thomas Wolfe. Reprinted with the Estate's permission.
>
> *Library of Congress Cataloging in Publication Data*
>
> Main entry under title:
>
> Thomas Wolfe interviewed, 1929–1938.
>
>   (Southern literary studies)
>   Includes index.
>   1. Wolfe, Thomas, 1900–1938—Interviews.
>   2. Novelists, American—20th century—Interviews.
>   3. Fiction—Authorship. I. Magi, Aldo P.
>   II. Walser, Richard Gaither, 1908–   . III. Series.
>   PS3545.O337Z8633 1985   813'.52   84-25083
>   ISBN 0-8071-1229-1

[i–vii] viii [ix–xi] xii–xiii [xiv–xv] xvi–xviii [ix–xx] [1] 2–4 [5] 6–11 [12] 13–20 [21] 22–26 [27] 28–30 [31] 32–33 [34] 35 [36] 37 [38–46] 47–50 [51] 52–53 [54] 55–57 [58] 59–64 [65–66] 67–69 [70] 71–73 [74] 75 [76] 77–79 [80] 81–82 [83] 84–86 [87] 88–90 [91] 92–96 [97] 98–99 [100] 101–102 [103] 104–106 [107] 108–110 [111] 112–120 [121] 122–129 [130–131] 132–135 [136–140]

[1–5]^{16}

Contents: p. i: 'Southern Literary Studies | Louis D. Rubin, Jr., Editor'; p. ii: blank; p. iii: half title; p. iv: blank; p. v: title; p. vi: copyright; pp. vii–viii: contents; p. ix: list of illustrations; p. x: blank; pp. xi–xiii: text, headed '[rule] | Preface and Acknowledgments | [rule]'; p. xiv: blank; pp. xv–xviii: text, headed '[rule] | Chronology | [rule]'; p. xix: half title; p. xx: blank; pp. 1–129: text, headed '[rule] | [bold face] New York University *Daily News,* [roman] October 29, 1929 | [rule]'; p. 130: blank; pp. 131–135: text, headed '[rule] | Index | [rule]'; pp. 136–140: blank.

Typography and paper: 6" (6½") × 4"; 36 lines per page. Running heads: rectos, dates of interviews; versos, 'Thomas Wolfe Interviewed'.

Binding: Grayish greenish yellow V cloth. Spine stamped in red vertically and horizontally: '[vertically] *Magi and Walser* Thomas Wolfe Interviewed,

Thomas Wolfe Interviewed
1929–1938

Edited by Aldo P. Magi and Richard Walser

Two Plays by Thomas Wolfe

Mannerhouse
A Play in a Prologue and Four Acts
Edited and Introduced by Louis D. Rubin, Jr. and John L. Idol, Jr.

This early play by Thomas Wolfe, completed in 1925, is a powerful and evocative account of the Civil War's devastating effect on the South and in particular on one southern family. Wolfe's use of sound, setting, and the techniques of expressionism and symbolism to convey mood and emotion shows a thorough knowledge of the possibilities of the dramatic form. Although Wolfe would find his true voice as a novelist, *Mannerhouse* clearly displays the mark of genius that would make him one of the greatest writers of the century.

Welcome to Our City
A Play in Ten Scenes
Edited and Introduced by Richard S. Kennedy

Written while Thomas Wolfe was a student at Harvard University's renowned 47 Workshop, *Welcome to Our City* is about a modern South overrun with boosterism and dedicated to greed. The action of the play centers on a scheme of the town fathers and real estate promoters of Altamont, a small southern city, to snatch up all the property in a centrally seated black district, evict the tenants, and build a white residential section in its place. Emotionally gripping and mockingly satiric, *Welcome to Our City* effectively captures the festering social climate of the 1920s.

Louisiana State University Press
Baton Rouge 70803

ISBN 0-8071-1229-1

Thomas Wolfe Interviewed, 1929–1938
Edited by Aldo P. Magi and Richard Walser

In *Thomas Wolfe Interviewed, 1929–1938*, Aldo P. Magi and Richard Walser have brought together twenty-five accounts of Thomas Wolfe talking to the press—ranging from the first interview he gave, a conversation with a student journalist for New York University's *Daily News*, to the last, an interview with the Portland *Sunday Oregonian* in July, 1938, only a few months before his death.

These encounters with the working press have an appealing intimacy rarely found in biographies or scholarly studies. Wolfe, always happy to meet with journalists, was ever ready to talk about the writing of *Look Homeward, Angel*, about Scribner's acceptance of the manuscript, and about the book's popular reception. "As my book began to grow before me, a wild sense of exultation and joyous elation seized me," he told an interviewer for the *Rocky Mountain News*. Walking along New York's Fifth Avenue with another interviewer just after *Look Homeward, Angel*'s appearance, Wolfe spotted a copy prominently displayed in a bookstore window and proudly pointed it out. "His eyes came away from the window unwillingly," the reporter noted. Nor did Wolfe shy away from addressing the outrage his first novel occasioned in his hometown. "If they think I have intended to make fun of my old home and my own people they have gone far wrong," he told an interviewer for the Asheville *Times*.

Wolfe talked about his southern upbringing, his education, his frequent trips to Europe, and his life in New York. He enjoyed discussing his favorite authors and books, as

---

well as what he himself planned to write in the future. Wolfe had tremendous faith in America's ability to produce a great national literature.

Readnotes and afterwords place each interview in perspective, brightening the reader's grasp of the varied situations in which Wolfe met with reporters. In some instances, the interviewers themselves reflect on their meetings with Wolfe. For these interviews the journalists had to tape recorders and did not conduct the sort of lengthy, in-depth interviews that have now become common. The interviews are, instead, often the products of several hours of questioning, put together from jotted-down notes and from the reporters' memories. Since most of these interviews have been buried in newspaper archives for decades, even veteran Wolfe scholars will find much here that is fresh and useful.

ALDO P. MAGI'S library of secondary Thomas Wolfe materials, numbering more than three thousand items, is recognized as the largest private collection of its kind in the world. He is associate editor of the *Thomas Wolfe Review* and is a trustee of the Thomas Wolfe Society.

RICHARD WALSER is professor emeritus of English at North Carolina State University. He is the author of several books and numerous articles on Thomas Wolfe and is one of the leading Wolfe scholars in the world.

Southern Literary Studies
Louis D. Rubin, Jr., Editor

Louisiana State University Press
Baton Rouge 70803

Dust jacket for A 28

1929–1938 [at bottom, horizontally] 1935 | [LSU seal] | 1985'. Light reddish brown endpapers. All edges trimmed. Green headbands and footbands.

Dust jacket: Front printed on yellowish gray in black and red: '[black rule] | [red lettering] Thomas Wolfe Interviewed | 1929–1938 | [black rule] | [black lettering] *Edited by Aldo P. Magi and Richard Walser* | [portrait of Wolfe in red by Thea Voelcker with the artists' signature in the lower right-hand corner]'. Spine printed vertically on yellowish gray in black and red: '[black lettering] *Magi and Walser* [red lettering] Thomas Wolfe Interviewed, 1929–1938 [black lettering] *Louisiana*'. Back: blurbs for *M* (A 14) and *WTOC* and biographical material for Magi and Walser.

Publication: Number of copies not determined. Copyright #TX-1-842-841. Published 24 November 1985. Price: $16.95.

Printing: Printed by Thomson-Shore, Dexter, Michigan.

Locations: CJ (dj), DLC (2 copies; 1 stamped 'DEC 2 6 1985' and 1 stamped 'JAN– 7 1985'), JI (dj).

A 29 THE HOUND OF DARKNESS

A 29
Only printing (1986)

The Hound of Darkness

Edited, with a Foreword, by
John L. Idol, Jr.

The Thomas Wolfe Society

1986

A 29: 10″ × 7″

> © 1986 The Thomas Wolfe Society
> All rights reserved
> Manufactured in the United States of America
>
> Approved by Mr. Paul Gitlin,
> Administrator, C.T.A., Estate of Thomas Wolfe
>
> *Permission:*
> The materials published herein come
> from the William B. Wisdom Collection
> and are printed for the first time
> by permission of Paul Gitlin and the
> Houghton Library, Harvard University.
>
> This edition of *The Hound of Darkness*
> is the seventh annual publication for
> members of the Thomas Wolfe Society.
>
> This is copy number _____
> in an edition of 600 copies.

[i–xi] xii–xix [xx] [1–3] 4–5 [6–7] 8–32 [33–35] 36–38 [39–41] 42–46 [47–49] 50–66 [67–69] 70 [71–73] 74 [75–77] 78 [79–81] 82–88 [89–91] 92–94 [95–97] 98–104 [105–107] 108–125 [126–127] 128 [129–131] 132–134 [135–140]

[1–5]^{16}

Contents: p. i: half title; p. ii 'THOMAS | WOLFE'; p. iii: title; p. iv: copyright; p. v: text, headed *'Acknowledgements'*; p. vi: blank; p. vii: dedication; p. viii: blank; p. ix: contents; p. x: blank; pp. xi–xix: text, headed 'Forward'; p. xx: blank; p. 1: half title; p. 2: blank; pp. 3–5: text, headed 'A Prologue to America'; p. 6: blank; pp. 7–32: text, headed 'The House at Malbourne'; pp. 33–34: blank; pp. 35–38: text, headed 'The Lovers'; pp. 39–40: blank; pp. 41–46: text, headed 'The Mexicans'; pp. 47–48: blank; pp. 49–66: text, headed 'The Newspaper'; pp. 67–68: blank; pp. 69–70: text, headed 'The House in Boston'; pp. 71–72: blank; pp. 73–74: text, headed 'The Whores'; pp. 75–76: blank; pp. 77–78: text, headed '[The Boy in Bed]'; pp. 79–80: blank; pp. 81–88: text, headed 'The Drug Store'; pp. 89–90: blank; pp. 91–94: text, headed 'The Seaman: Dere Ain't No | Decent Air in Brooklyn'; pp. 95–96: blank; pp. 97–104: text, headed: 'The Fantasies: Clara Kimball Young'; pp. 105–106: blank; pp. 107–125: text, headed 'The Wind from the West'; p. 126: blank; pp. 127–128: text, headed 'The Pencil Merchant'; pp. 129–130: blank; pp. 131–134: text, headed 'The Rock in Maine'; pp. 135–

A 29 *The Hound of Darkness*

136: blank; p. 137: 'Appendix'; p. 138: blank; p. 139: text, headed 'The Whorehouse Rag'; p. 140: blank.

13 skits, 1 fragment, and 1 song: "A Prologue to America" #, "The House at Malbourne",* "The Lovers",* "The Mexicans",* "The Newspaper" (see A 9 and A 10—retitled "Gentlemen of the Press"), "The House In Boston",* "The Whores",* "[The Boy in Bed]",* "The Drug Store",* "The Seaman: Dere Ain't No Decent Air in Brooklyn",* "The Fantasies: Clara Kimball Young",* "The Wind from the West",* "The Pencil Merchant",* "The Rock in Maine",* "The Whorehouse Rag".*

Typography and paper: 7½" (7⅞") × 4⅞"; 37 lines per page. Running heads: rectos, *'The Hound of Darkness'*; versos, *'Thomas Wolfe'*. Wove paper.

Binding: Black V cloth. Front goldstamped on a blindstamped rectangular panel: '[rule] | The Hound | of | Darkness | [rule] | THOMAS WOLFE | [rule]'; spine: goldstamped vertically: *'The Hound of Darkness* WOLFE [in two lines] Thomas Wolfe | Society'; spine: blindstamped Wolfe Society seal. White wove endpapers coated on verso of front paste-down and recto of free-front endpapers and on verso of free-back and recto of back paste-down endpapers with facsimile manuscript. All edges trimmed.

Publication: 600 copies. Published May 1986. Not for sale. Distributed to members of the Thomas Wolfe Society.

Locations: CJ, JI.

Binding for A 29

AA. Posthumously Published Collections

Posthumously collected volumes of Wolfe's writings published in the United States and Great Britain through 1985 which do not include any previously unpublished material by Wolfe.

AA 1 THE FACE OF A NATION
1939 (Simultaneous publications)

AA 1.1.a
[beneath woodcut of a man] THE FACE | OF A | NATION | *Poetical Passages* | *From the Writings* | *of* | THOMAS WOLFE | [decoration] | *Decorations by* | EDWARD SHENTON | [french rule] | *CHARLES SCRIBNER'S SONS* [bullet] *NEW YORK* | *1939*

On copyright page: 'CL'.

321 pp.

Contents: "America," "The Golden World," "Greeting and Farewell," "Fixity and Change," "We Shall Not Come Again," "The Unvisited World," "Where Now?" "Conversation by Moonlight," "Drunkenness," "April Night and Morning," "Euripides in the Wilderness," "O Young Love, Return," "Departure," "Journey to the North," "O Lost," "Who Has Known Fury?" "Man's Youth," "The Earth Flows By," "The Lost Land," "Lost Country of Youth," "Destiny," "Portrait," "Lonely Joy," "The Dream of Time," "The Heart of the Dark," "Hunger to Devour the Earth," "Coming of Spring," "Proud Cruel City," "The Secret Heart of Night," "The Hudson River," "Discovery of Catawba," "Springtime in New England," "Demoniac Ecstasy," "Remembered Faces," "Jewish Women," "The Inevitable Instant," "The World of First Light," "October Has Come Again," "Light of Fading Day," "The Sound of the Sea," "His Father's Hands," "Night," "Hymn to Death, Loneliness and Sleep," "Far Away Lay America," "Opulent Fantasies," "Old Men and Women," "Spring Night in the City," "Life's Hungry Man," "Echoes of Forgotten Time," "Voices of the Books," "Lost and Scattered," "Visions of Horror and of Delight," "The American Wilderness," "O Flower of Love," "Space and Movement," "Names of the Nation," "Spring Plowing," "Waters of Darkness," "Escape into the World," "Young, and Drunk, and Twenty," "Dreams of Guilt and Time," "The Four Lost Men," "Faces," "What Is This Memory?" "To Keep Time With," "Speaking Dust," "Return to America," "Herrick, Crashaw, Carew," "May Morning In the Park," "Food," "The Hills of Home." Excerpts from *LHA, OTATR, SOAN,* and *FDTM*.

Dust jacket.

Publication: 7,500 copies. Copyright #A135146. Published 2 October 1939. Date of contract: 26 May 1939. Royalty: 10% first 5,000, then 15%. Price: $2.75. Reprinted in 1949 and in 1953.

Printing: Printed and bound by Country Life Press, Garden City, New York.

Locations: CJ (dj), DLC (OCT 18 1939), EG (5 copies; 3 copies with dj and 1 copy dated 1949), MH, NcRSM (dj).

Salesman's dummy: includes excerpt from FOAN.

Title page: '[beneath woodcut of a man] THE FACE | OF A | NATION | *Poetical Passages* | *From the Writings* | *of* | THOMAS WOLFE | [decoration] | *Decorations by* | EDWARD SHENTON | [french rule] | *CHARLES SCRIBNER'S, SONS [bullet] NEW YORK* | *1939*'.

On copyright page: 'A'.

pp. 113–118.

Contents: "The Four Lost Men".

Binding: Black V cloth.

Location: MH.

AA 1.1.b

Identical to AA 1.1.a except for:

Title page: '[beneath woodcut of a man] THE FACE | OF A | NATION | *Poetical Passages* | *From the Writings* | *of* | [roman] THOMAS WOLFE | [decoration] *Decorations by* | EDWARD SHENTON | [french rule] | *THE LITERARY GUILD OF AMERICA, INC.* | *NEW YORK 1939*'.

Publication: Number of copies not determined.

Locations: NcRSM (2 copies with djs), ViU (2 copies).

Note one: A memo dated 6 November 1947 in the Scribners records indicates that FOAN had been printed three times prior to that date.

AA 2 STORIES BY THOMAS WOLFE
1944

[within quadruple-rules frame] Stories | *by* | THOMAS WOLFE | [decoration] | AVON BOOK COMPANY | Jo Meyers [bullet] E. B. Williams | 432 FOURTH AVENUE, NEW YORK 16, N.Y. | [rule] | *Published by special arrangement with* Harper & Brothers

Wrappers.

On copyright page: 'Copyright, 1944'.

135 pp.

Contents: "No Cure for It," "Gentlemen of the Press," "A Kinsman of His Blood," "Chickamauga," "The Return of the Prodigal," "The Lion at Morning," "The Battle of Hogwart Heights," "The Lost Boy." All are from *THB*.

Publication: Number of copies not determined. *Avon Modern Short Story Monthly* #17. Published 20 June 1944. Price: 25¢.

Locations: APM, CJ, EG, MH, MJB, NcA (2 copies), NcRSM (2 copies).

AA 3 A STONE, A LEAF, A DOOR
1945

A Stone, A Leaf, A Door | POEMS | BY THOMAS WOLFE | *Selected and Arranged in Verse by* | JOHN S. BARNES | [decoration] | *With a Foreword by* | LOUIS UNTERMEYER | *New York* | CHARLES SCRIBNER'S SONS | 1945

On copyright page: 'A'.

166 pp.

Contents: "A Stone, A Leaf, A Door," "Ben," "Yesterday, Remember?" "O Lost," "Artemidorus, Farewell!" "Royal Processional," "Magic," "Niggertown," "Gant," "Eugene," "Dance," "The Cock That Crows at Morning," "Play Us a Tune," "Father, I Know That You Live," "Yuh Musta Been Away," "In Silence," "Like the River," "The Way Things Are," "Pity," "Night," "Death, Loneliness, and Sleep," "As It Had Always Been," "Immortal Drunkenness," "Fountain," "This Is Man," "Ben, My Ghost," "Full with the Pulse of Time," "The Bridge," "That Sharp Knife," "Spring in the South," "New Orleans—River," "Come Back Again," "The Locomotive," "At Morning," "Where Are We to Seek?" "Light of Fading Day," "What Are We?" "The Great Ship," "April," "The Blazing Certitude," "Stranger than a Dream," "The Old House," "Spring," "Like the First Day of the World," "City April," "The Ghosts of Time," "Chance," "You Were Not Absent," "Old Men and Women," "To Keep Time With," "Plum Tree," "Moonlight," "Flood in Altamont," "Gant's Dream," "Gold and Sapphires," "The Proud Stars," "The Magic and the Loss," "Like the Light," "Judge Bland," "Never Opened, Never Found," "Some Things Will Never Change," "Brooklyn," "The Song of the Whole Land," "The Ship," "The Vision of the City," "The Railroad Station," "Going Home Again," "October," "The Silence of the House," "Time," "Burning in the Night," "Toward Which."

Publication: 3,000 copies. Copyright #A794. Published prior to 13 October 1945. Date of contract: 8 January 1945. Royalty: 5% to John S. Barnes on all copies sold in first seven years, after a sale of 750 copies; 10% to the estate of Thomas Wolfe on all copies sold in first seven years, and 15% thereafter.

Price: $2.50. Reprinted at least fifteen times prior to February 1970. Reprints noted: 1945 (omits 'A' on copyright page); 1948; 1950; 1954; February 1960 (with 'K-2.60[V]' on copyright page); and February 1970 (with 'O-2.70[V]' on copyright page). Printed at least three times in wrappers as *Scribner Library* #SL 283. Reprinted as a *Hudson River Edition* [c. 1980].

Dust jacket.

Printing: Printed and bound by the Scribner Press, New York City.

Locations: APM (2 copies; 1 copy with dj and 1 copy 'K-2.60[V]'), DLC (1 copy stamped 'OCT 13 1945' and reprint copy: 'O-2.70[V]'), InU Lilly (dj), MB (1948), MH, MJB (reprint), NcA (2 copies; 1 copy 1954), NcRSM (1945 printing without 'A'; 1954 printing in wrappers), PSt (dj), ViU (1950 reprint), ScCleU.

Note one: Information taken from a memo dated 6 November 1947 and from an unsigned letter to John S. Barnes dated 30 October 1945, both in the Scribner records, indicates that *ASALAD* went through five printings prior to 6 November 1947 and that the first three printings numbered 3,000 copies, 2,000 copies, and 5,000 copies, respectively.

AA 4 THE PORTABLE THOMAS WOLFE
1946

AA 4.1.a–b
First and second printings

The Portable | THOMAS WOLFE | *Edited by Maxwell Geismar* | [Viking Press seal over a rule] | *NEW YORK: THE VIKING PRESS* | 1946

On copyright page: 'PUBLISHED IN AUGUST, 1946'.

712 pp.

Contents: "Artemidorus, Farewell," "Jason's Voyage," "Love's Bitter Mystery," "The Quest of the Fair Medusa," "The Story of a Novel," "The Face of the War," "Only the Dead Know Brooklyn," "Dark in the Forest, Strange as Time," "Circus at Dawn," "In the Park," "Chickamauga." Excerpts from *LHA, OTATR, TWATR, YCGHA, SOAN, FDTM,* and *THB.*

Dust jacket.

Publication: Number of copies not determined. Copyright #A5505. Published prior to 28 August 1946. Royalty: 10% of 28% to Harper & Brothers; 90% of 28% to the Estate of Thomas Wolfe; 50% of 72% to Charles Scribners Sons; 50% of 72% to the Estate of Thomas Wolfe subject to 10% of 40% to Madeleine Boyd. Price: $2.00. Reprinted in August 1948.

Locations: CJ (dj), DLC (Aug. 28, 1946), EG (dj), InU Lilly (dj), MH, ViU (August 1948; rebound).

AA 4.1.c
Third printing

[within a wavy frame] THE INDISPENSABLE | [ornamental lettering] THOMAS WOLFE | [beneath frame] EDITED BY | MAXWELL GEISMAR | [diamond] | NEW YORK | THE BOOK SOCIETY | 1950

On copyright page: 'PUBLISHED IN AUGUST, 1946'.

Locations: APM, NcRSM.

AA 4.1.d
Fourth printing

Selections from the Works of | THOMAS WOLFE | *Edited by Maxwell Geismar* | [Heinemann seal] | [rule] | WILLIAM HEINEMANN LTD | MELBOURNE :: LONDON :: TORONTO

On copyright page: 'FIRST PUBLISHED 1952'.

Publication: Number of copies not determined. Published in 1952. Price: 12/6.

Locations: BL (25JUL52), InU Lilly (dj), MH, NcA (dj), NcRSM (2 copies).

AA 5 THOMAS WOLFE SHORT STORIES
1947

AA 5.1.a
First printing

THOMAS WOLFE | SHORT STORIES | *Vigil strange I kept on the field one night* | [Penguin seal] PENGUIN BOOKS, INC [bullet] NEW YORK

Wrappers.

On copyright page: 'FIRST PENGUIN BOOKS EDITION, SEPTEMBER, 1947'.

150 pp.

Contents: "The Men of Old Catawba," "The Four Lost Men," "Circus at Dawn," "The Bums at Sunset," "Only the Dead Know Brooklyn," "Death the Proud Brother," "Gulliver," *The Story of a Novel:* Selections from *FDTM* and the complete *SOAN*.

Publication: Number of copies not determined. Penguin #644. Published September 1947. Price: 25¢.

Printing: Not determined.

Locations: EG, MH, MJB, MoU, NcRSM (2 copies).

AA 5.1.b–c
Second and third printings

THOMAS WOLFE SHORT STORIES | Only The Dead | Know Brooklyn | [tapered rule] | *Selections from* | *FROM DEATH TO MORNING* | *plus* | *THE STORY OF A NOVEL* [Signet seal] | A SIGNET BOOK | Published by THE NEW AMERICAN LIBRARY.

Wrappers.

Publication: Number of copies not determined. Published in July 1949 as Signet #950. Reprinted in October 1952. Price: 25¢.

Locations: CJ (1952), Dr. Martin Luther College (1949), EG (2 copies 1952), MJB (1952), NcU (2 copies 1952).

AA 6 THE SHORT NOVELS OF THOMAS WOLFE
1961

THE SHORT NOVELS OF | [decoration] Thomas Wolfe | EDITED, | WITH AN INTRODUCTION | AND NOTES BY | *C. HUGH HOLMAN* | CHARLES SCRIBNER'S SONS [decoration] New York

On copyright page: 'A-2.61[H]'

323 pp.

Contents: "A Portrait of Bascom Hawke," "The Web of Earth," "No Door," " 'I Have a Thing to Tell You,' " "The Party at Jack's."

Dust jacket.

Publication: Number of copies not determined. Copyright #A497620. Published in February 1961. Price $4.50. Reprinted at least five times prior to February 1971. Reprints noted: 'D-2.69 [H]' [February 1969] and 'E-2.71 [H]' [February 1971]. Also reprinted as *Hudson River Edition* c. 1980.

Printing: Printed by the Haddon Craftsmen, Scranton, Pennsylvania.

Locations: BL (28FEB65), DLC (2 copies; both stamped 'APR 25 1961'), EG (dj), MH, MJB (dj), NcRSM, ScCleU (reprint: 'D-2.69[H]'), ViU (reprint: 'E-2.71[H]').

AA 7 THE THOMAS WOLFE READER
1962

THE | [six rules] | THOMAS WOLFE | [six rules] | READER | *Edited, with an Introduction and Notes,* by | C. HUGH HOLMAN | New York | [six rules] | CHARLES SCRIBNER'S SONS

On copyright page: 'A-4.62 [H]'.

690 pp.

Contents: Excerpts from *SOAN, LHA, OTATR, FDTM, TWATR, YCGHA,* and *THB;* a poem entitled "Toward Which"; and a letter to Maxwell Perkins dated 12 August 1938.

Dust jacket.

Publication: Number of copies not determined. Published in April 1962. Price: $7.50. Reprinted at least twice; once in January 1970.

Locations: DLC (JUL 13 1962), EG, JI (dj), MH, MJB (dj), NcRSM (3 copies: 1 copy 'A-4.62[H]'; 1 copy without code on copyright page; and 1 copy 'B-1.70[H]' in dj), ViU ('B-1.70 [H]').

AA 8 THE AUTOBIOGRAPHY OF AN AMERICAN NOVELIST
1983

THE | AUTOBIOGRAPHY | OF AN | AMERICAN | NOVELIST | [rule] | Thomas Wolfe | *Edited by Leslie Field* | HARVARD UNIVERSITY PRESS | Cambridge, Massachusetts | London, England | 1983

On copyright page: '10 9 8 7 6 5 4 3 2 1'.

152 pp.

Contents: *SOAN* and "Writing and Living."

Publication: Number of copies not determined. Published in May 1983 in cloth and in wrappers. Price: cloth, $15.00; wrappers $5.95.

Locations: APM, CJ (wrappers), DLC (MAY 31983), ScCleU.

Note one: Field's edition of *SOAN,* published here, uses the entirety of Wolfe's original seventy-four-page typescript, severely edited by Elizabeth Nowell for publication in *The Saturday Review of Literature,* as copy-text, rather than the typescript prepared by Wolfe later for book publication in the 1936 Scribners edition. Field's edition of "Writing and Living," published here, fills in some twenty-one 'hiatuses' in the 1964 Purdue University Studies edition. See A 5, A 9, C 53, and C 87.

B. First Book and Pamphlet Appearances

Titles in which material by Wolfe appears for the first time in a book or pamphlet. Previously published items are so identified. The first printings only of these titles are described, but retitled reprintings and selected reprintings are also noted.

B 1 CAROLINA FOLK-PLAYS (SECOND SERIES)
1924

SECOND SERIES | [rule] | CAROLINA | FOLK-PLAYS | Edited | With An Introduction on MAKING A FOLK THEATRE | By | FREDERICK H. KOCH | Founder and Director of The Carolina Playmakers | And Editor of the First Series of their plays | *Illustrated from photographs of the original productions of* | *the plays* | [Holt seal] | NEW YORK | HENRY HOLT AND COMPANY | 1924

"The Return of Buck Gavin," pp. 31–44. Previously unpublished.

A one-act play produced by the Carolina Playmakers at Chapel Hill, North Carolina, on 14 and 15 March 1919. Included in *Carolina Folk-Plays (First, Second, and Third Series)* (B10).

Locations: APM, InU Lilly, MH (2 copies), NcA, NcRSM (4 copies), NcU, ScCleU, ViU.

Note one: Reprinted at a later date with the year omitted from title page (MH, NcA).

B 2 MODERN AMERICAN PROSE
1934 (Simultaneous publications)

B 2.1.a

[within double-rules frame decorated at corners and in ornamental lettering] MODERN AMERICAN PROSE | *Edited by* | CARL VAN DOREN | HARCOURT, BRACE AND COMPANY | NEW YORK 1934

"A Portrait of Bascom Hawke," pp. 743–796. See C 19.

Locations: DLC (Aug 7 1934), MH.

B 2.1.b

Identical to B 2.1.a except for:

[within double-rules frame decorated at corners and in ornamental lettering] MODERN AMERICAN PROSE | *Edited by* | CARL VAN DOREN | THE LITERARY GUILD | NEW YORK 1934

Location: DLC.

B 3 EDITOR'S CHOICE
1934

[within double-rules frame] EDITOR'S | CHOICE | [decoration] | ALFRED DASHIELL | [G. P. Putnam seal] | G [bullet] P [bullet] PUTNAM'S SONS | NEW YORK

Published in 1934.

"The Web of Earth," pp. 33–111. See C 20.

Locations: DLC (OCT 27 1934), InU Lilly (dj), MH.

B 4 O. HENRY PRIZE STORIES OF 1934
1934

O. HENRY | MEMORIAL AWARD | [ornamental lettering] Prize Stories of 1934 | [roman] SELECTED AND EDITED BY | HENRY HANSEN | *Literary Editor of* | *the New York World-Telegram* | [Doubleday seal] | DOUBLEDAY, DORAN & COMPANY, INC. | GARDEN CITY, NEW YORK | 1934

"Boom Town," pp. 243–279. See C 26.

Locations: DLC (DEC 31 1934), InU Lilly (dj), MH.

B 5 O. HENRY PRIZE STORIES OF 1935
1935

O. HENRY | MEMORIAL AWARD | [ornamental lettering] Prize Stories of 1935 | [roman] *SELECTED AND EDITED BY* | *HARRY HANSEN* | *Literary Editor of the New York World-Telegram* | [Doubleday seal] | DOUBLEDAY, DORAN & COMPANY, INC. | GARDEN CITY, NEW YORK | 1935

"Only the Dead Know Brooklyn," pp. 265–273. See C 36.

Publication: Published 8 November 1935, 6 days prior to its publication in *FDTM*.

Locations: DLC (NOV 12 1935), MH, NcRSM.

B 6 PRESS TIME
1936

[within a frame of type ornaments and three rules] PRESS | TIME | *A BOOK OF* | *POST CLASSICS* | [rule] | [seal depicting a printing press] | [rule] | BOOKS, INC. | NEW YORK

Published in 1936.

First Book and Pamphlet Appearances 213

"An Interview with Thomas Wolfe" by May Cameron, pp. 247–252.

Largely written by Wolfe. See C 55.

Locations: APM, InU Lilly, MH, NcRSM, ViRCU.

B 7 PORTRAITS AND SELF-PORTRAITS
1936

PORTRAITS AND | SELF-PORTRAITS | COLLECTED AND ILLUSTRATED BY | GEORGES SCHREIBER | 1936 | HOUGHTON MIFFLIN COMPANY BOSTON | [gothic lettering] The Riverside Press Cambridge

"Thomas Wolfe," an autobiographical sketch, pp. 163–167. Previously unpublished. See B 21, B 49, B 50, C 136.

Locations: InU Lilly (dj), MH, NcA.

B 8 1936 ESSAY ANNUAL
1936

[decoration above four rules] | 1936 | ESSAY ANNUAL | A Yearly Collection of Signifi- | cant Essays, Personal, Critical, | Controversial, and Humorous | ERICH A. WALTER | *Department of English, University of Michigan* | [decoration] | SCOTT, FORESMAN AND COMPANY | *Chicago-Atlanta-Dallas-New York* | [decoration below four rules]

"His Father's Earth," pp. 104–114. See C 34.

Locations: APM, InU Lilly, MH, ViU.

B 9 POST STORIES OF 1937
1938

[within triple-rules frame in ornamental lettering] POST STORIES | OF 1937 | [Ben Franklin silhouette] | [roman] BOSTON | LITTLE, BROWN AND COMPANY | 1938

"The Child by Tiger," pp. 243–265. See C 76.

Location: MH, ScCoR.

B 10 CAROLINA FOLK-PLAYS (FIRST, SECOND, AND THIRD SERIES)
1941

[within double-rules frame] CAROLINA | FOLK-PLAYS | [rule] | FIRST, SECOND, AND THIRD SERIES | [decoration] | Edited and with an Introduction by | FREDERICK H. KOCH | *Founder and Director of* | *The Carolina Playmakers* | Foreward by | PAUL GREEN | [Holt seal] | NEW YORK | HENRY HOLT AND COMPANY

Published in 1941.

"The Third Night," pp. 125–143. Previously unpublished. See C 94.

Locations: MH, NcRSM (2 copies).

B 11 VOGUE'S FIRST READER
1942

Vogue's | *First* | Reader | [rule] | INTRODUCTION BY FRANK CROWNINSHIELD | *Julian Messner, Incorporated* [star] 1942 [star] *New York*

"A Prologue to America," pp. 13–20. See C 85. Only half of the original material is printed. See A 22 for first complete reprinting. See also A 29.

Reprinted in 1944 and 1948.

Locations: DLC, InU Lilly (dj), MH, MJB (1948).

B 12 THOMAS WOLFE A BIBLIOGRAPHY
1943

[purple lettering] THOMAS WOLFE | [black ornamental lettering] a Bibliography | [roman] by GEORGE R. PRESTON, JR. | [Boesen seal in purple] | CHARLES S. BOESEN | 270 Park Avenue *Publisher* New York, N.Y. | 1943

Facsimiles previously unpublished ms. page of "O Lost," p. 24, and quotes briefly from a conversation with Wolfe, p. 54. See D 11.

Locations: APM (2 copies; 1 copy 1979), EG (1979), InU Lilly, MJB, ScCleU.

Note one: Facsimile reprint in 1979 by Greenwood Press, Westport, Connecticut.

B 13 THE CRACK-UP
1945

[ornamental lettering] THE CRACK-UP | [roman] F. SCOTT FITZGERALD | With other Uncollected Pieces, | Note=Books and Unpublished Letters | Together with Letters to Fitz- | gerald from Gertrude Stein, Edith | Wharton, T. S. Eliot, Thomas Wolfe | and John Dos Passos | And Essays and Poems by Paul | Rosenfeld, Glenway Wescott, John | Dos Passos, John Peale Bishop and

| Edmund Wilson | *Edited by* [decoration] EDMUND WILSON | *A New Directions Book*

Published in 1945.

"A Letter from Thomas Wolfe," pp. 312–316. Previously unpublished. See *Letters*, pp. 641–645.

Locations: InU Lilly (dj), MH, NcA, ScCleU.

B 14 OF MAKING MANY BOOKS
1946

OF MAKING | MANY BOOKS | [rule] | *A Hundred Years of Reading, Writing and Publishing* | [rule] | by | ROGER BURLINGAME | MDCCC XLVI [Scribners seal] MDCCCC XLVI | [rule] | *NEW YORK* | CHARLES SCRIBNER'S SONS | 1946

Previously unpublished letter to John Hall Wheelock dated summer 1929 and undated letter to Mrs. J. M. Roberts, pp. 1–2, 40–42. See C 131.

Locations: APM (dj), InU Lilly (dj), NcA, NcRSM.

B 15 UNSEEN HARVESTS
1947

[within a double-rules frame] *Unseen Harvests* | A TREASURY OF TEACHING | *Edited by* | CLAUDE M. FUESS | *and* | EMORY S. BASFORD | THE MACMILLAN COMPANY | NEW YORK [bullet] 1947

"A Letter of Gratitude and Indebtedness," pp. 437–438. See C 131.

Letter to Frank Wells, Superintendent of Schools in Asheville, North Carolina.

Locations: InU Lilly (dj), ScCleU.

B 16 THOMAS WOLFE A CRITICAL STUDY
1947

THOMAS WOLFE | *A Critical Study* | BY | PAMELA HANSFORD JOHNSON | [Heinemann seal] | [rule] | WILLIAM HEINEMANN LTD | LONDON : : TORONTO

Published in 1947.

Quotes from undated letters to Mrs. J. M. Roberts, pp. 2–3, 4, 11, 12, 15, 37, 38, 107–108, and 129. See C 131.

Location: NcA.

Note one: Distributed by Scribners in New York and London in 1948 in a new edition and retitled *Hungry Gulliver An English Critical Appraisal of Thomas Wolfe* (APM, NcA). Republished in wrappers as *The Scribner Library* #SL 81 in January 1963, retitled *The Art of Thomas Wolfe* (APM).

B 17 TOM WOLFE'S "DIXIELAND"
1949

TOM | WOLFE'S | *"Dixieland"* | [portrait of a young Thomas Wolfe] | *By* LOLA LOVE McCOY

Published in 1949.

Wrappers.

Facsimiles inscription to Margaret Roberts dated 15 October 1929 in a copy of *LHA,* p. [11]. See C 137 and C 148.

Locations: APM, EG.

B 18 EDITOR TO AUTHOR
1950

EDITOR TO AUTHOR | THE LETTERS OF | MAXWELL E. PERKINS | *Selected and Edited, with Commentary* | *and an Introduction* | *by* | JOHN HALL WHEELOCK | [Scribners seal] | *CHARLES SCRIBNER'S SONS, NEW YORK* | *CHARLES SCRIBNER'S SONS, LTD., LONDON* | *1950*

"Letter to Maxwell Perkins," p. 141. See C 120, C 134, and *Letters,* pp. 777–778.

Locations: EG (dj), InU Lilly (dj), NcRSM.

Note one: Republished by Grosset & Dunlap as *Grosset's Universal Library* #UL-75.

B 19 THOMAS WOLFE: CAROLINA STUDENT
1950

Thomas Wolfe: Carolina Student | A BRIEF BIOGRAPHY | by AGATHA BOYD ADAMS | [decoration] | CHAPEL HILL | THE UNIVERSITY OF NORTH CAROLINA LIBRARY | 1950

Quotes from a *Tar Heel* editorial attributed to Wolfe, "Useful Advice to Candidates," p. 43 (see E 4), and, in passing, from letters and conversations. See C 143.

Locations: InU Lilly, NcRSM.

Note one: Reprinted in 1955 (APM).

B 20 SHERWOOD ANDERSON HIS LIFE AND WORK
1951

JAMES SCHEVILL | SHERWOOD | ANDERSON | His Life and Work | THE UNIVERSITY OF DENVER PRESS

Published in 1951.

Letter to Sherwood Anderson, pp. 325–326. Previously unpublished. See *Letters*, pp. 654–656, and C 124.

Locations: InU Lilly (dj), NcA, NcRSM, ScCleU.

B 21 THE ENIGMA OF THOMAS WOLFE
1953

THE ENIGMA of | *THOMAS WOLFE* | *Biographical and Critical Selections* | *Edited by RICHARD WALSER* | *Harvard University Press, Cambridge, 1953*

"Something of My Life," pp. 3–7. First book appearance of the complete essay, part of which appeared in 1936 in Georges Schreiber's *Portraits and Self-Portraits*. See B 7, B 49, B 50, C 136.

"Justice Is Blind," pp. 91–100. Previously unpublished.

Bishop, Don. "Tom Wolfe As A Student," pp. 8–17. Quotes briefly from an unidentified manuscript written by Wolfe "As editor of the newspaper," from conversations, and from articles in *The Tar Heel* that might have been written by Wolfe. See E 16.

Kennedy, Richard S. "Wolfe's Harvard Years," pp. 18–32. Quotes from an undated letter to Edwin Greenlaw, from Wolfe's Autobiographical Outline, from a letter to Miss MacReady of the Harvard Appointment Bureau dated 22 August, from a fall 1922 letter to Mrs. J. M. Roberts, and from a note to Professor Baker. A reworking of C 144.

Volkening, Henry T. "Penance No More," pp. 33–50. Quotes from conversations with and letters to Henry T. Volkening and from the inscription in Volkening's copy of *FDTM*. See C 100 and *Letters*, pp. 180–182, 194, 289–293.

Braswell, William. "Thomas Wolfe Lectures and Takes A Holiday," pp. 64–76. Quotes from three letters to Herbert J. Muller, from a letter "to his host in Lafayette," from Wolfe's letter to the editor of *The Nation* (see C 89), and from conversations. See C 111.

Locations: APM (dj), InU Lilly (dj), NcRSM (2 copies), ScCleU.

B 22 THOMAS WOLFE AT WASHINGTON SQUARE
1954

THOMAS WOLFE | AT | WASHINGTON SQUARE | [on light tan Washington Square Monument] BY | THOMAS CLARK POLLOCK | AND OSCAR CARGILL | [beneath monument] New York University Press | WASHINGTON SQUARE [bullet] NEW YORK | [tapered rule] | London: Geoffrey Cumberlege Oxford University Press | 1954

Published in January 1954.

Quotes from conversations with Wolfe, facsimiles Wolfe's previously unpublished comments on a student paper, prints a previously unpublished letter to Russell Kraus dated 7 February.

Locations: APM (dj), CJ (dj with slipcase), InU Lilly (dj), NcA, NcRSM.

Note one: Distributed with *The Correspondence of Thomas Wolfe and Homer Andrew Watt* as a "Limited Edition" boxed set. See A 17.1.a, *Note one.*

Note two: Second printing in July 1954 (CJ [dj]).

B 23 AUTHORS AT WORK
1957

Authors at Work | AN ADDRESS DELIVERED BY | Robert H. Taylor | AT THE OPENING OF AN EXHIBITION | OF LITERARY MANUSCRIPTS | AT THE GROLIER CLUB | TOGETHER WITH A CATALOGUE OF THE EXHIBITION BY | Herman W. Liebert | AND FACSIMILES OF MANY | OF THE EXHIBITS | [ornamental rule] | New York [bullet] The Grolier Club [bullet] 1957

Published 1 November 1957.

Facsimiles a page from Wolfe's Autobiographical Outline and a manuscript page from *LHA*. Previously unpublished.

Locations: InU Lilly, NcA.

B 24 THOMAS WOLFE: A BIOGRAPHY
1960

[ornamental lettering] Thomas Wolfe | [roman] A BIOGRAPHY | BY | [ornamental lettering] Elizabeth Nowell | GARDEN CITY, NEW YORK | *Doubleday & Company, Inc.* | 1960

Quotes in passing from previously unpublished conversations, reminiscences, and letters.

First Book and Pamphlet Appearances

Locations: APM (dj), ScCleU.

Note one: Also a Book-of-the-Month Club Selection (CJ). Printed by Heinemann (London, Melbourne, and Toronto) in 1961 (CJ) and reprinted by Greenwood Press (Westport, Connecticut) in 1972 (NcA).

B 25 THOMAS WOLFE OCTOBER RECOLLECTIONS
1961

JONATHAN DANIELS | THOMAS WOLFE | *October Recollections* | [decoration] | BOSTICK & THORNLEY, PUBLISHERS | *Columbia, South Carolina*

Published in 1961.

Quotes briefly from undated letter to Jonathan Daniels, p. 13. Previously unpublished.

Locations: APM, InU Lilly, ScCleU.

B 26 THOMAS WOLFE AND HIS FAMILY
1961

THOMAS WOLFE | and HIS FAMILY | BY MABEL WOLFE WHEATON WITH LeGETTE BLYTHE | DOUBLEDAY & COMPANY, INC., GARDEN CITY, NEW YORK 1961

Quotes from conversations with Wolfe, from a previously unpublished letter to Fred Wolfe dated 3 May, pp. 227–228, and from previously unpublished inscriptions in Fred Wolfe's copies of *FDTM* and *OTATR*, p. 160.

Locations: APM (dj), EG, NcRSM.

B 27 THE WINDOW OF MEMORY
1962

[ornamental lettering] THE | WINDOW OF | MEMORY | [wavy line] *The Literary Career of Thomas Wolfe* | [wavy line] | by | RICHARD S. KENNEDY | "You want to make a perfect thing, but I want | to get the whole wilderness of the American | continent into my work." | —Thomas Wolfe to John Hall | Wheelock in conversation. | CHAPEL HILL | THE UNIVERSITY OF NORTH CAROLINA PRESS

Published in 1962.

Quotes at length from and prints previously unpublished letters, manuscripts, and notebooks. Prints the rough outline for *TWATR*, pp. 415–437.

Locations: APM (dj), CJ (wrappers), InU Lilly, NcA (2 copies), ScCleU.

Note one: A reduced photo-offset reprint was distributed in wrappers in 1968 containing 'A PREFACE TO THE 1968 PRINTING' (p. x). Some material on pages 222 and 223 in this printing has been reset.

B 28 THE NORTH CAROLINA MISCELLANY
1962

[two-page title page] [decoration] The | *North Carolina* | Miscellany | edited by | RICHARD WALSER | CHAPEL HILL | THE UNIVERSITY OF NORTH CAROLINA PRESS | *drawings by* PAUL GRAY [decoration]

Published in 1962.

"Return," pp. 168–173. See C 70 and D 6.

Location: NcU.

B 29 MEETING TWO AMERICAN GIANTS
1962

Meeting | two | american | giants | MARGINAL NOTES | BY | H. M. LEDIG-ROWOHLT | ROWOHLT

Wrappers.

Published in 1962.

Colophon: 'Printed in Germany 1962 | by Clausen & Bosse, Leck [virgule] Schleswig'.

Quotes in passing from conversations with Wolfe and briefly from a note Wolfe left in H. M. Ledig-Rowohlt's office, p. 24. See C 142.

Location: NcU.

B 30 WILLKOMMEN IN ALTAMONT! HERRENHAUS
1962

THOMAS WOLFE | Willkommen | in Altamont! | Herrenhaus | ZWEI DRAMEN | [rule] | Die Herren | von der Presse | EINE SZENE | Im Anhang | Horst Frenz [angle bracket] Thomas Wolfe | als Dramatiker [angle bracket] | und Briefe zur Entstehungsgeschichte | der Dramen | [Rowohlt seal] | ROWOHLT

Wrappers: #516 on spine.

Published in 1962.

The first book appearance of "Welcome to Our City." In German. Also contains *Mannerhouse*. See A 13, A 14, A 23, and C 151.

Location: APM.

B 31 SELECTIONS FROM THE TWENTIETH CENTURY
1964

[two-page title page] AN EXHIBITION SELECTIONS FROM THE TWENTIETH CENTURY | [ornamental lettering] A | Creative Century | [roman] COLLECTIONS AT THE UNIVERSITY OF TEXAS | HELD IN NOVEMBER 1964 AT THE ACADEMIC CENTER & UNDERGRADUATE LIBRARY: THE UNIVERSITY OF TEXAS

Prints the inscription to Harold Butterfield in a copy of *LHA* dated 29 October 1929, p. 67.

Location: NcU.

B 32 THOMAS WOLFE MEMOIR OF A FRIENDSHIP
1965

[ornamental lettering] THOMAS WOLFE | [roman] MEMOIR OF A FRIENDSHIP | by Robert Raynolds | [decoration] UNIVERSITY OF TEXAS PRESS | AUSTIN & LONDON

Published in 1965.

Includes printings of Wolfe's inscription in Raynolds's copy of *FDTM,* pp. 3 and 146; excerpt from a Wolfe letter dated 19 July 1933, p. 52; excerpt from a Wolfe letter dated 9 October 1933, p. 100; excerpt from a Wolfe letter dated 29 March 1935, p. 128; Wolfe's inscription in Raynolds's copy of *OTATR,* p. 129; and a Wolfe letter dated 21 June 1938. All previously unpublished.

Locations: APM (dj), MJB, NcRSM, ScCleU.

B 33 THOMAS WOLFE
1968

THOMAS | WOLFE | [rule] [three decorations] BY [three decorations] [rule] | *Andrew . Turnbull* | [decoration] *New York* [decoration] | CHARLES SCRIBNER'S SONS

Published in February 1968.

Quotes in passing and in notes from previously unpublished letters, manuscripts, and reminiscences.

Locations: APM (dj), CJ, InU Lilly (dj), NcRSM (3 copies), ScCleU.

Note one: Republished in wrappers as *Pocket Books* #78011 in July 1969.

B 34 THE HOUGHTON LIBRARY 1942–1967
1967

THE | HOUGHTON | LIBRARY | 1942–1967 | [red lettering] | *A Selection of Books and Manuscripts* | *in Harvard Collections* | [black lettering] CAMBRIDGE | The Harvard College Library | MCMLXVII

Facsimiles a previously unpublished leaf from one of Wolfe's notebooks and an inscription in a copy of *LHA* to Aline Bernstein dated 3 October 1929, pp. 118–119. See C 133.

Locations: InU Lilly (dj), MJB, PSt.

B 35 THOMAS WOLFE'S ALBATROSS
1968

Paschal Reeves | [blue lettering] Thomas Wolfe's Albatross: | *Race and Nationality in America* | [black lettering] UNIVERSITY OF GEORGIA PRESS [bullet] Athens

Published in 1968.

Quotes in passing from the following unpublished fragments and manuscripts: "Niggertown," "Passage to England," "Autobiographical Notebook," "O Lost," "The October Fair," unpublished passages of *OTATR*, manuscripts and typescripts for *SOAN*, manuscripts and typescripts for *TWATR*, manuscripts and typescripts for *YCGHA*, notes and sketches for the posthumous books, rejected passages from the posthumous books, pocket notebooks, and Wolfe's letters to Aline Bernstein.

Locations: APM (dj), NcA, NcRSM.

B 36 DUKEDOM LARGE ENOUGH
1969

David A. Randall | [increasing and decreasing rule with decorations at both ends] DUKEDOM LARGE ENOUGH | —*my library Was dukedom large enough*—| THE TEMPEST, ACT I, SCENE 2 | [Random House Seal] | RANDOM HOUSE *NEW YORK*

Published in 1969.

First Book and Pamphlet Appearances 223

Prints a four-part letter to Aline Bernstein dated 1 December [1930], pp. 249–252.

Location: ViU.

B 37 WORKS IN PROGRESS
1970

WORKS IN | PROGRESS | NUMBER ONE | Book trade distributed by | Doubleday & Company, Inc. | The Literary Guild of America, Inc. | New York, N.Y.

Published in 1970.

Quotes from *The Notebooks of Thomas Wolfe,* edited by Richard Kennedy and Paschal Reeves, pp. 177–191. Previously unpublished. See A 21.

Locations: APM, MJB, NcU.

B 38 A CENTURY OF COLLEGE HUMOR
1971

[ornamental lettering] A | Century | of | College | Humor | [within double-rules frame and with drawings of men in the lower left-hand corner] Cartoons, [a woman's face in multiple exposure] Stories, | [drawing of a man and woman] Poems, Jokes and [drawing of a professor holding a hoop and a student jumping through it] | Assorted [drawing of a car] Foolishness from | Over 95 Campus Magazines, | Edited by Dan Carlinsky | [beneath frame] [Random House seal] | RANDOM HOUSE [virgule] NEW YORK

Published in 1971.

"The Streets of Durham," pp. 52–53. See C 11 and D 12.

Locations: NcRSM, ViU.

B 39 THOMAS WOLFE AND THE GLASS OF TIME
1971

Thomas Wolfe and | the Glass of Time | edited by Paschal Reeves | University of Georgia Press | Athens

Published in 1971.

Prints previously unpublished letter to Mrs. William E. Dodd dated 13 June 1935, pp. 158–159.

Location: NcA.

B 40 ASHEVILLE AND THOMAS WOLFE
1972

[facsimile of hand lettering] ASHEVILLE AND THOMAS WOLFE: | A STUDY IN CHANGING ATTITUDES | [drawing of the Old Kentucky Home] | by Betty Lynch Williams | 1971

Published in 1972.

Wrappers.

Quotes from a previously unpublished letter to J[ack]. M. Westall dated 14 February 1938, p. 26.

Locations: APM, EG.

B 41 JOHNNY PARK TALKS OF THOMAS WOLFE
1973

[drawing of steeples] | [ornamental lettering JOHNNY PARK TALKS OF THOMAS WOLFE | By | William J. Cocke | Author and Publisher | P.O. Box 7421 | Asheville, N.C. 28807 | 1973

Wrappers.

Quotes from a previously unpublished letter to Park dated 28 November 1926, pp. 20–22, and from a 28 October 1929 telegram to Mabel Wolfe Wheaton, p. 23.

Locations: APM, NcA.

B 42 THE ROMANTIC EGOISTS
1974

[ornamental lettering] THE | ROMANTIC | EGOISTS | *EDITED BY* | [roman] MATTHEW J. BRUCCOLI | SCOTTIE FITZGERALD SMITH | AND | JOAN P. KERR | *ART EDITOR* | MARGARETA F. LYONS | [decoration] | *CHARLES SCRIBNER'S SONS* [virgule] *New York*

Published in 1974.

Facsimiles March 1934 TLS from Wolfe to F. Scott Fitzgerald, p. 201. See B 47.

Locations: InU Lilly, MJB.

Note one: 500 numbered copies of a limited issue in slipcase were signed by Scottie Fitzgerald Smith.

B 43 THE FIRST FIREFLY
1974

The First Firefly | [tapered rule] | *New Poems | and Prose* | [tapered rule] | Melville Cane | [Harcourt Brace Jovanovich seal] | *Harcourt Brace Jovanovich, Inc., New York*

Published in 1974.

"Thomas Wolfe: A Memoir," pp. 37–49.

Prints two previously unpublished letters to Melville Cane: one undated and the other dated 22 July 1930. Also quotes, in passing, from conversations. See C 162.

Location: NcU.

B 44 THOMAS WOLFE UNDERGRADUATE
1977

Richard Walser | *Thomas Wolfe Undergraduate* | "These were the golden years" | —*Look Homeward, Angel* | Durham, N.C. | Duke University Press | 1977

Quotes in passing from previously unpublished letters to family members and from conversations.

Locations: APM (dj), NcRSM, ScCleu.

B 45 MAX PERKINS EDITOR OF GENIUS
1978

[within single-rules frame] MAX PERKINS | [rule] | Editor of Genius [virgule] A. Scott Berg | [rule] | [caricature of Perkins with caricatures of Fitzgerald, Hemingway, and Wolfe in the background] | [rule] | *Thomas Congdon Books* [Congdon seal] E.P. DUTTON [bullet] *New York*

Published in 1978.

Quotes from previously unpublished Wolfe manuscripts.

Dust jacket.

Location: CJ.

Note one: Republished in a 640-page edition as *Pocket Books* #82719-7 in October 1979.

B 46 THOMAS WOLFE'S PENNSYLVANIA
1978

[blue lettering] THOMAS WOLFE'S | PENNSYLVANIA | [black lettering] Richard Walser | [with superimposed 'C's] *Croissant* | & | *Company* | *Athens, Ohio*

Wrappers.

Published in 1978.

Quotes in passing from a conversation between Wolfe and his cousin Jim Wolfe, and, at length from a previously unpublished letter to Jim Wolfe dated 5 April 1938, p. 10.

Locations: APM, EG, ScCleU.

B 47 CORRESPONDENCE OF F. SCOTT FITZGERALD
1980

Correspondence of | F. SCOTT FITZGERALD | [tapered rule] | Edited by | MATTHEW J. BRUCCOLI | and MARGARET M. DUGGAN | with the assistance of | Susan Walker | [Random House seal] | RANDOM HOUSE NEW YORK

Published in 1980.

First printing of March 1934 TLS from Wolfe to F. Scott Fitzgerald facsimiled in B 42, p. 332.

Locations: CJ (dj), InU Lilly (dj).

B 48 THOMAS WOLFE THE DISCOVERY OF A GENIUS
1981

THOMAS WOLFE | THE DISCOVERY | OF A GENIUS | BY | MADELEINE BOYD | EDITED | BY | ALDO P. MAGI | WITH AN INTRODUCTION | BY | ELIZABETH EVANS | THE THOMAS WOLFE SOCIETY | 1981.

Wrappers.

Prints the inscription by Wolfe in Madeleine Boyd's copy of *LHA*, p. 11.

350 copies printed by the Erie Bay Company, Sandusky, Ohio.

Locations: CJ, DLC (May 15 1981).

B 49 DICTIONARY OF LITERARY BIOGRAPHY
VOLUME NINE: AMERICAN NOVELISTS, 1910–1945
1981

Dictionary of Literary Biography [bullet] Volume Nine | American Novelists, 1910–1945 | Part 3: Mari Sandoz—Stark Young | Edited by James W. Martine | *Saint Bonaventure University* | A Bruccoli Clark Book | Gale Research Company [bullet] Book Tower [bullet] Detroit, Michigan 48226 | 1981

Facsimiles typescript page of Wolfe's "Autobiographical Statement," p. 176. See B 7, B 21, B 50, and C 136.

Location: ScCleU.

B 50 DICTIONARY OF LITERARY BIOGRAPHY:
DOCUMENTARY SERIES
1982

DICTIONARY OF LITERARY BIOGRAPHY | DOCUMENTARY SERIES | AN ILLUSTRATED CHRONICLE | VOL. [drawing of a typewriter within a circle] TWO | James Gould Cozzens | James T. Farrell | William Faulkner | John O'Hara | John Steinbeck | Thomas Wolfe | Richard Wright | EDITED BY MARGARET A. VAN ANTWERP | A BRUCCOLI CLARK BOOK | GALE RESEARCH COMPANY BOOK TOWER | DETROIT, MICHIGAN 48226

Published in 1982.

Facsimiles part of a holograph letter to Wolfe's mother dated May 1923; Wolfe's holograph map of Asheville; a page from Wolfe's autobiographical outline for *LHA;* a four-page excerpt from a letter to George McCoy; Wolfe's corrections of a galley for *OTATR;* the inscription in Wolfe's copy of *OTATR;* a revised galley proof from "The Web of Earth"; a revised typescript page from Wolfe's "Autobiographical Statement" (see B 7, B 21, B 49, and C 136); a revised typescript page from Wolfe's "Writing and Living"; Wolfe's last letter to Maxwell Perkins; and manuscript pages from *YCGHA,* pp. 337, 341, 342, 346, 352, 355, 359, 365, 376, 380, 381, and 392.

Locations: APM, ScCleU.

B 51 THOMAS WOLFE: A HARVARD PERSPECTIVE
1983

THOMAS WOLFE [colon composed of two diamonds] | A Harvard Perspective | [two rules] | edited by | Richard S [diamond shaped period] Kennedy | [two rules] | [with superimposed 'C's] *Croissant* | & | *Company* | *Athens, Ohio*

Published in 1983.

Quotes from a partially unpublished letter to Aline Bernstein dated 18, 25, and 26 November 1928 and from the inscription in Aline Bernstein's copy of *OTATR;* facsimiles a page from "O Lost," two pages of Wolfe's Rough Outline for *TWATR*, seven typescript pages from *TWATR*, and two typescript pages from *YCGHA*, pp. 21, 88, and 97–108.

Location: ScCleU.

B 52 THOMAS WOLFE THE FINAL JOURNEY
1984

[ornamental lettering] Thomas Wolfe | [roman] THE FINAL JOURNEY | *BY* | BRIAN F. BERGER | WITH A REMEMBRANCE | *BY* | EDWARD M. MILLER | [Willamette River Press seal] | *WILLAMETTE RIVER PRESS* | WEST LINN, OREGON | 1984

Limited edition of 750 copies; 700 for sale. Distributed with a facsimile of a previously unpublished 5 July [1938] one-page holograph letter from Wolfe to Edward M. Miller written on the letterhead of the New Washington Hotel in Seattle. The facsimile is folded and inserted into an envelope pasted to the back paste-down endpaper. See C 166.

Locations: CJ (dj), ScU.

C. First-Appearance Contributions to Magazines and Newspapers

First publication in magazines and newspapers of previously unpublished material by Wolfe. All signed unless otherwise indicated.

C1
"A Field in Flanders." *The University of North Carolina Magazine,* n.s. 35 (November 1917), 77.

Poem. See *YCGHA,* 711.

C2
"To France." *The University of North Carolina Magazine,* n.s. 35 (December 1917), 165.

Poem.

C3
"The Challenge." *The University of North Carolina Magazine,* n.s. 35 (March 1918), 223–224.

Poem. See *YCGHA,* 710–711.

C4
"A Cullenden of Virginia." *The University of North Carolina Magazine,* n.s. 35 (March 1918), 234–239.

Short story.

C5
"To Rupert Brooke." *The University of North Carolina Magazine,* n.s. 35 (May 1918), 314–315.

Poem. See D5.

C6
"The Drammer." *The Magazine* (University of North Carolina), n.s. 36 (April 1919), 72–74.

Poem.

C7
"An Appreciation." *The Magazine* (University of North Carolina), n.s. 36 (May 1919), [79].

Signed 'THOMAS CLAYTON.'

Poem.

C 8
"Deferred Payment." *The Magazine* (University of North Carolina), 36 (June 1919), 139–153.

Play.

C 9
"Russian Folk Song." *The Magazine* (University of North Carolina), 36 (June 1919), 191.

Signed 'Thomas Clayton'.

Poem.

C 10
"The Creative Movement in Writing." *The Tar Heel* (University of North Carolina), 14 June 1919, p. 2.

Article.

C 11
"The Streets of Durham, or, Dirty Work at the Crossroads." *University of North Carolina Tar Baby*, 1 (18 November 1919), 4–5, 14.

Play.

See B 38 and D 12. *Not seen.*

C 12
"Concerning Honest Bob." *The Magazine* (University of North Carolina), n.s. 37 (May 1920), 251–261.

Signed 'T. C. Wolfe'.

Play.

C 13
"In Devising Torture Cruelties Nordic Race Has Demonstrated The Superiority It Boasts Of: London Tower." *Asheville Citizen,* 19 July 1925, p. 44.

Article.

See D 13.

C 14
"An Angel on the Porch." *Scribner's Magazine,* 86 (August 1929), 205–210.

Story incorporated into *LHA,* 99–100, 262–269.

C 15
Savino, Guy. "Thomas Wolfe, W.S.C. English Instructor, Author of Much Acclaimed First Novel." *Daily News* (New York University), 29 October 1929.

Interview. Entry based on an unpaginated clipping.

C 16
Cooper, Lee. "Wolfe Denies 'Betraying' Asheville." *The Asheville Times,* 4 May 1930, pp. B1, B4.

Interview.

C 17
"Younghill Kang Distills Riches of Experience." *The New York Evening Post,* 4 April 1931, p. 5D.

Review of Younghill Kang's *The Grass Roof.*

C 18
Starkey, Marion L. "Thomas Wolfe from North Carolina." *Boston Evening Transcript,* 26 September 1931, Book Section, pp. 1–2.

Interview.

C 19
"A Portrait of Bascom Hawke." *Scribner's Magazine,* 91 (April 1932), 193–198, 239–256.

Story incorporated into *OTATR,* 104–111, 116–130, 136–150, 177–186, 192. See B 2.

C 20
"The Web of Earth." *Scribner's Magazine,* 92 (July 1932), 1–5, 43–64.

Story incorporated into *FDTM,* 212–304. See B 3.

C 21
"The Train and the City." *Scribner's Magazine,* 93 (May 1933), 285–294.

Story incorporated into *TWATR,* 441–449; *OTATR,* 407–419; *YCGHA,* 3–4. See D 15.

C 22
"Death the Proud Brother." *Scribner's Magazine,* 93 (June 1933), 333–338, 378–388.

Story incorporated into *FDTM,* 17–70.

C 23
"No Door: A Story of Time and the Wanderer." *Scribner's Magazine,* 94 (July 1933), 7–12, 46–56.

Story incorporated into *FDTM,* 1–14; *OTATR,* 2, 90–93, 327–334, 601–608, 611–613; and *YCGHA,* 37–44.

C 24
"The Four Lost Men." *Scribner's Magazine,* 95 (February 1934), 101–108.

Story incorporated into *FDTM,* 114–133.

C 25
"The Sun and the Rain." *Scribner's Magazine*, 95 (May 1934), 358–360.

Story incorporated into *OTATR*, 797–802.

C 26
"Boom Town." *The American Mercury*, 32 (May 1934), 21–39.

Story incorporated into *YCGHA*, 88–120, 142–146. See B 4.

C 27
"The House of the Far and Lost." *Scribner's Magazine*, 96 (August 1934), 71–81.

Story incorporated into *OTATR*, 619–627, 637–652.

C 28
"Dark in the Forest, Strange as Time." *Scribner's Magazine*, 96 (November 1934), 273–278.

Story incorporated into *FDTM*, 98–113.

C 29
"The Names Of The Nation." *Modern Monthly*, 8 (December 1934), 598–605.

Story incorporated into *OTATR*, 861–870.

C 30
"For Professional Appearance." *Modern Monthly*, 8 (January 1935), 660–666.

Story incorporated into *OTATR*, 165–175.

C 31
"One of the Girls in Our Party." *Scribner's Magazine*, 97 (January 1935), 6–8.

Story incorporated into *FDTM*, 155–163.

C 32
Vanderbilt, Sanderson. "Thomas Wolfe Cuts 2d Book to 450,000 Words." *New York Herald Tribune*, 18 February 1935, p. 13.

Interview which also prints a note written by Wolfe to Sanderson.

C 33
"Circus at Dawn." *Modern Monthly*, 9 (March 1935), 19–21, 52.

Story incorporated into *FDTM*, 205–211.

First Appearances in Magazines and Newspapers

C 34
"His Father's Earth." *Modern Monthly*, 9 (April 1935), 99–104.

Story incorporated into *TWATR*, 86–90. See B 8.

C 35
"Old Catawba," *Virginia Quarterly Review*, 11 (April 1935), 228–238.

Story incorporated into *FDTM*, 185–187, 195–204.

C 36
"Only the Dead Know Brooklyn." *The New Yorker*, 11 (15 June 1935), 13–14.

Story incorporated into *FDTM*, 91–97. See B 5.

C 37
"Polyphemus." *The North American Review*, 240 (June 1935), 20–26.

Story incorporated into *FDTM*, 187–195.

C 38
"In the Park." *Harper's Bazaar*, 68th year (June 1935), 54–55, 104, 106, 108.

Story incorporated into *FDTM*, 169–184.

C 39
"The Face Of The War." *Modern Monthly*, 9 (June 1935), 223–231, 247.

Story incorporated into *FDTM*, 71–90.

C 40
"Gulliver, The Story of a Tall Man." *Scribner's Magazine*, 97 (June 1935), 328–333.

Story incorporated into *FDTM*, 134–149. See *Notebooks*, 1:37–41.

C 41
"Arnold Pentland." *Esquire*, 3 (June 1935), 26, 150–152.

Story incorporated as "A Kinsman of His Blood" into *THB*, 66–76.

C 42
Anonymous. "Brevity To Be Goal of Thomas Wolfe." *The New York Times*, 5 July 1935, p. 11.

Interview.

C 43
Anonymous. "People." *Time*, 26 (15 July 1935), 44–45.

Quotes from Wolfe's interview with reporters upon his arrival in Manhattan after four months abroad.

C 44
"Cottage by the Tracks." *Cosmopolitan,* 99 (July 1935), 48–49, 176.

Story incorporated, as "The Far and the Near," into *FDTM,* 164–168.

C 45
Anonymous. "Write Hard and at Home Advises Author at C.U." *Rocky Mountain News,* 8 August 1935, p. 16.

Interview.

C 46
Kerr, David. "Frost, Wolfe Pack House, McNeal, Baker Considered Most Helpful To Writers." *The Silver and Gold* (University of Colorado), 8 August 1935, pp. 1, 4.

Article quoting from Wolfe's lecture at the Sixth Annual Writer's Conference in Boulder, Colorado.

C 48
Crossen, Forrest. "Future of Writers Conference Discussed by Faculty Members." *Boulder Daily Camera,* 12 August 1935, p. 3.

Article quoting statements made by Wolfe about the Sixth Annual Writer's Conference in Boulder, Colorado.

C 48
"Good Reading." *New York Herald Tribune,* 17 August 1935, p. 9.

Lewis Gannett's column, "Books and Other Things," quoting comments made by Wolfe in a letter to Lewis Gannet.

Wolfe's complete letter, which Gannet used, is printed in *Letters,* 479–480.

C 49
Hynds, Reed. "Thomas Wolfe Visits City—Says He'll Write a 'Really Great' Book." *St. Louis Star-Times,* 20 September 1935.

Interview. Unpaginated clipping noted.

C 50
"The Bums at Sunset." *Vanity Fair,* 45 (October 1935), 30, 62.

Story incorporated into *FDTM,* 150–154.

C 51
Hazen, David W. "Author To End Series in Oregon." *The Morning Oregonian* (Portland), 18 October 1935, p. 4.

Interview.

First Appearances in Magazines and Newspapers 237

C 52
Bigart, Homer. "Thomas Wolfe At 35 Is Tired of Being a Legend." *New York Herald Tribune,* 3 November 1935, p. 5.

Interview.

C 53
"The Story of a Novel." *Saturday Review of Literature,* 13 (14 December 1935), 3–4, 12, 14, 16; (21 December 1935), 3–4, 15; (28 December 1935), 3–4, 14–16.

Essay expanded by Wolfe and printed as SOAN. See A 5, A 9, and AA 8 *Note one.*

C 54
"Thomas Wolfe on 'What a Writer Reads.' " *Book Buyer,* 1 (December 1935), 13–14.

Article.

C 55
Cameron, May. "Thomas Wolfe Talks About His Contemporaries and Predicts a Bright Future for Our Writers." *New York Post,* 14 March 1936, p. 15.

Interview. See B 6.

C 56
"The Bell Remembered." *The American Mercury,* 38 (August 1936), 457–466.

Story incorporated into "The Bell Strikes Three" and "The Lost Day" in *THB,* 327–348.

C 57
H. H. "Wir Sprachen Thomas Wolfe." *Berliner Tageblatt* (Morning Edition), 5 August 1936, p. 2.

Interview.

C 58
"Fame and the Poet." *The American Mercury,* 39 (October 1936), 149–154.

Short Story.

C 59
Sancton, Thomas. "Thomas Wolfe Revisits City Whose Spirit He Portrayed in First Successful Novel." *Times-Picayune New Orleans State,* 3 January 1937, pp. 1, 14.

Interview.

C 60
Stevenson, Paul. "Thomas Wolfe, Noted Author, Visiting Here." *The Sunday American* (Atlanta, Ga.), 17 January 1937, pp. 4A and 7A.

Interview.

C 61
Fuhrman, Lee. " 'Of Time and the River's' Author Hopes for Time to Read 'Gone.' " *Atlanta Constitution,* 17 January 1937, p. 6C.

Interview.

C 62
Anonymous. "Wolfe Revisits Student Scene." *News and Observer* (Raleigh, N.C.), 23 January 1937, p. 5.

Interview.

C 63
Crawley, Oliver. "Thomas Wolfe Comes Back." *The State* (Raleigh, N.C.), 27 February 1937, p. 9.

Quotes from Wolfe's talk to Phillips Russell's creative writing class at Chapel Hill.

C 64
"I Have a Thing to Tell You: (Nun will ich ihnen 'was sagen)." *The New Republic,* 90 (10 March 1937), 132–136; (17 March 1937), 159–164; and (24 March 1937), 202–207.

Story incorporated into YCGHA, 634–651, 655, 663–704, 743.

C 65
[Armstrong, Anne W.]. "Thos. Wolfe, Famous Author, Visitor Here." *Bristol News* (Bristol, Va.), 30 April 1937, pp. 1, 8.

Interview.

C 66
Anonymous. "Thomas Wolfe Welcomed By Friends Here." *The Asheville Times,* 4 May 1937, pp. 1, 15.

Interview.

C 67
Anonymous. "Wolfe Tells Club Members He Plans To Return To City." *The Asheville Times,* 4 May 1937, p. 15.

Interview.

First Appearances in Magazines and Newspapers 239

C 68
Anonymous. "Thos. Wolfe Comes Home For First Time Since Writing Novel." *Asheville Citizen,* 4 May 1937, pp. 1–2.

Interview.

C 69
Anonymous. "Wolfe Home With Avid Views of Life." *Daily News* (Asheville, N.C.), 7 May 1937, pp. 1, 16.

Interview.

C 70
"Thomas Wolfe Describes His Feelings at Being Home Again." *Asheville Citizen-Times,* 16 May 1937, p. 1B.

Article written by Wolfe for the *Asheville Citizen-Times* and entitled "Return." See B 28 and D 6.

C 71
"Mr. Malone." *The New Yorker,* 13 (29 May 1937), 22–27.

Story incorporated into *TWATR,* 525–536.

C 72
"Oktoberfest." *Scribner's Magazine,* 101 (June 1937), 27–31.

Story incorporated into *TWATR,* 662–672.

C 73
" 'E, A Recollection." *The New Yorker,* 13 (17 July 1937), 22–26.

Story incorporated into *YCGHA,* 513–527.

C 74
"April, Late April." *The American Mercury,* 42 (September 1937), 87–97.

Story incorporated into *TWATR,* 441–452.

C 75
Anonymous. "Wolfe Leaves After Summer Visit Here; Finishes New Story." *Asheville Citizen,* 3 September 1937, p. 9.

Article quoting Wolfe.

C 76
"The Child by Tiger." *The Saturday Evening Post,* 210 (11 September 1937), 10–11, 92, 94, 97–98, 100, 102.

Story incorporated into *TWATR,* 132–156. See B 9.

C 77
Hayes, Harold. "Wolfe Plans Novel Patterned After Swift's Famous Satire." *Roanoke World-News*, 11 September 1937, p. 2

Interview.

C 78
"Katamoto." *Harper's Bazaar*, 70th year (October 1937), 74–75, 132, 134–135.

Story incorporated into *YCGHA*, 28–36.

C 79
Carraway, Gertrude S. "Thomas Wolfe, 37 Today, Plans Early Return to Native Mountains to Live." *Charlotte Observer*, 3 October 1937, sec. 3, p. 5.

Interview.

C 80
"The Lost Boy." *Redbook*, 70 (November 1937), 25–28, 80–90.

Story incorporated into *THB*, pp. 1–42.

C 81
Anonymous. "News Items from Institute Members." *National Institute News Bulletin* (National Institute of Arts and Letters), 3 (1937), 2–8.

Brief, untitled statement by Wolfe about his writing.

C 82
Anonymous. "News Items from Institute Members." *National Institute News Bulletin* (National Institute of Arts and Letters), 4 (1938), 2–12.

Brief, untitled statement by Wolfe about his writing.

C 83
"Chickamauga." *The Yale Review*, 27 (Winter 1938), 274–298.

Story incorporated into *THB*, 77–107.

C 84
"The Company." *The New Masses*, 11 January 1938, pp. 33–38.

Story incorporated into *YCGHA*, 129–140.

C 85
"A Prologue To America." *Vogue*, 91 (1 February 1938), 63–66, 150–152, 161.

Story incorporated into *TWATR*, 474–475, and *YCGHA*, 429–431, 506–508. See A 22, A 29, and B 11.

First Appearances in Magazines and Newspapers 241

C 86
Anonymous. "How to Keep Out of War." *The Nation*, 146 (2 April 1938), 376–378.

Wolfe wrote a section of this article, pp. 377–378. See *Letters*, 735–736.

C 87
Anonymous. "Writers Have Their Place In World, Says T. Wolfe." *Exponent* (Purdue University), 20 May 1938, p. 1.

Prints a small portion of Wolfe's speech, "Writing and Living," delivered at a literary banquet at Purdue on 19 May 1938. See A 19 and AA 8.

C 88
Houston, K. C. "Beauty, Size of Campus Impress Visiting Speaker." *Exponent* (Purdue University), 20 May 1938, p. 1.

Interview.

C 89
"Franco Prepares for Tourists." *The Nation*, 146 (21 May 1938), 598.

Letter to the Editor. See B 21 and *Letters*, pp. 752–754.

C 90
Wayne, Frances. "T. E. [sic] Wolfe, 'Wordiest Author,' Pays Visit To Denver On Whim." *Denver Post*, 25 May 1938, p. 13.

Interview.

C 91
Anonymous. "Author Wolfe Visits Seattle; He's Just as Big as His Books." *Seattle Post-Intelligencer*, 17 June 1938, p. 5.

Interview.

C 92
Hazen, David W. "Thomas Wolfe: He Writes 'Em Standing Up." *The Sunday Oregonian* (Portland, Ore.), 3 July 1938, p. 11.

Interview.

C 93
[Koch, Frederick H.]. "Thomas Wolfe: Playmaker." *The Carolina Play-Book*, 11 (September 1938), 65–69.

Article quoting briefly from an autobiographical sketch written in 1919 (see C 154) and from letters dated 10 January [1925] and 9 October 1933. See *Letters*, 383–384.

C 94
"The Third Night: A Play of the Carolina Mountains." *The Carolina Play-Book*, 11 (September 1938), 70–75.

Play originally produced at the University of North Carolina 12 October 1919. See *TWN*, v. 2, no. 2 (Fall 1978), p. 42, and B 10.

C 95
McCoy, George. "A Giant Has Fallen." *Asheville Citizen-Times*, 18 September 1938.

Article printing excerpts from letters to McCoy dated 17 August 1929, 3 November 1929, and 3 April 1930. Unpaginated clipping noted.

C 96
Stoney, George. "Eugene Returns to Pulpit Hill." *The Carolina Magazine*, 68 (October 1938), 11–14.

Article quoting from Wolfe's talk to Phillips Russell's class at Chapel Hill.

C 97
Aswell, Edward C. "Thomas Wolfe's Unpublished Works." *The Carolina Magazine*, 68 (October 1938), 19–20.

Article quoting from a letter to Aswell dated December 1937 and from conversations.

C 98
"Look Howeward, Angel." *Omnibook*, 1 (December 1938), 193–320.

Abridgement of *LHA*. See A 2.1.a *Note two*.

C 99
Anonymous. "The Tributary Theatre." *Theatre Arts Monthly*, February 1939, p. 150.

Article quoting in passing from an undated letter from Wolfe to Professor Koch.

C 100
Volkening, Henry. "Thomas Wolfe: Penance No More." *Virginia Quarterly Review*, 15 (Spring 1939), 196–215.

Article quoting from conversations with Wolfe, from letters from Wolfe dated 4 July 1929, 9 August 1929, July 1930, September 1930, and January 1931, and from the inscription in Volkening's copy of *FDTM*.

See B 21, and *Letters*, 181, 194–197, 289–293.

First Appearances in Magazines and Newspapers 243

C 101
"Portrait of a Literary Critic: A Satire." *The American Mercury*, 46 (April 1939), 429–437.

Article incorporated into *THB*, 150–161.

C 102
"The Party at Jack's." *Scribner's Magazine*, 105 (May 1939), 14–16, 40, 42–49, 58–62.

Story incorporated into *YCGHA*, scattered from pp. 196–322.

C 103
Anonymous. "An American Author's Testament." *The Daily Worker* (New York), 15 May 1939, p. 7.

Prints an undated letter to "one of the editors of Harper Brothers". Compare to "Author's Note" in *TWATR* and to *Letters*, 710–719.

C 104
"A Western Journey." *The Virginia Quarterly Review*, 15 (Summer 1939), 335–357.

Excerpts from the notes later published as *A Western Journal* (A 16).

C 105
"Three O'Clock." *North American Review*, 247 (Summer 1939), 219–224.

Story incorporated into *TWATR*, 17–21.

C 106
"The Winter Of Our Discontent." *The Atlantic Monthly*, 163 (June 1939), 817–823.

Story incorporated into *TWATR*, 414–426. Republished in 1948 as "Portrait of a Player," in *The Theater Annual: 1947*, 43–54.

C 107
"The Golden City." *Harper's Bazaar*, 72nd year (June 1939), 42–43, 100, 102–103.

Story incorporated into *TWATR*, 220–232 and into "The Enchanted City" (C 110).

C 108
"The Birthday." *Harper's Magazine*, 179 (June 1939), 19–26.

Story incorporated into *TWATR*, 346–358.

C 109
Vining, Lou Nyrtis. "Thomas Wolfe—In Memorian." *Writer's Digest,* 19 (July 1939), 47–50.

Article quoting from an interview with Wolfe at the Rocky Mountain Writer's Conference in summer 1935.

C 110
"Enchanted City." *Reader's Digest,* 35 (October 1939), 132–135.

Story reworking material appearing in *TWATR,* 220–232, and in "The Golden City" (C 107).

C 111
Braswell, William. "Thomas Wolfe Lectures and Takes a Holiday." *College English,* 1 (October 1939), 11–22.

Article quoting from three letters to Herbert J. Muller, from a letter to Wolfe's "Lafayette Host," and from conversations. See B 21.

C 112
Flaccus, Kimball. "The Poet's Life." *Voices,* 99 (Autumn 1939), 45–48.

Article printing the inscription in Flaccus's copy of *LHA.*

C 113
"The Hollyhock Sowers." *The American Mercury,* 50 (August 1940), 401–405.

Story incorporated into *YCGHA,* 605–611.

C 114
"Dark Messiah." *Current History and Forum,* 51 (August 1940), 29–32.

Story incorporated into *YCGHA,* 621–633.

C 115
"Nebraska Crane." *Harper's Magazine,* 181 (August 1940), 279–285.

Story incorporated into *YCGHA,* 55–69.

C 116
"So This Is Man." *Town and Country,* 95 (August 1940), 28, 69–70.

Essay subsequently incorporated into *YCGHA,* 432–436, 501–505. See D 1.

C 117
"The Promise of America." *Coronet,* 8 (September 1940), 9–12.

Essay incorporated into *YCGHA,* 505–508. See D 7.

First Appearances in Magazines and Newspapers 245

C 118
Basso, Hamilton. "Thomas Wolfe: A Summing Up." *The New Republic*, 103 (23 September 1940), 422–523.

Article quoting from a letter to Hamilton Basso dated July 1937 and from a postcard mailed from Yellowstone Park in 1938.

C 119
"The Hollow Men." *Esquire*, 14 (October 1940), 27, 115–116.

Story reworking material in *YCGHA*, 460–479.

C 120
"The Last Letter of Thomas Wolfe." *The Carolina Play-Book*, 14 (September 1941), 65.

Letter dated 12 August 1938 addressed to Maxwell Perkins. See B 18, C 131, and *Letters*, 777–778.

C 121
"The Anatomy of Loneliness." *The American Mercury*, 53 (October 1941), 467–475.

Story incorporated into *THB*, 186–197, as "God's Lonely Man." See D 4.

C 122
"The Lion At Morning." *Harper's Bazaar*, 74th year (October 1941), pp. 66–67, 110–112, 114, 116.

Story incorporated into *THB*, 162–185.

C 123
"The Plumed Knight." *Town and Country*, 96 (October 1941), 74, 100–103.

Story incorporated into *THB*, 264–276.

C 124
"A Letter From Thomas Wolfe." *Story*, 19 (September–October 1941), 68–69.

Letter to Sherwood Anderson dated 22 September 1937. See *Letters*, 654–656, and B 20.

C 125
"The Hills Beyond." *Omnibook*, 4 (January 1942), 129–160.

Excerpts from *THB*, 201–217, 222–234, 240–252, 264–280, 287–297, 299–309, 327–348.

C 126
Koch, Frederick, "Thomas Wolfe: Playmaker." *Carolina Play-Book,* 16 (March–June 1943), 7–12.

Article quoting from previously unpublished letters and from conversations with Wolfe.

C 127
"The Man Who Lives with His Idea." *Carolina Play-Book,* 16 (March–June 1943), 15–22.

Tribute to Frederick H. Koch and the Carolina Playmakers, written about 1923. Includes a facsimile of a manuscript page.

C 128
"Letter to Proff Koch," *Carolina Play-Book,* 16 (March–June 1943), 23–26.

Letter to Frederick H. Koch dated 26 November 1920. See *Letters,* 9–13.

C 129
Blythe, Legette. "Strictly Personal." *The Saturday Review of Literature,* 28 (25 August 1945), 18–19.

Article printing letter to Legette Blythe c. 13 January 1935. See *Letters,* 430–431.

C 130
Davis, Ruth. "Strictly Personal." *The Saturday Review of Literature,* 29 (5 January 1946), 13, 14, 31–32.

Article printing Julia Wolfe's talk to John Skally Terry's class at New York University on 30 November 1945. Quotes from conversations with Wolfe and from the inscription in Julia Wolfe's copy of *FDTM.*

C 131
"Writing Is My Life: Letters of Thomas Wolfe," *Atlantic Monthly,* 178 (December 1946), 60–66; "Writing is my life: Munich and New York," 179 (January 1947), 39–45; "Writing is my Life: The Novelist Under Fire," 179 (February 1947), 55–61.

Articles printing 18 letters to Mrs. J. M. Roberts, Asheville, North Carolina, 1920–1938, and a letter to Frank Wells.

See B 14, B 15, B 16, and *Letters,* 16–17, 23–26, 33–35, 57–60, 66–68, 94–96, 109–110, 111–112, 121–122, 134–135, 162–172, 197–199, 219–221, 517–522, 708–709, 728–731, 736–740, 747–749.

C 132
Carpenter, Frederic I. "Thomas Wolfe: The Autobiography of An Idea." *University of Kansas City Review,* 12 (Spring 1946), 179–187.

Article quoting from the manuscript of *Mannerhouse.*

First Appearances in Magazines and Newspapers 247

C 133
Anonymous. "Other Gifts." *Harvard Alumni Bulletin,* 49 (22 February 1947), 421.

Article facsimiling inscription from Wolfe to Aline Bernstein dated 3 October 1929 appearing in MH copy of *LHA.* See   B 34.

C 134
Anonymous. "The Last Letter of Thomas Wolfe and the Reply to It." *Harvard Library Bulletin,* 1 (Autumn 1947), 278–279.

Article printing and facsimiling four-page letter to Maxwell Perkins dated 12 August 1938. See B 18, C 120, and *Letters,* 777–778.

C 135
"Old Man Rivers." *Atlantic Monthly,* 180 (December 1947), 92–104.

Story.

C 136
"Something of My Life." *Saturday Review of Literature,* 31 (7 February 1948), 6–8.

The original sketch submitted for use in Georges Schreiber's *Portraits and Self-Portraits* (1936), 163–167. Contains a facsimile of a typescript page by Wolfe. See B 7 and B 21.

C 137
Hutsell, James. "Thomas Wolfe and 'Altamont.'" *The Southern Packet,* 4 (April 1948), 1–10.

Article facsimiling a 1929 telegram from Wolfe to Mabel Wheaton, an inscription to Margaret Roberts dated 15 October 1929 in a copy of *LHA* (see B 17 and C 148), and, with photographs in the foreground obscuring most of it, an unidentified manuscript page.

C 138
Dickson, Frank A. "Thomas Wolfe Started His Hard Work Early." *The Independent* (Anderson, S.C.), 17 July 1948, p. 5.

Article printing and facsimiling a letter to Effie Wolfe Gambrell dated 16 May 1909. Also prints 2 letters, one written in 1908 and the other dated 23 October 1908. Part two of a ten-part series.

C 139
Dickson, Frank A. "Wolfe Play To Be In N.Y.; Will Appear In Book Form." *The Independent* (Anderson, S.C.), 7 August 1948, p. 5.

Quotes from the previously unpublished manuscript forward to "Buck Gavin." Part five of a ten-part series.

C 140
Dickson, Frank A. "Wyler Will Direct Motion Picture of Famous Novel." *The Independent* (Anderson, S.C.), 21 August 1948, p. 5.

Prints telegram to Mabel Wolfe Wheaton dated 28 October 1929. Part seven of a ten-part series.

C 141
"Alles war so ganz anders." *Der Monat,* 1 (October 1948), 67–68.

Article printing German translation of letters to Heinz Ledig dated 10 June 1936. See *Letters,* 524–527.

C 142
Ledig-Rowohlt, H[einz]. M[aria]. "Thomas Wolfe in Berlin." *Der Monat,* 1 (October 1948), 69–77.

Article quoting from conversations with Wolfe, from a letter to Ledig-Rowohlt c. 22 June 1936, and from undated notes from Wolfe.

Translated in *The American Scholar,* 22 (Spring 1953), 185–201. See B 29.

C 143
Adams, Agatha Boyd. "Thomas Wolfe at Chapel Hill." *The Carolina Quarterly,* 2 (December 1949), 21–29.

Article quoting in passing from undated letters and conversations. See B 19.

C 144
Kennedy, Richard S. "Thomas Wolfe at Harvard, 1920–1923." *Harvard Library Bulletin,* 4 (Spring and Autumn 1950), 172–190; 304–319.

Article quoting from a letter to Edwin Greenlaw dated March or April 1922, from the autobiographical notebook, from Wolfe's application to the Graduate School at Harvard dated August 1920, from a theme written by Wolfe at Harvard entitled "The Supernatural in the Poetry and Philosophy of Coleridge," from a letter to Merlin Taylor dated summer 1921, from a letter to Horace Williams written in 1922, from an untitled paper on folk plays, from a letter to Elizabeth Cattelle dated 18 November 1934, from a letter to Frederick H. Koch dated 26 November 1920, from a letter to Miss MacReady of the Harvard Appointment Bureau dated 22 August 1922, and from other unpublished manuscript materials. See B 21.

C 145
Adams, Agatha Boyd. "Thomas Wolfe: The Friendliness of A Lonely Man." *The Carolina Quarterly,* 2 (May 1950), 16–22.

Article quoting in passing from Wolfe's letters to Albert Coates and from conversations.

C 146
Meade, Robert D., ed. " 'You Can't Escape Autobiography': New Letters of Thomas Wolfe." *Atlantic Monthly,* 186 (November 1950), 80–83.

Article printing letters written in the winter of 1932 to Julian R. Meade, Danville, Virginia. See *Letters,* 319–324, 336–340, 342–343.

C 147
"Notes from *A Western Journal.*" *Holiday,* 10 (July 1951), 102–107.

Excerpts from *A Western Journal,* illustrated with photographs. See A 16.

C 148
McCoy, George W. "Asheville and Thomas Wolfe." *The North Carolina Historical Review,* 30 (April 1953), 200–217.

Article quoting from a letter written to McCoy dated 17 August 1929, from the inscription in Margaret Roberts's copy of *LHA* dated 15 October 1929 (facsimiled in B 17 and C 137), from a letter to McCoy dated 3 November 1929, from a letter dated 22 March 1932, and from a letter to Mabel Wheaton dated 4 May 1937.

C 149
Flaccus, Kimball. "Gotham Gambit: Memories of Thomas Wolfe and Others." *Dartmouth Alumni Magazine,* 49 (December 1956), 24–27.

Article printing inscription in Flaccus's copy of *FDTM* dated 5 December 1935, a letter to Flaccus dated 22 February 1934, and a letter to Flaccus dated c. 8 June 1937.

C 150
Harris, Arthur S. "Thomas Wolfe's Papers." *Worcester Sunday Telegram Feature Parade Section,* 10 February 1957, p. 5.

Article facsimiling a manuscript page of *LHA.*

C 151
"Welcome to Our City." *Esquire,* 48 (October 1957), 58–83.

First publication of this play, written while Wolfe was at Harvard. See A 23 and B 30.

C 152
Delakas, Daniel L. "Thomas Wolfe and Anatole France." *Comparative Literature,* 9 (Winter 1957), 33–50.

Article quoting from Wolfe's notebooks and unpublished manuscript material. See *Notebooks,* 149–150.

C 153
Watts, Georgia. "An Afternoon With Thomas Wolfe." *Writer's Digest,* 39 (February 1959), 30–34.

Article quoting in passing from conversations with Wolfe and briefly from an undated letter to Frederick H. Koch.

C 154
"A Previously Unpublished Statement By Thomas Wolfe." *Carolina Quarterly,* 11 (Spring 1960), 9–10.

Prints a biographical statement prepared as a class assignment for Professor Koch's playwriting class in 1919. See C 93.

C 155
Thornton, Mary Lindsay, ed. " 'Dear Mabel,' Letters of Thomas Wolfe to His Sister, Mabel Wolfe Wheaton." *South Atlantic Quarterly,* 60 (Autumn 1961), 469–483.

Twelve letters dated 24 December 1922, [summer 1924], 9 October [1927], 21 January 1929, 27 September 1929, 17 October 1929, 5 May 1930, 22 May 1930, 14 October 1931, 28 April 1932, 10 June 1933 and 14 August 1933.

C 156
Skipp, Francis E. "The Editing of *Look Homeward, Angel*." *The Papers of the Bibliographical Society of America,* 57 (First Quarter 1963), 1–13.

Article quoting from Wolfe's Pocket Notebooks, from a typescript version of *LHA,* and from a previously unpublished section of a letter to Elizabeth Nowell dated 23 April 1935.

C 157
Kennedy, Richard S. "Thomas Wolfe and the American Experience." *Modern Fiction Studies,* 11 (Autumn 1965), 219–233.

Article quoting previously unpublished manuscript material from the Notebooks.

C 158
Blythe, LeGette. "About Tom Wolfe." *The Miscellany* (Davidson College), 2 (December 1966), 40–47.

Article facsimiling and printing an autograph note Blythe received attached to a TLS from William Weber at Scribners dated 4 January 1935.

C 159
Skipp, Francis E. "Thomas Wolfe, Max Perkins, and Politics." *Modern Fiction Studies,* 13 (Winter 1967/68), 503–511.

Article quoting from TL to Hamilton Basso c. 13 July 1937 and, briefly, from Wolfe's notebooks.

C 160
Schmid, Hans. "A Note on Thomas Wolfe's *Oktoberfest*-Letter." *Harvard Library Bulletin*, 18 (October 1970), 367–370.

Article quoting from sections of Wolfe's 4 October–20 October 1928 letter to Aline Bernstein which were deleted or damaged in transmission in Nowell's *Letters*, 142–148.

C 161
Anonymous. "Thomas Wolfe Letter To Be Donated To Library." *The Robesonian* (Rowland, N.C.), 21 February 1971.

Article printing a letter to William N. Cox dated 9 February 1938. Unpaginated clipping noted.

C 162
Cane, Melville. "Thomas Wolfe: A Memoir." *The American Scholar*, 41 (Autumn 1972), 637–642.

Article quoting from conversations with Wolfe, from an undated letter and from a letter dated 22 July 1930. See B 43.

C 163
Miehe, Patrick. "The Outline of Thomas Wolfe's Last Book." *Harvard Library Bulletin*, 21 (October 1973), 400–401.

Article facsimiling two pages of the rough outline of *TWATR* and suggesting that they are actually the work of Edward Aswell. See C 164.

C 164
Kennedy, Richard S. "Thomas Wolfe's Last Manuscript." *Harvard Library Bulletin*, 23 (April 1975), 203–211.

Article responding to C 163, quoting from Wolfe's rough outline for *TWATR*. Facsimiles three chapter title pages and two pages from the rough outline of *TWATR*.

C 165
Coates, Albert. "Tom Wolfe As I Remember Him." *Alumni Review* (University of North Carolina at Chapel Hill), 64 (November 1975), 2–8.

Article printing four letters to Albert Coates: two undated and two dated 1923 and 1936, respectively.

C 166
Edward M. Miller, "The Western Journey: Prelude and Aftermath." *The Thomas Wolfe Newsletter*, 1 (Spring 1977), 20–22.

Article printing letter from Wolfe to Edward Miller dated 5 July [1938]. See B 52.

C 167
Green, Charmian. "Wolfe's Stonecutter Once Again: An Unpublished Episode." *Mississippi Quarterly,* 30 (Fall 1977), 611–623.

Article printing a dramatic sequence from a sixteen-page Wolfe manuscript written sometime between 1920 and 1923.

C 168
Pritchard, Billy. "Junk Dealer Finds Wolfe Letters in Household Purchases." *Asheville Citizen-Times,* 30 October 1977, p. C 1.

Article facsimiling two letters to George McCoy; one undated, probably written in 1922, and one dated 16 February 1934.

C 169
"Confessio Amoris." *Thomas Wolfe Newsletter,* 3 (Fall 1979), pp. 42–43.

Facsimile of the manuscript page (p. 42) and a calligraphic copy made by Charles T. Mayer (p. 43) tentatively dated Paris, 1930. See D 9 and D 10.

C 170
North, Caroline. "Thomas Wolfe in New Orleans: Letters of William H. Fitzpatrick to Andrew Turnbull." *The Thomas Wolfe Review,* 4 (Spring 1980), 17–21.

Article quoting from Wolfe's inscription in William Fitzpatrick's copies of *LHA* and *SOAN,* both dated 6 January 1936 (p. 18).

C 171
Halberstadt, John. "The Making of Thomas Wolfe's Posthumous Novels." *The Yale Review,* 70 (October 1980), 74–94.

Undocumented article that primarily paraphrases Wolfe material. Halberstadt uses quotation marks around single words and brief phrases for emphasis as well as for quotation, making it difficult to determine what, if any, material is previously unpublished. However, in an article published in the January–February 1982 issue of *Harvard Magazine* ("The 'Creative Editing' of Thomas Wolfe," 41–42, 44–46), Halberstadt writes of the *Yale Review* article: "I quoted fewer than ten words of Wolfe's that had not been previously published."

C 172
Idol, John, Jr. "Thomas Wolfe and T. S. Eliot: The Hippopotamus and the Old Possum." *The Southern Literary Journal,* 13 (Spring 1981), 15–26.

Article quoting briefly from the unpublished manuscript of *Welcome To Our City.*

C 173
Walser, Richard. "The McCoy Papers." *The Thomas Wolfe Review,* 5 (Spring 1981), 1–6.

Article printing four paragraphs from a letter to George McCoy dated 3 October 1929.

C 174
Trotti, John Boone. "Thomas Wolfe: The Presbyterian Connection." *Journal of Presbyterian History,* 59 (Winter 1981), 517–542.

Article quoting briefly from Wolfe's unpublished "Reflections on Religion" and from the Autobiographical Outline.

C 175
Kennedy, Richard S. "The 'Wolfegate' Affair." *Harvard Magazine,* 84 (Sept.–Oct. 1981), 48–53.

Facsimiles two pages from the typescript of *The Web and the Rock.*

C 176
Kennedy, Richard S. "Thomas Wolfe and Elizabeth Nowell: A Unique Relationship." *South Atlantic Quarterly,* 81 (Spring 1982), 202–213.

Article quoting briefly from letters to Elizabeth Nowell dated 29 December 1937 and 19 June 1938.

C 177
Idol, John, Jr. "Ernest Hemingway and Thomas Wolfe." *The South Carolina Review,* 15 (Fall 1982), 24–31.

Article quoting briefly from Wolfe's manuscript draft of an unpublished review of *A Farewell to Arms.*

C 178
Kennedy, Richard S. "Thomas Wolfe At New York University." *The Thomas Wolfe Review,* 6 (Fall 1982), 1–10.

Article quoting from a letter to Walter Bonime dated 20 September 1927, from marginalia in textbooks used by Wolfe at New York University, from assignments prepared by Wolfe for his students at New York University, from a note listing modern American authors scrawled in 1928 on the back of an examination paper, and from an inscription to James B. Munn appearing in a copy of a typescript of *Mannerhouse.*

C 179
Anonymous. "Wolfe Calls: Questions and Answers." *The Thomas Wolfe Review,* 6 (Fall 1982), 62–64.

Query facsimiling a card written by Wolfe.

C 180
Stutman, Suzanne. "The Wolfe-Bernstein Letters." *The Thomas Wolfe Review,* 7 (Fall 1983), 1–13.

Article quoting from letters to Aline Bernstein dated 20 October 1926, 15 November 1928, 9 August 1928, 27 August 1928, 27 September 1926, 25 September 1926, 9 November 1926, 5 June 1926, 2 October 1926, 26 August 1926, 25 October 1926, 11–12 August 1928, 10 November 1926, 12 August 1928, 27 August 1928, and August 1931.

C 181
Anonymous. "Wolfe Trails: News and Notes." *The Thomas Wolfe Review,* 7 (Fall 1983), 51–57.

Article quoting briefly from Wolfe's 18 April 1923 response to a Chapel Hill questionnaire.

C 182
Scribner, Charles, III. "Crying Wolfe." *Vanity Fair,* 46 (October 1983), 60–61.

Article including first printing of Wolfe's "Last Poem." Contains partially obscured facsimiles of typescript. See C 183.

C 183
Scribner, Charles, III. "Crying Wolfe." *Princeton University Library Chronicle,* 45 (Spring 1984), 225–229.

Article including complete facsimile of Wolfe's "Last Poem." See C 182.

C 184
Lewis, Phyllis H. "Thomas Wolfe's *Welcome to Our City*: An Angry Young Southerner Looks Back." *The Thomas Wolfe Review,* 8 (Spring 1984), 20–26.

Article quoting from the expanded typescript of *WTOC* [Harvard Univ. Library *46AM-7 (13, 14)] and not from the shorter version, edited by Richard S. Kennedy and published by LSU Press in 1983.

C 185
DiGiovanni, Nicholas. " 'Country Cousin' Mary Large Recalls Author Thomas Wolfe." *The Democrat* (Flemington, N.J.), 22 March 1984, p. 12.

Article printing telegram to Mary Mitchell Westall, c. 19 September 1937; quoting from a letter to Jack Westall dated 14 February 1938; facsimiling an undated letter (partially obscured) and the envelope in which it came addressed to Jack Westall; and quoting from conversations.

C 186
Kennedy, Richard S. "What the Galley Proofs of Wolfe's *Of Time and the River* Tell Us." *The Thomas Wolfe Review,* 9 (Fall 1985), 1–8.

Article quoting from a letter to Fred Wolfe dated 13 July 1934, the galley proofs of *OTATR,* and Wolfe's markings on the galley proofs of *OTATR.*

C 187
Mills, Michael S. "From *O Lost* to *Look Homeward, Angel:* A Generic Shift." *The Thomas Wolfe Review,* 10 (Spring 1986), 64–72.

Quotes from the manuscript of *O Lost.*

D. Keepsakes

Separately printed small items with limited numbers of copies not offered for sale, intended for private distribution, and printing previously published material by Wolfe.

D1 WHAT IS MAN?
[*1942*]

[embossed ornamental lettering within a blindstamped frame] What | Is | Man?

Published in 1942.

Colophon: 'COLOPHON | "What is Man?" is an excerpt from the book "You Can't | Go Home Again" by Thomas Wolfe, here presented | in the handwriting of R. Hunter Middleton for his | friend James T. Mangan. Done in Chicago, January, | 1942 | The binding of this book, is the work of Albert Kner.'

Not paginated.

$[1]^{10}$

Binding: Cover title; dark blue stiff laid wrappers, saddlebound.

Publication: 100 copies.

Printing: See colophon.

Locations: APM, MH, NcA, NRSM, ViU.

Note: Prints passage from YCGHA, 432–436. See C 116.

D2 AMERICA
[*1942*]

[swelled rule in red] | AMERICA | [tapered rule in red] | BY | THOMAS WOLFE

Published in 1942.

On colophon: '150 copies were privately printed and presented | to the friends of the Greenwood Press of San | Mateo, California. | January 1942 Copy No. '.

1–11[12]

$[1]^6$

Binding: Cover title; wrappers, saddlebound.

Unprinted glassine dust jacket.

Publication: See colophon.

Printing: See colophon.

Locations: APM, CSFU, InU Lilly, MH (dj).

Note: Prints a short poetical passage from *OTATR, 155–160.*

D 3 FROM OF TIME AND THE RIVER AMERICA
1942

[black lettering] *From Of Time and the River* | [ornamental red lettering] America | [black lettering] *By Thomas Wolfe* | PRIVATELY PRINTED [star] CHICAGO | [red rule] | *1942*

Published in April 1942.

[1–8] 9–26 [27–32]

[1]¹⁶

Binding: Very deep red V cloth. Front goldstamped vertically from bottom to top along spine: 'A [star] M [star] E [star] R [star] I [star] C [star] A' and horizontally 'BY THOMAS WOLFE'.

Dust jacket.

Publication: Number of copies not determined.

Printing: Designed by Norman Forgue and his class in typography and design at the Harrison Commercial Art Institute and printed at the Norman Press in Chicago.

Locations: APM (dj), NcA, NcRSM, ViU.

Note: Prints a short poetical passage from OTATR, 155–160.

D 4 GOD'S LONELY MAN
1947

[red lettering] [diamond] THOMAS WOLFE [diamond] | [black lettering] GOD'S | LONELY | MAN | *An Autobiographical Sketch* | SAN JOSE COLLEGE LABORATORY PRESS | [diamond] 1947 [diamond]

Colophon: 'This book, like many books produced for the pleasure of the | maker, was a long time a-making. The text was set and most | of the presswork completed in 1945. The title-page was set and | printed in early 1947, and the binding was completed in May | of this year. The type used is Goudy's Deepdene, with accents | in Bernhard's Modern Roman. The edition consists of thirty copies only, on Ivory Laid Strathmore Text'.

Keepsakes 261

[i–vi] 1–16 [17–22]

[1]⁴ [2]⁶ [3]⁴

Binding: Very deep red V cloth with white V-cloth shelfback. Front stamped in white: 'GOD'S | LONELY | MAN'.

Publication: Prints passage from *THB*, 186–197. See C 121.

Printing: See colophon.

Location: InU Lilly.

Note: See A 9 and C 121.

D 5 TO RUPERT BROOKE
1948

TO | RUPERT BROOKE | [rule] | THOMAS WOLFE | [rule] | 1948

Colophon: 'One hundred copies | [rule] | Privately Printed | by LECRAM PRESS | for | RICHARD JEAN PICARD | [rule] | Noel 1948'.

Not paginated.

[1]⁴

Binding: Yellowish white wrappers. Front recto: 'TO | RUPERT BROOKE | [rule] | THOMAS WOLFE | [rule] | 1948'. All edges trimmed.

Publication: See colophon.

Printing: See colophon.

Locations: APM, BL (15MAY65), DLC, InU Lilly, MH, NcA, NcU, ViU (2 copies).

Note: See C 5.

D 6 RETURN
[*1976*]

[facsimiled manuscript page printed in dark blue on light blue] Return | by | Thomas Wolfe | I have been seven years [written above crossed out 'long'] from | home, but now I have come | back again. And what is | there to say? | Time passes, + puts better—debate. [crossed out 'There was a time'] | There is too [written beneath illegible crossed out word] much to say, there is [illegible crossed out words] so | much to say that must be spoken

Published in 1976.

Not paginated.

[1]⁸

Binding: Cover title; light blue stiff wove wrappers, saddlebound.

Publication: Number of copies not determined.

Printing: Not determined.

Locations: APM, CJ, NcRSM.

Note: Edited by Myra Champion for the Thomas Wolfe Memorial. Prints an article first appearing in the *Asheville Citizen-Times* (see C 70). See B 28.

D 7 THE PROMISE OF AMERICA
[*1977*]

[within an ornamental frame] THE PROMISE OF AMERICA | By | *Thomas Wolfe*

Published in 1977.

Single 8⅜" × 5½" sheet printed on recto and verso.

Head title.

Publication: Number of copies not determined.

Printing: Printed by Aldo P. Magi and distributed at the Thomas Wolfe Festival at St. Mary's College in Raleigh, North Carolina, on 24 and 25 October 1977.

Locations: APM, NcRSM.

Note: Prints an essay originally printed in *Coronet* (see C 117) and later incorporated into *YCGHA*, 505–508.

D 8 TIME... THOMAS WOLFE
[*1978*]

[printed on blue in ornamental red letters with a drawing of Wolfe] Time... | Thomas Wolfe

Published in 1978.

Colophon: 'A Remembrance..... Thomas Wolfe Fest, St. Mary's College, Raleigh, North Carolina | October 1 and 2, 1978.'

Not paginated.

Single sheet of 10½" × 6⅜" laid paper, white on one side and blue on the other, folded once to produce four pages.

Keepsakes 263

Publication: 150 numbered copies, not for sale, distributed on 1 and 2 October 1978 at the Thomas Wolfe Fest at St. Mary's College, Raleigh, North Carolina.

Printing: Not determined.

Locations: APM (2 copies), CJ, NcRSM, NcU.

Note: Edited by Aldo P. Magi. Prints one passage from *YCGHA* and two passages from *TWATR*.

D 9 CONFESSIO AMORIS
[*1979*]

[in calligraphy] Confessio Amoris

Published in 1979.

On verso: 'THOMAS WOLFE | FEST | October 28 and 29, 1979 | Sarah Graham Kenan Library | St. Mary's College | Raleigh, North Carolina | COMPLIMENTS OF: | *The Thomas Wolfe Newsletter* | Department of English | University of Akron | Akron, OH 44325'.

Single 9" × 5¾" sheet of laid paper printed on recto and verso.

Head title.

Publication: Number of copies not determined.

Printing: Privately printed by the Thomas Wolfe Society from plates prepared for *The Thomas Wolfe Newsletter* in Fall 1979. See C 169 and D 10.

Locations: CJ, JI, NcRSM.

D 10 CONFESSIO AMORIS
[*1979*]

[in calligraphy] CONFESSIO AMORIS

Published in 1979.

Broadside; 9" × 6".

Head title.

Publication: Number of copies not determined.

Printing: Calligraphy by Michael W. Hughey of Asheville, North Carolina.

Location: NcA.

Note: See C 169 and D 9.

D 11 THE PROEM TO "O LOST" – THOMAS WOLFE
[*1979*]

[lettered vertically from bottom to top along the left-hand margin in medium gray] THE PROEM TO "O LOST" – THOMAS WOLFE [drawing of a medium gray angel at center]

Published in 1979.

On colophon: 'The proem to "O Lost" is a special publication for | members of The Thomas Wolfe Society and | commemorates the fiftieth anniversary of the | publication of [bold face] Look Homeward, Angel.'

Not paginated.

Single rectangular sheet of 18″ × 9″ laid paper, white on one side and pale yellow on the other, folded horizontally in thirds to produce six pages.

Publication: 300 numbered copies. Edited by John L. Idol, Jr., and Aldo P. Magi and distributed to members of the Thomas Wolfe Society in 1979.

Printing: Not determined.

Locations: APM (2 copies), CW, JI, NcU.

Note: Facsimiles a holograph page of "O Lost" as it appears in the ledger in the William B. Wisdom Collection at Harvard University. See B 12.

D 12 THOMAS WOLFE'S DISCOVERY OF AMERICA
[*1980*]

[printed in blue beneath red and blue American flag] Thomas Wolfe's | DISCOVERY | OF | AMERICA

Published in 1980.

Single coated sheet folded once distributed by the Thomas Wolfe Memorial.

Publication: Number of copies not determined.

Printing: Not determined.

Locations: APM, NcU.

Note: Prints passages from *YCGHA*.

D 13 THE LONDON TOWER
1980

[blue lettering] LONDON TOWER | Thomas Wolfe | *The Thomas Wolfe Society* | 1980

On colophon: 'Edited and prepared for publication in this form by Aldo P. Magi. . . .'

Keepsakes 265

Not paginated.

[1]⁶

Binding: Yellowish white wrappers, saddlebound. Front printed in dark blue on medium blue drawing of the London Tower: 'LONDON TOWER | Thomas Wolfe'. Inside wrappers, front and back, contain medium blue drawings of the London Tower.

Publication: 300 copies printed for distribution to members of the Thomas Wolfe Society.

Printing: Not determined.

Locations: APM (2 copies), JI, NcRSM.

Note: Prints an article originally appearing in *The Asheville Citizen* (see C 13).

D 14 THE STREETS OF DURHAM
[*1982*]

[ornamental lettering] The Streets | of | Durham | Thomas Wolfe | [Wolfe's head seal] | [roman] WOLFE'S HEAD PRESS | RALEIGH

Published in 1982.

On copyright page: 'Limited to three hundred fifty copies | none of them for sale | for distribution only to members of the | Thomas Wolfe Society | Dept. English, University of Akron, Akron OH 44325'.

[1–8] 9 [10] 11–14 [15–18] 19–26 [27–28]

Perfect-bound pamphlet.

Binding: Dark orangish yellow wrappers: '[within ornamental frame in ornamental letters] The Streets of | Durham | [masks of comedy and tragedy]'. Spine printed vertically: 'THE STREETS OF DURHAM THOMAS WOLFE'. All edges trimmed.

Publication: See copyright.

Locations: APM, CJ, CW, NcRSM.

Note: Prints a play originally printed in the *University of North Carolina Tar Baby*. See B 38 and C 11.

D 15 THE TRAIN AND THE CITY
1984

The Train and the City | *by* | *Thomas Wolfe* | With an Introduction by | Richard S. Kennedy | The Thomas Wolfe Society | 1984

One copyright page: 'This edition of "The Train and the City" is the fifth in a series of annual | publications for the members of the Thomas Wolfe Society.'

[i–iv] 1–27 [28]

[1]^{16}

Binding: Light blue wrappers, saddlebound, with photograph of New York City skyline on front. Front printed in light blue on photograph: 'The Train and the City | *Thomas Wolfe*'. All edges trimmed.

Publication: 450 copies distributed to members of the Thomas Wolfe Society.

Printing: Not determined.

Locations: APM, NcA, NcRSM.

Note: See C 21.

E. Putative First Appearances by Wolfe

Titles in which material attributed to Wolfe appears for the first time in a book, pamphlet, newspaper, or magazine.

E 1
"A Carolina Man." *The Tar Heel* (University of North Carolina), 11 October 1919, p. 2.

Unsigned article attributed to Wolfe by Agatha Boyd Adams. See B 19 and C 143.

E 2
"Clean Sportsmanship." *The Tar Heel* (University of North Carolina), 25 October 1919, p. 2.

Unsigned article attributed to Wolfe by Agatha Boyd Adams. See B 19 and C 143.

E 3
"Ye Who Have Been There Only Know." *The Tar Heel* (University of North Carolina), 13 December 1919, p. 2.

Unsigned article attributed to Wolfe by Agatha Boyd Adams. See B 19 and C 143.

E 4
"Useful Advice to Candidates." *The Tar Heel* (University of North Carolina), 28 February 1920, p. 2.

Unsigned article attributed to Wolfe by Agatha Boyd Adams. See B 19 and C 143.

E 5
"Athletic Courtesy and Lack of It." *The Tar Heel* (University of North Carolina), 24 April 1920, p. 2.

Unsigned article attributed to Wolfe by Agatha Boyd Adams. See B 19 and C 143.

E 6
Hughes, Aline. "Tarheels in New York." *The State* (Raleigh, N.C.), 29 December 1934, p. 25.

Article quoting briefly from conversations with Wolfe.

E 7
Bridgers, Ann Preston. "Thomas Wolfe: Legends of a Man's Hunger in His Youth." *The Saturday Review of Literature,* 11 (6 April 1935), 599, 609.

Article quoting briefly from conversations Wolfe had with Ann Bridgers and Dorothy and Dubose Heyward, with Jonathan Daniels, and with John Terry Skally. Also quotes from memory an undated letter to Helen Arthur.

E 8
Ehrsam, Theodore G. "I Knew Thomas Wolfe." *The Book Collector's Journal,* 1 (June 1936), pp. 1, 3.

Article quoting briefly from a conversation Ehrsam had with Wolfe while in Wolfe's class at New York University.

E 9
Miller, Edward M. "Gulping The Great West." *The Oregonian* (Portland, Oregon), 31 July and 7 August 1938, pp. 1, 9; 6.

Article quoting from conversations Miller had with Wolfe while traveling with him in the Northwest.

E 10
Bates, Ernest Sutherland. "Thomas Wolfe." *The Modern Quarterly,* 11 (Fall 1938), 86–89.

Article quoting briefly from conversations with Wolfe.

E 11
Forsythe, Robert [Kyle Crichton]. "Forsythe's Page." *The New Masses,* 29 (27 September 1938), 14.

Article quoting briefly from conversations with Wolfe.

E 12
Perkins, Maxwell. "Scribner's and Tom Wolfe." *The Carolina Magazine,* 68 (October 1938), 15–17.

Article quoting from conversations with Wolfe. See B 21.

E 13
Perkins, Maxwell. "Thomas Wolfe A Writer for the People of His Time and Tomorrow." *Wings* (The Literary Guild), 13 (October 1939), 4–9.

Essay on Wolfe quoting briefly from conversations with him. Distributed by the Literary Guild of America on 2 October 1939 with their selection *The Face of a Nation.*

E 14
Cannon, Bernard. "Memories of Thomas Wolfe as Told by Fred Wolfe to Bernard Cannon Expressly for the Journal." *The Wofford Journal* (Wofford College), 51 (May 1941), 3, 4, 19.

Article paraphrasing Wolfe's inscription in Fred Wolfe's copy of *FDTM* and quoting from conversations.

E 15
Daniels, Jonathan. "Poet of the Boom." In *Tar Heels* (Dodd & Mead, 1941), pp. 218–235.

Article quoting briefly from conversations with Wolfe. See B 21.

E 16
Bishop, Don. "Thomas Wolfe." *The Carolina Magazine*, 71 (March 1942), 28–35, 47–48.

Article quoting briefly from conversations with Wolfe. See B 21.

E 17
Powell, Desmond. "Of Thomas Wolfe." *Arizona Quarterly*, 1 (Spring 1945), 28–36.

Article quoting from conversations with Wolfe during the summer of 1935.

E 18
Whitson, Max. "Tom Wolfe's Cabin." *The State* (Raleigh, N.C.), 12 January 1946, p. 5.

Article quoting from conversations with Wolfe during the summer of 1937.

E 19
Armstrong, Anne W. "As I Saw Thomas Wolfe." *Arizona Quarterly*, 2 (Spring 1946), 5–15.

Article quoting from conversations with Wolfe.

E 20
Middlebrook, L. Ruth. "Reminiscences of Thomas Wolfe." *American Mercury*, 63 and 64 (November 1946 and April 1947), 544–549; 413–420.

Article quoting briefly from conversations with Wolfe.

E 21
Norwood, Hayden. *The Marble Man's Wife*. New York: Scribners, 1947.

Biography of Wolfe's mother, Julia, quoting in passing from conversations with Wolfe.

E 22
Dickson, Frank A. "Wolfe Found Life Not All Bad, Not All Good." *The Independent* (Anderson, S.C.), 24 July 1948, p. 5.

Article quoting from a conversation Wolfe had with his sister, Mabel Wolfe Wheaton. Part three of a ten-part series.

E 23
Dickson, Frank A. "Wolfe Described Teacher As 'Mother' Of His Spirit." *The Independent* (Anderson, S.C.), 31 July 1948, p. 5.

Article quoting from a conversation Wolfe had with his sister, Mabel Wolfe Wheaton. Part four of a ten-part series.

E 24
Dickson, Frank A. "Noted Wolfe Home May Be Transformed Into Museum." *The Independent* (Anderson, S.C.), 4 September 1948, p. 5.

Article quoting from a conversation Wolfe had with Edward C. Aswell. Part nine of a ten-part series.

E 25
Aswell, Edward, and John Skally Terry. "En Route to a Legend." *The Saturday Review of Literature,* 31 (27 November 1948), 7–9, 34–36.

Article quoting briefly from a spring 1934 phone call to Terry.

E 26
Meyerhoff, Hans. "Death of a Genius: The Last Days of Thomas Wolfe." *Commentary,* 13 (January 1952), 44–51.

Article quoting briefly from conversations Wolfe had with his sister.

E 27
Anonymous. "Thomas Wolfe: Biography in Sound." *The Carolina Quarterly,* 9 (Fall 1956), 5–19.

Script for an NBC Radio Broadcast in which friends and family quote in passing from conversations with Wolfe.

E 28
Nowell, Elizabeth. "The Death of Thomas Wolfe." *Esquire,* 53 (April 1960), 144–147.

Article quoting in passing from conversations.

E 29
Bell, Alladine. "T. Wolfe of 10 Montague Terrace." *The Antioch Review,* 20 (Fall 1960), 377–390.

Article quoting from conversations.

Putative First Appearances

E 30
Crichton, Kyle. *Total Recoil*. Garden City, New York: Doubleday, 1960.

Book quoting in passing from conversations.

E 31
Eaton, Clement. "Student Days with Thomas Wolfe." *The Georgia Review*, 17 (Summer 1963), 146–155.

Article quoting briefly from conversations with Wolfe.

E 32
Angoff, Charles. "Thomas Wolfe and the Opulent Manner." *Southwest Review*, 48 (Winter 1963), vi–vii, 81–92.

Article quoting from conversations Wolfe had with Angoff and Elizabeth Nowell about the publication of "Boom Town."

E 33
Spearman, Walter. *The Carolina Playmakers*. Chapel Hill, N.C.: The University of North Carolina Press, 1970.

Book quoting from conversations between Wolfe and Professor Frederick H. Koch, pp. 10–13.

E 34
West, Luke. " 'Which of Us Has Known His Brother?' " *The State* (Columbia, S.C.), 31 January 1971, p. 2E.

Article quoting from conversations between Wolfe and his brother Fred Wolfe.

E 35
Cox, W[illiam]. N. "Cox's Reference Notes." *The Robesonian* (Rowland, N.C.), 21 February 1971.

Article quoting briefly from conversations with Wolfe. Unpaginated clipping noted.

E 36
Griffin, John C. "Thomas Wolfe Remembered: An Evening With Fred-Luke." *The Lance* (University of South Carolina at Lancaster), 4 (Spring 1975), 17–20, 32–34.

Article quoting in passing from conversations between Wolfe and his brother Fred Wolfe.

E 37
Cadle, Dean, and Richard Reed. "Thomas Wolfe at 75." *Appalachian Heritage*, 3 (Summer 1975), 45–58.

Interview with Fred Wolfe quoting in passing from conversations with his brother.

E 38
Gould, Elaine Westall. *Look Behind You, Thomas Wolfe.* Hicksville, N.Y.: Exposition Press, 1976.

Book quoting in passing from conversations.

E 39
Phillipson, John. "Thomas Wolfe Visits Vermont: A Retrospect." *The Thomas Wolfe Newsletter,* 1 (Spring 1977), 13–19.

Article quoting from conversations.

E 40
Little, Elizabeth T. "A Brief Recollection of Thomas Wolfe." *The Thomas Wolfe Newsletter,* 2 (Fall 1978), 16–17.

Article quoting from conversations.

E 41
Hoagland, Clayton, and Kathleen Hoagland. *Thomas Wolfe Our Friend 1933–1938.* Edited by Aldo P. Magi and Richard Walser. Athens, Ohio: Croissant & Company, 1979.

Book quoting in passing from conversations.

E 42
Marx, Samuel. *Thomas Wolfe and Hollywood.* Athens, Ohio: Croissant & Company, 1980.

Pamphlet quoting from a conversation Wolfe had with Samuel Marx and Jean Harlow at MGM.

E 43
Pegram, Addie Bradshaw. "Anecdote: Wolfe on the Telephone." *The Thomas Wolfe Newsletter,* 4 (Spring 1980), 42.

Anecdote quoting from a telephone conversation between Wolfe and his mother, overheard by the author.

E 44
Jordan, John Y. "Thomas Wolfe Remembered—III." *The Thomas Wolfe Newsletter,* 4 (Spring 1980), 43–44.

Article quoting from conversations.

E 45
Anonymous. "He Wolfed His Meal." *The Thomas Wolfe Newsletter,* 4 (Fall 1980), 54.

Anecdote quoting from conversation with Wolfe.

E 46
Tennant, Charles G. "Thomas Wolfe Remembered—IV." *The Thomas Wolfe Newsletter,* 4 (Fall 1980), 41–44.

Article quoting from conversations.

E 47
Anonymous. "Wolfe the Reviser." *The Thomas Wolfe Review,* 5 (Spring 1981), 66.

Article quoting briefly from a conversation with Gladys Coates.

E 48
Jones, H. G., ed. *Thomas Wolfe of North Carolina.* Chapel Hill, N.C.: North Caroliniana Society and the North Carolina Collection, 1982.

Book quoting in passing from conversations Wolfe had with schoolmates, pp. 51–90.

Appendix / Index

Appendix
Principal Works About Thomas Wolfe

Adams, Agatha Boyd. *Thomas Wolfe: Carolina Student, A Brief Biography*. Chapel Hill: University of North Carolina Library, 1950.
Austin, Neal F. *A Biography of Thomas Wolfe*. Austin, Texas: Roger Beacham, 1968.
Boyd, Madeleine. *Thomas Wolfe: The Discovery of a Genius*, ed. Aldo P. Magi. The Thomas Wolfe Society, 1981.
Evans, Elizabeth. *Thomas Wolfe*. New York: Ungar, 1984.
Field, Leslie A. *Thomas Wolfe: Three Decades of Criticism*. New York: New York University Press, 1968.
Holman, C. Hugh. *The Loneliness at the Core: Studies in Thomas Wolfe*. Baton Rouge: Louisiana State University Press, 1975.
. *Thomas Wolfe*. Minneapolis: University of Minneapolis Press, 1960.
. *The World of Thomas Wolfe*. New York: Scribners, 1962.
Johnson, Elmer D. *Thomas Wolfe: A Checklist*. Kent State University Press, 1970.
Johnson, Pamela Hansford. *Thomas Wolfe: A Critical Study*. London: Heinimann, 1947. Republished in New York by Scribners in 1948 as *Hungry Gulliver: An English Critical Appraisal of Thomas Wolfe* and in 1963 as *The Art of Thomas Wolfe*.
Jones, H. G. *Thomas Wolfe of North Carolina*. Chapel Hill, N.C.: North Caroliniana Society and the North Carolina Collection of UNC, Chapel Hill, 1982.
Kennedy, Richard S., ed. *Thomas Wolfe: A Harvard Perspective*. Athens, Ohio: Croissant, 1983.
The Window of Memory: The Literary Career of Thomas Wolfe. Chapel Hill: University of North Carolina Press, 1962. Rev. Ed. 1968.
Marx, Samuel. *Thomas Wolfe and Hollywood*. Athens, Ohio: Croissant & Co., 1980.
McElderry, Bruce R., Jr. *Thomas Wolfe*. New York: Twayne, 1964.
Norwood, Hayden. *The Marble Man's Wife*. New York: Scribners, 1947.
Nowell, Elizabeth. *Thomas Wolfe: A Biography*. Garden City, N.Y.: Doubleday & Company, 1960.
Phillipson, John S. *Critical Essays on Thomas Wolfe*. Boston, Mass.: G. K. Hall, 1985.
. *Thomas Wolfe: A Reference Guide*. Boston, Mass.: G. K. Hall, 1977.
Pollock, Thomas Clark, and Oscar Cargill. *Thomas Wolfe at Washington Square*. New York: New York University Press, 1954.

Preston, George. *Thomas Wolfe: A Bibliography*. New York: Charles S. Boesen, 1943.

Reeves, Paschal. *Guide to Thomas Wolfe*. Columbus, Ohio: Merrill, 1972.

——. *Thomas Wolfe and the Glass of Time*. Athens: University of Georgia Press, 1971.

——. *Thomas Wolfe's Albatross: Race and Nationality in America*. Athens: University of Georgia Press, 1968.

Rubin, Louis D., ed. *Thomas Wolfe: A Collection of Critical Essays*. Englewood Cliffs, N.J.: Prentice-Hall, 1973.

——. *Thomas Wolfe: The Weather of His Youth*. Baton Rouge: Louisiana State University Press, 1955.

Turnbull, Andrew. *Thomas Wolfe*. New York: Scribners, 1967.

Walser, Richard, ed. *The Enigma of Thomas Wolfe: Biographical and Critical Selections*. Cambridge, Mass.: Harvard University Press, 1953.

——. *Thomas Wolfe: An Introduction and Interpretation*. New York: Barnes and Noble, 1961.

——. *Thomas Wolfe Undergraduate*. Durham, N.C.: Duke University Press, 1977.

Watkins, Floyd C. *Thomas Wolfe's Characters: Portraits from Life*. Norman: University of Oklahoma Press, 1957.

Wheaton, Mabel Wolfe, and LeGette Blythe. *Thomas Wolfe and His Family*. Garden City, N.Y.: Doubleday, 1961.

Index

"About Tom Wolfe," C 158
Adams, Agatha Boyd. B 19, C 143, C 145, E 1–E 5
Adams, J. Donald, A 9.1.a
Alumni Review (University of North Carolina at Chapel Hill), C 165
"America," AA 1
America, D 2
The American Mercury, C 26, C 56, C 58, C 74, C 101, C 113, C 121, E 20
The American Scholar, C 142, C 162
"An American Author's Testament," C 103
"The American Wilderness," AA 1
"An Afternoon With Thomas Wolfe," C 153
"The Anatomy of Loneliness," C 121
Anderson, Sherwood, B 20, C 124
"Anecdote: Wolfe on the Telephone," E 43
"An Angel on the Porch," C 14
Angoff, Charles, E 32
The Antioch Review, E 29
Appalachian Heritage, E 37
"An Appreciation," C 7
"April," AA 3
"April, Late April," C 74
"April Night and Morning," AA 1
Arizona Quarterly, E 17, E 19
Armstrong, Anne W., C 65, E 19
"Arnold Pentland," C 41
"Artemidorus, Farewell!" AA 3, AA 4
The Art of Thomas Wolfe, B 16 *Note one*
Arthur, Helen, E 7
"Asheville and Thomas Wolfe," C 148
Asheville and Thomas Wolfe, B 40
Asheville Citizen, C 13, C 68, C 74, D 13 *Note one*
Asheville Citizen-Times, C 70, C 95, C 168, D 6 *Note one*
The Asheville Times, C 16, C 66, C 67
"As I Saw Thomas Wolfe," E 19

"As It Had Always Been," AA 3
Aswell, Edward C., A 4.1.d *Note one*, A 8.1.a *Note two*, A 8.1.n *Note one*, A 8.2.a, A 9, A 9.1.a *Note two*, A 23 *Note one*, A 24 *Note two*, C 97, C 163, E 25
"Athletic Courtesy and Lack of It," E 5
Atlanta Constitution, C 61
Atlanta Journal, A 8.1.a, A 9.1.a
Atlantic Monthly, C 106, C 131, C 135, C 146
"At Morning," AA 3
Authors at Work, B 23
"Author's Note," C 106
"Author To End Series in Oregon," C 51
"Author Wolfe Visits Seattle; He's Just as Big as his Books," C 91
Autobiographical Notebook, B 35
Autobiographical Outline, B 23, B 50, C 174
The Autobiography of an American Novelist, AA 8
"Autobiographical Statement," B 49, B 50
Avon Book Company, AA 2
Avon Books, A 9.2
Avon Modern Short Story Monthly, AA 2

Baker, George Pierce, A 23 *Note one*, B 21
Ballinger, A 1.1.b
Bantam Books, A 2.9.a
Barnes, John S., AA 3
Basford, Emory S., B 15
Basso, Hamilton, C 118, C 159
Bostick & Thornley, B 25
Bates, Ernest Sutherland, E 10
"The Battle of Hogwart Heights," AA 2
"Beauty, Size of Campus Impress Visiting Speaker," C 88
Beer, Thomas, A 2.1.a
Bell, Allandine, E 29
"The Bell Remembered," C 56

"The Bell Strikes Three," C 56
"Ben," AA 3
Benet, Stephen Vincent, A 9.1.a
"Ben, My Ghost," AA 3
Berg, A. Scott, B 45
Berger, Brian F., B 52
Bernstein, Aline, A 2.1.a *Note three*, A 4.1.a$_1$ *Note one*, A 26, A 27, B 34–B 36, B 51, C 133, C 160, C 179
Berliner Tageblatt, C 57
Beyond Love and Loyalty, A 25
Bigart, Homer, C 52
"The Birthday," C 108
Bishop, Don, B 21, E 16
Black Archer Press, A 10
"The Blazing Certitude," AA 3
Blumenthal, Joseph, A 17.1.a
Blythe, LeGette, B 26, C 129, C 158
Bonime, Walter, C 178
Book Buyer, C 54
The Book Collector's Journal, E 8
Book-of-the-Month Club, A 2.6.c, A 3.1.z, B 24
Book-of-the-Month Club News, A 3.1.a *Note one*
Books, Inc., B 6
The Book Society, AA 4
"Boom Town," B 4, C 26, E 32
Boston Evening Transcript, C 18
Boulder Daily Camera, C 47
"The Boy in Bed," A 29
Boyd, Madeleine, AA 4, B 48
Braswell, William, A 7.1.i, A 19, B 21, C 111
"Brevity To Be Goal of Thomas Wolfe," C 42
"The Bridge," AA 3
Bridgers, Ann Preston, E 7
"A Brief Recollection of Thomas Wolfe," E 40
Bristol News (Bristol, Va.), C 65
"Brooklyn," AA 3
Buccaneer Books, A 2.13
"Buck Gavin," C 139
Buffalo Evening News, A 8.1.a
"The Bums at Sunset," A 4, AA 5, C 50
Burlingame, Roger, B 14
"Burning in the Night," AA 3
Butterfield, Harold, B 31
Bruccoli, Matthew J., B 42, B 47
Bruccoli Clark, B 49, B 50

Cadle, Dean, E 37
Cameron, May, B 6, C 55
Canby, Henry Seidel, A 4.1.a$_1$, A 9.1.a, A 13.1.a
Cane, Melville, B 43, C 162
Cannon, Bernard, E 14
Cargill, Oscar, A 17, B 22
Carlinsky, Dan, B 38
Carolina Folk-Plays (First, Second, and Third Series), B 1, B 10
Berliner Tageblatt, C 57
Carolina Folk-Plays (Second Series), B 1
The Carolina Magazine, C 96, C 97, E 12, E 16
"A Carolina Man," E 1
The Carolina Play-Book, C 93, C 94, C 120, C 126, C 127, C 128
Carolina Playmakers, B 1
The Carolina Playmakers, E 33
The Carolina Quarterly, C 143, C 145, C 154, E 27
Carpenter, Frederic I., C 132
Carraway, Gertrude S., C 79
Cattelle, Elizabeth, C 144
A Century of College Humor, B 38
"The Challenge," C 3
Chamberlain, John, A 3.1.a
Champion, Myra, D 6 *Note one*
"Chance," AA 3
Charles S. Boesen, A 15, B 12
Charles Scribner's Sons, A 2.1, A 2.2.a, A 2.4, A 2.6, A 2.9.b, A 2.11, A 3.1, A 3.2.a *Note one*, A 3.4, A 3.6, A 4.1.a$_1$, A 4.1.a$_2$ *Note one*, A 4.1.b, A 4.1.c, A 4.1.e–f, A 4.4, A 5.1.a$_1$, A 5.1.a$_2$ *Note one*, A 5.1.a$_3$, A 5.1.b–h, A 11, A 18, AA 1, AA 3, AA 4, AA 6, AA 7, AA 8 *Note one*, B 14, B 16 *Note one*, B 18, B 33, B 42, E 21
Charlotte Observer, C 79
Chase, Richard, A 7.3, A 7.4.a, A 8.3.a–e
Chicago Tribune, A 11.1.a
"Chickamauga," A 9, AA 2, AA 4, C 83
"The Child by Tiger," B 9, C 76
"City April," AA 3
"Circus at Dawn," A 4, AA 4, AA 5, C 33
Cincinnati Enquirer, A 8.1.a
Clausen & Bosse, Leck/Schleswig, B 29
Clayton, Thomas (pseud. for Thomas Wolfe), C 7, C 9
"Clean Sportsmanship," E 2
Cleveland News, A 8.1.a, A 9.1.a

Index

Coates, Albert, C 145, C 165
Coates, Gladys, E 47
Cocke, William J., B 41
"The Cock That Crows at Morning," AA 3
College English, C 111
"Come Back Again," AA 3
"Coming of Spring," AA 1
Commentary, E 26
"The Company," C 84
Comparative Literature, C 152
"Concerning Honest Bob," C 12
"Confessio Amoris," C 169
Confessio Amoris, D 9, D 10
"Conversation by Moonlight," AA 1
Cooper, Lee, C 16
Coronet, C 117, D 7 *Note one*
Correspondence of F. Scott Fitzgerald, B 47
The Correspondence of Thomas Wolfe and Homer Andrew Watt, A 17, B 22 *Note one*
Cosmopolitan, C 44
"Cottage by the Tracks," C 44
Coughlan, Robert, A 18.2.a
" 'Country Cousin' Mary Large Recalls Author Thomas Wolfe," C 185
"Cox's Reference Notes," E 35
Cox, William N., C 161, E 35
The Crack-Up, B 13
Crawley, Oliver, C 63
" 'The Creative Editing' of Thomas Wolfe," C 171
"The Creative Movement in Writing," C 10
Crichton, Kyle, E 11, E 30
The Crisis in Industry, A 1
Croissant & Company, A 22, B 46, B 51, E 41, E 42
Crossen, Forrest, C 47
Crowninshield, Frank, B 11
"Crying Wolfe," C 182, C 183
Current History and Forum, C 114
"A Cullenden of Virginia," C 4

Daily News (Asheville, N.C.), C 69
Daily News (New York University), C 15
The Daily Worker, (New York), C 103
"Dance," AA 3
Daniels, Jonathan, B 25, E 7, E 15
"Dark in the Forest, Strange as Time," A 4, AA 4, C 28

"Dark Messiah," C 114
Darrow, Whitney, A 4.1.d *Note one*
Dartmouth Alumni Magazine, C 149
Dashiell, Alfred, A 5.1.a$_1$, A 5.1.c–d, B 3
Davis, Ruth, C 130
" 'Dear Mabel,' Letters of Thomas Wolfe to His Sister, Mabel Wolfe Wheaton," C 154
"Death, Loneliness, and Sleep," AA 3
"Death of a Genius: The Last Days of Thomas Wolfe," E 26
"The Death of Thomas Wolfe," E 28
"Death the Proud Brother," A 4, AA 5, C 22
"Deferred Payment," C 8
Delakas, Daniel L., C 152
Dell, A 7.3, A 8.3.a–e
The Democrat (Flemington, N.J.), C 185
"Demoniac Ecstasy," AA 1
Denver Post, C 90
"Departure," AA 1
Der Monat, C 142
"Destiny," AA 1
Dickson, Frank A., C 138–C 140, E 22–E 25
Dictionary of Literary Biography Documentary Series, B 50
Dictionary of Literary Biography Volume Nine: American Novelists, 1910–1945, B 49
Dieter, George, A 7.1.a *Note one*
DiGiovanni, Nicholas, C 185
"Discovery of Catawba," AA 1
Dodd, Mrs. William E., B 39
Dodd & Mead, E 15
Donald, David, A 25.1.a
Doubleday, E 30
Doubleday, Doran & Company, Inc., B 4, B 5, B 24, B 26, B 37
"The Drammer," C 6
"The Dream of Time," AA 1
"Dreams of Guilt and Time," AA 1
"The Drug Store," A 29
"Drunkenness," AA 1
Duggan, Margaret, B 47
Dukedom Large Enough, B 36
Duke University Press, B 44

" 'E, A Recollection," C 73
"The Earth Flows By," AA 1
Eaton, Clement, E 31

"Echoes of Forgotten Time," AA 1
"The Editing of *Look Homeward, Angel*," C 156
Editions for the Armed Services, A 2.3, A 3.3
Editor's Choice, B 3
Editor to Author, B 18
Ehrsam, Theodore G., E 8
"The Enchanted City," C 107, C 110
The Enigma of Thomas Wolfe, B 21
"En Route to a Legend," E 25
E. P. Dutton, B 45
"Ernest Hemingway and Thomas Wolfe," C 177
"Escape into the World," AA 1
Esquire, A 23 *Note one*, C 41, C 119, C 151, E 28
"Eugene," AA 3
"Eugene Returns to Pulpit Hill," C 96
"Euripides in the Wilderness," AA 1
Evans, Elizabeth, B 48
An Exhibition Selections From The Twentieth Century, B 31
Exponent (Purdue University), C 87, C 88
Exposition Press, E 38

The Face of a Nation, A 11.1.a, AA 1, E 13
"The Face of the War," A 4, AA 4, C 39
"Faces," AA 1
Fadiman, Clifton, A 5.1.a₁, A 8.1.a, A 9.1.a, A 13.1.a
"Fame and the Poet," C 58
"The Fantasies: Clara Kimball Young," A 29
"The Far and the Near," A 4, C 44
"Far Away Lay America," AA 1
A Farewell to Arms," C 176
"Father, I Know That You Live," AA 3
"A Field in Flanders," C 1
Field, Leslie, A 19, AA 8
The First Firefly, B 43
Fitzgerald, F. Scott, B 13, B 42, B 47
"Fixity and Change," AA 1
Flaccus, Kimball, C 112, C 149
"Flood in Altamont," AA 3
Forgue, Norman, D 3
"Food," AA 1
"For Professional Appearance," C 30

The Forum and Century, A 3.1.d *Note one*
Forsythe, Robert, E 11
"Forsythe's Page," E 11
"Fountain," AA 3
"The Four Lost Men," A 4, AA 1, AA 5, C 24
Four Square Books, A 2.7
"Franco Prepares for Tourists," C 89
The Franklin Library, A 2.10, A 2.12, A 4.4
Franklin Mint Corporation, A 4.4
Frere-Reeves, A. S., A 2.1.e, A 3.2.a *Note one*, A 4.1.a₂ *Note one*, A 8.2.a *Note one*
From Death to Morning, A 4, AA 1, AA 4, AA 5, AA 7, B 5, C 20, C 22, C 23, C 24, C 28, C 31, C 33, C 35–C 40, C 44, C 50; Consul Edition, A 4.3; Franklin Library, A 4.4; Hudson River Editions, A 4.1.f; Scribner Library, A 4.1.e; Scribner Library of Contemporary Classics, A 4.1.f
From Of Time and the River America, D 3
"From *O Lost* to *Look Homeward, Angel*," C 187
"Frost, Wolfe Pack House, McNeal, Baker Considered Most Helpful To Writers," C 46
Fuess, Claude M., B 15
Fuhrman, Lee, C 61
"Full with the Pulse of Time," AA 3
"Future of Writers Conference Discussed by Faculty Members," C 47

Gale Research, B 49, B 50
Gambrell, Effie, A 11.1.a *Note one*, C 138
Gannett, Lewis, C 48
"Gant," AA 3
"Gant's Dream," AA 3
Garden City, A 7.1.e
Garden City Books, A 3.1.p, A 8.1.n, A 9.1.f
Garden City Publishing, A 2.1.l
Geismar, Maxwell, AA 4
"Gentlemen of the Press," A 9, A 29, AA 2
Gentlemen of the Press, A 10
Geoffrey Cumberlege Oxford University Press, A 17.1.a, B 22
George, Daniel, A 18.2

Index

The Georgia Review, E 31
"The Ghosts of Time," AA 3
"A Giant Has Fallen," C 95
"God's Lonely Man," A 9, C 121
God's Lonely Man, D 4
Goethe, Johann Wilhelm von, A 3.1.a, A 3.2.a
"Going Home Again," AA 3
"Gold and Sapphires," AA 3
"The Golden City," C 107, C 110
"The Golden World," AA 1
"Good Reading," C 48
Gorseline, Douglas W., A 2.4, A 2.12
"Gotham Gambit: Memories of Thomas Wolfe and Others," C 149
Gould, Elaine Westall, E 38
G. P. Putnam's Sons, B 3
The Grass Roof, C 17
Gray, Paul, B 28
The Greatest Books of the Twentieth Century, A 2.12
"The Great Ship," AA 3
Green, Charmian, C 167
Green, Paul, B 10
Greenlaw, Edwin, B 21, C 144
Greenwood Press, B 12 Note one, B 24
Greenwood Press of San Mateo, California, D 2
"Greeting and Farewell," AA 1
Griffin, John C., E 36
The Grolier Club, B 23
Grosset & Dunlap, A 2.1.k, A 3.1.j, A 3.1.n Note one, A 4.1.d, A 7.1.g, A 8.1.q, A 8.1.t, B 18
Grosset's Universal Library, A 7.1.g, A 8.1.q, B 18
"Gulliver," A 4, AA 5
"Gulliver, The Story of a Tall Man," C 40
"Gulping The Great West," E 9

Halberstadt, John, C 171
Hansen, Harry, A 2.1.a, A 4.1.a₁, A 8.1.a, B 5
Harcourt, Brace and Company, B 2
Harcourt Brace Jovanovich, Inc., B 43
Harlow, Jean, E 42
Harper & Brothers, A 7.1.a–d, A 7.1.h–k, A 8.1.a–h, A 8.1.k–m, A 8.1.o–p, A 8.1.r, A 9.1.a–b, A 9.1.d–e, A 9.1.g–h, A 13.1, AA 2

Harper Crest Library Editions, A 7.1.m
Harper Modern Classics, A 7.1.i, A 8.1.m
Harper & Row, A 7.1.l–n, A 7.4.b, A 8.1.s, A 8.1.u, A 8.4.b–f, A 9.1.i–k, A 9.4, A 9.5
Harper's Bazaar, C 38, C 78, C 107, C 122
Harper's Magazine, C 108, C 115
Harris, Arthur S., C 150
Harvard Alumni Bulletin, C 133
The Harvard College Library, B 34
Harvard Library Bulletin, C 134, C 144, C 160, C 163, C 164
Harvard Magazine, C 171, C 175
Harvard University Prss, AA 8, B 21
Hayes, Harold, C 77
Hazen, David W., C 51, C 92
"The Heart of the Dark," AA 1
Heinemann. See William Heinemann
Heller, Franklin, A 13.1.a Note two
Hemingway, Ernest, C 175
Henry Holt and Company, B 1, B 10
"Herrick, Crashaw, Carew," AA 1
"He Wolfed His Meal," E 45
Heyward, Dorothy, E 7
Heyward, Dubose, E 7
H. H., C 57
"His Father's Earth," B 8, C 34
"His Father's Hands," AA 1
The Hills Beyond, A 9, A 10 Note one, AA 2, AA 4, AA 7, C 41, C 56, C 80, C 83, C 101, C 121, C 122, C 123, C 125; New Avon Library, A 9.2; Lion Library Edition, A 9.3.a; Perennial Library Edition, A 9.3.a; A Plume Book, A 9.6.b; Pyramid Books Edition, A 9.3.b–c; Signet Classic, A 9.6.a
"The Hills of Home," AA 1
Hoagland, Clayton, E 41
Hoagland, Kathleen, E 41
Holding On For Heaven, A 27
Holiday, C 147
"The Hollow Men," C 119
"The Hollyhock Sowers," C 113
Holman, C. Hugh, A 3.4, A 12, AA 6, AA 7
The Houghton Library 1942–1967, B 34
Houghton Mifflin Company, B 7
The Hound of Darkness, A 29
"The House at Malbourne," A 29
"The House In Boston," A 29

House of Books, Ltd., A 6
"The House of the Far and Lost," C 27
Houston, K. C., C 88
"How to Keep Out of War," C 86
"The Hudson River," AA 1
Hudson River Editions, A 2.6.b, A 3.1.v, A 4.1.f, A 5.1.i, AA 3, AA 6
Hughes, Aline, E 6
Hughey, Michael W., D 10
"Hunger to Devour the Earth," AA 1
Hungry Gulliver An English Critical Appraisal of Thomas Wolfe, B 16 *Note one*
Hutsell, James K., C 137
"Hymn to Death, Loneliness and Sleep," AA 1
Hynds, Reed, C 49

Idol, John L., Jr., A 14, A 24, C 172, C 177, D 11
" 'I Have a Thing to Tell You,' " AA 6
"I Have a Thing to Tell You: (Nun will ich ihnen 'was sagen)," C 64
"I Knew Thomas Wolfe," E 8
"Immortal Drunkenness," AA 3
The Independent (Anderson, S.C.), C 138–C 140, E 22–E 25
The Indispensable Thomas Wolfe, AA 4.1.c
"In Devising Torture Cruelties Nordic Race Has Demonstrated The Superiority It Boasts of: London Tower," C 13
"The Inevitable Instant," AA 1
Inscriptions: B 17, B 50; to Aline Bernstein, B 34, B 51, C 133; to Madeleine Boyd, B 48; to Harold Butterfield, B 31; to William H. Fitzpatrick, C 170; to Kimball Flaccus, C 112, C 149; to James B. Munn, C 178; to Robert Raynolds, B 32; to Margaret Roberts, C 137, C 148; to Henry T. Volkening, B 21; to Fred Wolfe, B 26, E 14; to Julia Wolfe, C 130
"In Silence," AA 3
Interviews, A 14, B 6, C 15, C 16, C 18, C 32, C 42, C 43, C 45, C 49, C 51, C 52, C 55, C 57, C 59, C 61, C 62, C 65, C 66, C 68, C 69, C 76, C 79, C 88, C 90, C 91, C 92, C 109
"An Interview with Thomas Wolfe," B 6
"In the Park," A 4, AA 4, C 38

Jack, Peter Munro, A 4.1.a$_1$, A 5.1.a$_1$
"Jason's Voyage," AA 4
"Jewish Women," AA 1
Johnny Park Talks of Thomas Wolfe, B 41
Johnson, Pamela Hansford, B 16
Jones, H. G., E 48
Jordan, John Y., E 44
Journal of Presbyterian History, C 174
"Journey to the North," AA 1
"Judge Bland," AA 3
Julian Messner, Incorporated, B 11
"Junk Dealer Finds Wolfe Letters in Household Purchases," C 168
"Justice Is Blind," B 21

Kang, Younghill, C 17
"Katamoto," C 78
Kennedy, Richard S., A 2.6.a *Note one,* A 2.6.b *Note one,* A 2.6.c *Note two,* A 2.10 *Note two,* A 3.1.z *Note two,* A 21, A 23, A 25–A 27, B 21, B 27, B 37, B 51, C 144, C 157, C 164, C 175, C 176, C 178, C 184, C 186, D 15
Kerr, David, C 46
Kerr, Joan P., B 42
"A Kinsman of His Blood," A 9, AA 2, C 41
Klavins, Uldis, A 4.4
Koch, Frederick H., B 1, B 10, C 93, C 99, C 126–C 128, C 144, C 153, C 154, E 33
Kraus, Russell, B 22
K-19: Salvaged Pieces, A 24
The Lance (University of South Carolina at Lancaster), E 36
Landsborough Publications Limited, A 2.7
Large, Mary, C 184
"Last Country of Youth," AA 1
"The Last Land," AA 1
"The Last Letter of Thomas Wolfe," C 120
"The Last Letter of Thomas Wolfe and the Reply to It," C 134
"Last Poem," C 182, C 183
Latimer, Margery, A 2.1.a
Laurel Editions, A 7.3, A 8.3.a–e
Lawrence, Elizabeth, A 13.1.a *Note one*
Lecram Press, D 5
Lectures, C 46, C 87

Index

Ledig-Rowohlt, Heinz Maria, B 29, C 142
"A Letter from Thomas Wolfe," B 13, C 124
"A Letter of Gratitude and Indebtedness," B 15
Letters: B 19, B 24, B 27, B 33, B 44, C 126, C 143, C 162; to Sherwood Anderson, B 20, C 124, to Helen Arthur, E 7; to Edward C. Aswell, C 97; to Hamilton Basso, C 118, C 159; to Aline Bernstein, B 35, B 36, B 51, C 160, C 179; to Legette Blythe, C 129; to Walter Bonime, C 177; to Melville Cane, B 43; to Elizabeth Cattelle, C 144; to Albert Coates, C 145, C 165; to William J. Cocke, B 41; to William N. Cox, C 161; to Jonathan Daniels, B 25; to Mrs. William E. Dodd, B 39; to the editor of *The Nation*, B 21, C 89; to F. Scott Fitzgerald, B 13, B 42, B 47; to Kimball Flaccus, C 149; to Effie Gambrell, C 138; to Lewis Gannett, C 48; to Edwin Greenlaw, B 21, C 144; to "his host in Lafayette," B 21, C 111; to Frederick H. Koch, C 93, C 99, C 128, C 144, C 153; to Russell Kraus, B 22; to Heinz Maria Ledig-Rowohlt, C 142; to Miss MacReady, C 144; to George McCoy, B 50, C 95, C 148, C 168, C 173; to Julian R. Meade, C 146; to Edward M. Miller, B 52, C 166; to Herbert J. Muller, B 21, C 111; to Elizabeth Nowell, C 156, C 176; to "one of the editors of Harper Brothers," C 103; to Maxwell Perkins, AA 7, B 18, B 50, C 120, C 134; to Robert Raynolds, B 32; to Mrs. J. M. Roberts, B 14, B 16, B 21, C 131; to Merlin Taylor, C 144; to Henry T. Volkening, B 21, C 100; to Frank Wells, B 15; to Jack M. Westall, B 40, C 183; to Mabel Wheaton, C 148, C 155; to John Hall Wheelock, B 14; to Horace Williams, C 144; to Fred Wolfe, B 26, C 185; to Jim Wolfe, B 46; to Julia Wolfe, B 50
The Letters of Thomas Wolfe, A 18.1
The Letters of Thomas Wolfe to His Mother, A 12, A 20.1.a, A 25.1.a
"Letter to Maxwell Perkins," B 18
"Letter to Proff Koch," C 128

Lewisohn, Miss, A 13.1.b, A 13.2.a
Lewis, Phyllis H., C 184
Lewis, Sinclair, A 2.1.a, A 3.1.a, A 3.2.a
Liebert, Herman W., B 23
"Life's Hungry Man," AA 1
"Light of Fading Day," AA 1, AA 3
"Like the First Day of the World," AA 3
"Like the Light," AA 3
"Like the River," AA 3
Linder, Leo H., A 24 *Note one*
"The Lion at Morning," A 9, AA 2, C 122
Lion Books, A 9.3.a
Lion Library Editions, A 9.3.a
The Literary Guild, B 2.1.b, E 13
The Literary Guild of America, AA 1.1.b, B 37
Little Brown, and Company, A 2.1.a *Note four*, B 9
Little, Elizabeth T., E 40
"The Locomotive," AA 3
London Times Literary Supplement, A 4.1.a₁
The London Tower, D 13
"Lonely Joy," AA 1
Look Behind You, Thomas Wolfe, E 38
"Look Homeward, Angel," C 98
Look Homeward, Angel, A 2, A 3.1.a, A 3.1.z *Note two*, A 3.6, A 4.2, A 7.2.a, A 8.1.a, A 8.2.a *Note one*, A 8.2.a, A 13.2.a, AA 1, AA 4, AA 7, B 17, B 23, B 50, C 14, C 98, C 187; Bantam Books, A 2.9.a–c; De Luxe Illustrated Edition, A 2.4.f; 50th Anniversary Edition, A 2.6.c; A Four Square Book, A 2.7; The Greatest Books of the Twentieth Century, A 2.12; Hudson River Edition, A 2.6.b; Modern Library Giant, A 2.1.i; The 100 Greatest Masterpieces of American Literature, A 2.10; Scribner Illustrated Edition, A 2.12; Scribner Library, A 2.6.a; Scribner Library Edition, A 2.11; Scribner Library of Contemporary Classics, A 2.6.a; Scribner's Classics, A 2.9.d–f; A Signet Book, A 2.5.a–b; Signet Modern Classic, A 2.8; The Southern Classics Library, A 2.4.h
"Lost and Scattered," AA 1
"The Lost Boy," A 9, AA 2, C 80
The Lost Boy, A 9.5
"The Lost Day," C 56

Louisiana State University Press, A 14, A 23, A 28
"The Lovers," A 29
"Love's Bitter Mystery," AA 4
Lyons, Margareta, B 42

The Macmillan Company, B 15
The Magazine (University of North Carolina), C 6–C 9, C 12
Magi, Aldo P., A 22, A 28, B 48, D 7, D 8 *Note one*, D 11, D 13, E 41
"Magic," AA 3
"The Magic and the Loss," AA 3
"The Making of Thomas Wolfe's Posthumous Novels," C 171
"Mr. Malone," C 71
Mangan, James T., D 1
Mannerhouse, B 30, C 132
Mannerhouse: A Play in a Prologue and Four Acts, A 14, A 28
Mannerhouse: A Play in a Prologue and Three Acts, A 13
"Man's Youth," AA 1
"The Man Who Lives With His Idea," C 127
Mann, James B., C 177
The Marble Man's Wife, E 21
Martine, James W., B 49
Marx, Samuel, E 42
Max Perkins Editor of Genius, B 45
"May Morning In the Park," AA 1
Mayer, Charles T., C 169
McCoy, George W., B 50, C 95, C 148, C 168, C 173
McCoy, Lola Love, B 17
"The McCoy Papers," C 173
Meade, Julian R., C 146
Meeting Two American Giants, B 29
"Memories of Thomas Wolfe as Told by Fred Wolfe to Bernard Cannon Expressly for the Journal," E 14
"The Men of Old Catawba," A 4, AA 5
"The Mexicans," A 29
Meyerhoff, Hans, E 26
Meyers, Jo, AA 2
Middlebrook, L. Ruth, E 20
Middleton, R. Hunter, D 1
Miehe, Patrick, C 163
Miller, Edward M., B 52, C 166, E 9
Mills, Michael S., C 187
The Miscellany (Davidson College), C 158

Mississippi Quarterly, C 167
Modern American Prose, B 1
Modern Book Collecting for the Impecunious Amateur, A 2.1.a *Note four*
Modern Fiction Studies, C 157, C 159
Modern Library, A 2.1.i
Modern Library Giant, A 2.1.i
Modern Monthly, C 29, C 30, C 33, C 34, C 39
The Modern Quarterly, E 10
"Moonlight," AA 3
The Morning Oregonian, C 51
The Mountains, A 20
Muller, Herbert J., B 21, C 111
Munn, James B., C 178
My Other Loneliness, A 25.1.a, A 26

NBC Radio, E 27
"Names of the Nation," AA 1
"The Names of the Nation," C 29
National Institute of Arts and Letters, C 81, C 82
National Institute News Bulletin, C 81, C 82
The Nation, B 21, C 86, C 89
"Nebraska Crane," C 115
"Never Opened, Never Found," AA 3
New American Library, A 2.5.a–b
New American Library, A 7.4.a, A 8.4.a, A 9.6.a–b
New Avon Library, A 9.2
New Directions Books, B 13
New English Library, A 2.8
"New Orleans—River," AA 3
The New Masses, C 84, E 11
The New Republic, A 2.1.h, A 2.1.k, C 64, C 118
The New York Evening Post, C 17
New York Herald Tribune, A 11.1.a, C 32, C 48, C 52
New York Herald Tribune Books, A 9.1.a
New York Post, A 8.1.a, A 9.1.a, C 55
The New York Times, A 8.1.a, A 11.1.a, C 42
The New York Times Book Review, A 3.1.b *Note one*, A 3.1.c *Note one*, A 3.1.f *Note one*, A 3.1.g *Note one*
New York University Press, A 17, B 22
The New Yorker, C 36, C 71, C 73
"News Items from Institute Members," C 81, C 82

News and Observer (Raleigh, N.C.), C 62
"The Newspaper," A 29
"Niggertown," AA 3, B 35
"Night," AA 1, AA 3
1936 Essay Annual, B 8
"No Cure for It," A 9, AA 2
"No Door," A 4, AA 6, C 23
"No More Rivers," A 25
The North American Review, C 37, C 105
North, Caroline, C 170
The North Carolina Historical Review, C 148
The North Carolina Miscellany, B 28
North Caroliniana Society and the North Carolina Collection, E 48
A Note on Experts: Dexter Vespasian Joyner, A 6
"A Note on Thomas Wolfe . . . by Edward C. Aswell," A 9
"A Note on Thomas Wolfe's *Oktoberfest*-Letter," C 160
Notebooks, C 152, C 157
The Notebooks of Thomas Wolfe, A 21, B 37
"Noted Wolfe Home May Be Transformed Into Museum," E 25
"Notes from *A Western Journal*," C 147
Nowell, Elizabeth, A 18, A 25, AA 8 *Note one*, B 24, C 156, C 176, E 28, E 32
Norwood, Hayden, E 21

"O Flower of Love," AA 1
O. Henry Memorial Award Prize Stories of 1934, B 4
O. Henry Memorial Award Prize Stories of 1935, B 5
"O Lost," AA 1, AA 3, B 12, B 35, B 51, C 187, D 11
"O Young Love, Return," AA 1
"October," AA 3
"October has Come Again," AA 1
"The October Fair," B 35
Of Making Many Books, B 14
"Of Thomas Wolfe," E 17
Of Time and the River, A 2.6.c *Note two*, A 2.11, A 3, A 4.1.a₁, A 4.2.a, A 4.1.a₂ *Note one*, A 5.1.a₃, A 8.1.a, A 13.2.a, AA 1, AA 4, AA 7, B 35, B 50, C 19, C 21, C 23, C 25, C 27, C 29, C 30, C 186, D 2 *Note one*, D 3 *Note one*, D 8 *Note one*; Editions for the Armed Services, A 3.3; Hudson River Edition, A 3.1.v; Penguin Modern Classics, A 3.5; Scribner Library, A 3.1.y, A 3.4; The Scribner Library of Contemporary Classics, A 3.1.aa–bb
" ' Of Time and the River's' Author Hopes for Time to Read 'Gone,' " C 61
"Oktoberfest," C 72
"Old Catawba," C 35
"The Old House," AA 3
"Old Man Rivers," C 135
"Old Men and Women," AA 1, AA 3
Omnibook, A 2.1.a *Note two*, C 98, C 125
The 100 Greatest Masterpieces of American Literature, A 2.10
"One of the Girls in Our Party," A 4, C 31
"On Leprechauns," A 9
"Only the Dead Know Brooklyn," A 4, AA 4, AA 5, B 5, C 36
"Opulent Fantasies," AA 1
The Oregonian (Portland, Ore.), E 9
"Other Gifts," C 133
Outlet Book Company, A 4.1.b *Note two*
"The Outline of Thomas Wolfe's Last Book," C 163
Oxford University Press, A 17.1.a, B 22
Oxmoor House, A 2.4.h

Palaemon Press, A 1.1.c
The Papers of the Bibliographical Society of America, C 156
Park, Johnny, B 41
"The Party at Jack's," AA 6, C 102
"Passage to England," B 35
Pearson, Norman Holmes, A 20.1.a
Pegram, Addie Bradshaw, E 43
"Penance No More," B 21
"The Pencil Merchant," A 29
Penguin, A 2.14, A 7.5
Penguin Books, A 3.5, A 8.5.a–b, AA 5.1.a
Penguin Modern Classics, A 3.5, A 7.5, A 8.5.a–b
"People," C 43
Perennial Fiction Library, A 7.1.n
Perennial Library, A 7.4.b, A 8.4.b–f
Perennial Library Editions, A 9.4, A 9.5
Perkins, Maxwell E., A 2.4.b, A 2.4.d, A 2.4.e, A 2.4.g, A 3.1.a, A 3.3 *Note one*,

A 4.1.a₂ *Note one*, A 5.1.c *Note one*, A 10, AA 7, B 18, B 50, C 120, C 134, E 12, E 13
Philadelphia Public Ledger, A 2.1.a
Phillipson, John, E 39
Picard, Richard Jean, D 5
"Pity," AA 3
"Play Us a Tune," AA 3
Plume Books, A 9.6.b
"The Plumed Knight," C 123
"Plum Trees," AA 3
Pocket Books, B 33, B 45
"Poet of the Boom," E 15
"The Poet's Life," C 112
Poli, Joseph, A 4.1.b *Note one*, A 3.1.n *Note one*
Pollock, Thomas Clark, A 17, B 22
"Polyphemus," C 37
The Portable Thomas Wolfe, AA 4
"Portrait," AA 1
"Portrait of a Literary Critic," A 9
"Portrait of a Literary Critic: A Satire," C 101
"Portrait of a Player," C 105
"A Portrait of Bascom Hawke," AA 6, B 2, C 19
Portraits and Self-Portraits, B 7, B 21, C 136
Post Stories of 1937, B 9
Powell, Desmond, E 17
Press Time A Book of Post Classics, B 6
Preston, George R., Jr., A 4.1.b *Note two*, A 8.1.a *Note one*, B 12
"A Previously Unpublished Statement By Thomas Wolfe," C 154
Priestley, J. B., A 7.2.a, A 8.2.a
Princeton University Library Chronicle, C 183
Pritchard, Billy, C 168
The Proem To "O Lost," D 11
Prolegomena to Thomas Wolfe's A Crisis in Industry, A 1.1.b
"A Prologue to America," A 29, B 11, C 85
A Prologue to America, A 22
"The Promise of America," C 117, D 7
"Proud Cruel City," AA 1
"The Proud Stars," AA 3
Providence Journal, A 8.1.a
Purdue University Studies, AA 8 *Note one*, A 19

Pyramid Books, A 9.3.b–c
Pyramid Books Editions, A 9.3.b–c

"The Quest of the Fair Medusa," AA 4

"The Railroad Station," AA 3
Randall, David A., B 36
Random House, B 36, B 38, B 47
Rascoe, Burton, A 4.1.a₁, A 5.1.a₁, A 8.1.a, A 9.1.a
Raynolds, Robert, B 32
Reader's Digest, C 110
Redbook, C 80
Reed, Richard, E 37
Reeves, Paschal, A 21, A 23, B 35, B 37, B 39
"Reflections on Religion," C 174
Reingold, Alan, A 2.10
"Remembered Faces," AA 1
"Reminiscences of Thomas Wolfe," E 20
"Return," B 28, C 70
Return, D 6
"The Return of Buck Gavin," B 1
"The Return of the Prodigal," A 9, AA 2
"Return to America," AA 1
Reviews (by Thomas Wolfe): of *A Farewell to Arms*, C 176, of *The Grass Roof*, C 17
Roanoke World-News, C 77
Roberts, Margaret (Mrs. J. M.), B 14, B 16, B 17, B 21, C 131, C 137, C 148
The Robesonian (Rowland, N.C.), C 161, E 35
"The Rock in Maine," A 29
Rocky Mountain News, C 45
The Romantic Egoists, B 42
Rose, William H., Jr., A 8.1.n *Note one*
Ross, Mrs. C. Reid, A 12
Ross, Sue Fields, A 12
Rowohlt, B 29, B 30
"Royal Processional," AA 3
Rubin, Louis D., A 2.4.h, A 14
Russell, Phillips, C 63, C 96
"Russian Folk Song," C 9
Ryan, Pat M., A 20

San José College Laboratory Press, D 4
Sancton, Thomas, C 59
Savino, Guy, C 15
The Saturday Evening Post, C 76

Index

The Saturday Review of Literature,
  A 3.1.e *Note one,* A 5.1.a, *Note one,*
  A 11.1.a, AA 8 *Note one,* C 53, C 129,
  C 130, C 136, E 7, E 25
Schevill, James, B 20
Schmid, Hans, C 160
Schreiber, Georges, B 7, B 21, C 136
Scott, Foresman and Company, B 8
Scribner, Charles, III, C 182, C 183
Scribner Illustrated Editions, A 2.12
Scribner Library, A 2.6.a, A 3.1.y, A 3.4, A 4.1.e, B 16 *Note one*
Scribner Library Editions, A 2.11
Scribner Library of Contemporary Classics, A 2.6.a, A 3.1.aa–dd, A 4.1.f
"Scribner's And Tom Wolfe," C 12
Scribners Classics, A 2.9.b
Scribner's Magazine, C 14, C 19, C 20–C 25, C 27, C 28, C 31, C 40, C 72, C 102
"The Seaman: Dere Ain't No Decent Air in Brooklyn," A 29
Seattle Post-Intelligencer, C 91
"The Secret Heart of Night," AA 1
Selected Letters of Thomas Wolfe, A 18.2
Selections from the Works of Thomas Wolfe, AA 4.1.d
Shenton, Edward, AA 1
Sherwood Anderson His Life and Work, B 20
"The Ship," AA 3
The Short Novels of Thomas Wolfe, AA 6
Signet, A 8.4.a
Signet, A 7.4.a
Signet Books, AA 5.1.b–c
Signet Books, A 2.5.a–b
Signet Classics, A 9.6.a
Signet Modern Classics, A 2.8, A 7.4.a, A 8.4.a
"The Silence of the House," AA 3
The Silver and Gold (University of Colorado), C 46
Skally, John Terry, E 7
Skipp, Francis E., C 156, C 159
Smith, Scottie Fitzgerald, B 42
"Something of My Life," B 21, C 136
"Some Things Will Never Change," AA 3
"The Song of the Whole Land," AA 3
"So This Is Man," C 116
"The Sound of the Sea," AA 1
South Atlantic Quarterly, C 155, C 176
The South Carolina Review, C 177
The Southern Classics Library, A 2.4.h
The Southern Literary Journal, C 172
Southern Literary Studies, A 14, A 28
Southern Living Gallery, A 2.4.h
The Southern Packet, C 137
"Space and Movement," AA 1
"Speaking Dust," AA 1
Spearman, Walter, E 33
"Spring," AA 3
"Spring in the South," AA 3
"Spring Night in the City," AA 1
"Spring Plowing," AA 1
"Springtime in New England," AA 1
Starkey, Marion L., C 18
The State (Columbia, S.C.), E 34
The State (Raleigh, N.C.), C 63, E 6, E 18
Stern, Philip Van Doren, A 3.3 *Note one*
Stevens, George, A 8.1.a
Stevenson, Paul, C 60
St. Louis Star-Times, C 49
"A Stone, A Leaf, A Door," AA 3
A Stone, A Leaf, A Door, AA 3
Stoney, George, C 96
Stories by Thomas Wolfe, AA 2
Story, C 124
"The Story of a Novel," C 53
The Story of a Novel, A 5, A 11.1.a, A 16.1.a, AA 1, AA 4, AA 5, AA 7, AA 8, B 35, C 53; Hudson River Editions, A 5.1.i
"Stranger than a Dream," AA 3
"The Streets of Durham," B 38
The Streets of Durham, D 14
"The Streets of Durham, or, Dirty Work at the Crossroads," C 11
"Strictly Personal," C 129, C 130
"Student Days With Thomas Wolfe," E 31
Stutman, Suzanne, A 26, A 27, C 180
"The Sun and the Rain," C 25
The Sunday American (Atlanta, Ga.), C 60
The Sunday Oregonian (Portland, Or.), C 92
Sunday Times, A 4.2.a
Sun Dial Press, A 3.1.m, A 3.1.n *Note one,* A 7.1.f, A 8.1.i–j, A 9.1.c
"The Supernatural in the Poetry and Philosophy of Coleridge," C 144

Tar Heel, B 19
The Tar Heel (University of North Carolina), B 21, C 10, E 1–E 5
Tar Heels, E 15
"Tarheels in New York," E 6
Taylor, Merlin, C 144
Telegrams: to Mary Mitchell Westall, C 184; to Mabel Wolfe Wheaton, C 137, C 140
Tennant, Charles G., E 46
Terry, John Skally, A 11, C 130, E 25
"T.E. Wolfe, 'Wordiest Author,' Pays Visit to Denver on Whim," C 90
"That Sharp Knife," AA 3
The Theater Annual: 1947, C 105
Theatre Arts Monthly, C 99
"The Third Night," B 10
"The Third Night: A Play of the Carolina Mountains," C 94
"This Is Man," AA 3
Thomas Congdon Books, B 45
"Thomas Wolfe," B 7, E 10, E 16
Thomas Wolfe, B 33
Thomas Wolfe: A Bibliography, A 4.1.b Note two, B 12
Thomas Wolfe A Biography, B 24
Thomas Wolfe A Critical Study, B 16
Thomas Wolfe A Harvard Perspective, B 51
"Thomas Wolfe: A Memoir," B 43, C 162
"Thomas Wolfe and 'Altamont,'" C 137
"Thomas Wolfe and Anatole France," C 152
"Thomas Wolfe and Elizabeth Nowell: A Unique Friendship," C 176
Thomas Wolfe and His Family, B 26
Thomas Wolfe and Hollywood, E 42
"Thomas Wolfe and the American Experience," C 157
Thomas Wolfe and the Glass of Time, B 39
"Thomas Wolfe and the Opulent Manner," E 32
"Thomas Wolfe and T. S. Eliot: The Hippopotamus and the Old Possum." C 172
"Thomas Wolfe: A Summing Up," C 118
"Thomas Wolfe at Chapel Hill," C 143
"Thomas Wolfe at Harvard, 1920–1923," C 144
"Thomas Wolfe At New York University," C 178

"Thomas Wolfe at 75," E 37
"Thomas Wolfe At 35 Is Tired of Being a Legend," C 52
Thomas Wolfe at Washington Square, B 22
"Thomas Wolfe A Writer for the People of His Time and Tomorrow," E 13
"Thomas Wolfe: Biography in Sound," E 27
Thomas Wolfe: Carolina Student, B 19
"Thomas Wolfe Comes Back," C 63
"Thomas Wolfe Cuts 2d Book to 450,000 Words," C 32
"Thomas Wolfe Describes his Feelings at Being Home Again," C 70
The Thomas Wolfe Fest, D 8, D 9
The Thomas Wolfe Festival, D 7
"Thomas Wolfe from North Carolina," C 18
"Thomas Wolfe: He Writes 'Em Standing Up," C 92
"Thomas Wolfe in Berlin," C 142
"Thomas Wolfe—In Memoriam," C 109
"Thomas Wolfe in New Orleans: Letters of William H. Fitzpatrick to Andrew Turnbull," C 170
Thomas Wolfe Interviewed, A 14
Thomas Wolfe Interviewed 1922–1938, A 28
"Thomas Wolfe Lectures and Takes A Holiday," B 21, C 111
"Thomas Wolfe: Legends of a Man's Hunger in His Youth," E 7
"Thomas Wolfe Letter to Be Donated To Library," C 161
"Thomas Wolfe, Max Perkins, and Politics," C 159
Thomas Wolfe Memoir of a Friendship, B 32
The Thomas Wolfe Memorial, D 6 Note one
Thomas Wolfe Newsletter, C 94, C 166, C 169, D 9, E 39, E 40, E 43–E 46
"Thomas Wolfe, Noted Author, Visiting Here," C 60
Thomas Wolfe October Recollections, B 25
Thomas Wolfe of North Carolina, E 48
"Thomas Wolfe on 'What a Writer Reads,'" C 54
Thomas Wolfe Our Friend 1933–1938, E 41

Index

"Thomas Wolfe: Penance No More," C 100
"Thomas Wolfe: Playmaker," C 93, C 126
Thomas Wolfe's Purdue Speech "Writing and Living", A 19
The Thomas Wolfe Reader, AA 7
"Thomas Wolfe Remembered—III,'" E 44
"Thomas Wolfe Remembered—IV," E 46
"Thomas Wolfe Remembered: An Evening With Fred-Luke," E 36
The Thomas Wolfe Review, A 2.10 *Note two*, A 2.6.a *Note one*, A 2.6.b *Note one*, A 2.6.c *Note two*, A 3.1.z *Note two*, , C 170, C 173, C 178–C 181, C 184, C 186–C 187, E 47
"Thomas Wolfe Revisits City Whose Spirit He Portrayed in First Successful Novel," C 59
Thomas Wolfe's Albatross, B 35
Thomas Wolfe's Discovery of America, D 12
Thomas Wolfe Short Stories, AA 5
Thomas Wolfe Short Stories Only the Dead Know Brooklyn, AA 5.1.b–c
"Thomas Wolfe's Last Manuscript," C 164
Thomas Wolfe's Letters To His Mother, A 11
The Thomas Wolfe Society, A 24, A 27, A 29, B 48, D 9, D 11, D 13–D 15
"Thomas Wolfe's Papers," C 150
Thomas Wolfe's Pennsylvania, B 46
"Thomas Wolfe Started His Hard Work Early," C 138
"Thomas Wolfe's Unpublished Works," C 97
"Thomas Wolfe's *Welcome to Our City*: An Angry Young Southerner Looks Back," C 184
"Thomas Wolfe Talks About His Contemporaries and Predicts a Bright Future for Our Writers," C 55
"Thomas Wolfe: The Autobiography of An Idea," C 132
Thomas Wolfe The Discovery of a Genius, B 48
Thomas Wolfe The Final Journey, B 52
"Thomas Wolfe: The Friendliness of A Lonely Man," C 145
"Thomas Wolfe: The Presbyterian Connection," C 174

"Thomas Wolfe: 37 Today, Plans Early Return to Native Mountains to Live," C 79
Thomas Wolfe Undergraduate, B 44
"Thomas Wolfe Visits City—Says He'll Write a 'Really Great' Book," C 49
"Thomas Wolfe Visits Vermont: A Retrospect," E 39
"Thomas Wolfe Welcomed By Friends Here," C 66
"Thomas Wolfe, W. S. C. English Instructor, Author of Much Acclaimed First Novel," C 15
Thornton, Mary Lindsay, C 155
"Thos. Wolfe Comes Home For First Time Since Writing Novel," C 68
"Thos. Wolfe, Famous Author, Visitor Here," C 65
"Three O'Clock," C 105
"Time," AA 3
Time, C 43
Times, A 4.2.a
Times-Picayune New Orleans State, C 59
Time . . . Thomas Wolfe, D 8
"To France," C 2
"To Keep Time With," AA 1, AA 3
"Tom Wolfe As A Student," B 21
"Tom Wolfe As I Remember Him," C 165
"Tom Wolfe's Cabin," E 18
Tom Wolfe's "Dixieland," B 17
"To Rupert Brooke," C 5
To Rupert Brooke, D 5
Total Recoil, E 30
"Toward Which," AA 3, AA 7
Town and Country, C 116, C 123
"The Train and the City," C 21
The Train and the City, D 15
"The Tributary Theatre," C 99
Trotti, John Boone, C 174
Turnbull, Andrew, B 33
"T. Wolfe of 10 Montague Terrace," E 29

The University of Denver Press, B 20
University of Georgia Press, B 35, B 39
University of Kansas City Review, C 132
The University of North Carolina Department of Philosophy, A 1
University of North Carolina Library, B 19
The University of North Carolina Magazine, C 1–C 5

The University of North Carolina Press,
    A 12, A 20, A 21, A 25, A 26, B 27, B 28,
    E 33
University of North Carolina Tar Baby,
    C 11, D 14 *Note one*
University of Pittsburgh Press, A 16
The University of Texas, B 31
University of Texas Press, B 32
Unseen Harvests, B 15
Untermeyer, Louis, AA 3
"The Unvisited World," AA 1
"Useful Advice to Candidates," B 19,
    E 4

Van Antwerp, Margaret A., B 50
Vanderbilt, Sanderson, C 32
Van Doren, Carl, A 3.1.a, A 4.1.a$_1$, B 2
Vanity Fair, C 50, C 182
Viking Press, AA 4
Vining, Lou Nyrtis, C 109
Virginia Quarterly Review, C 35, C 100,
    C 104
"The Vision of the City," AA 3
"Visions of Horror and of Delight," AA 1
Vogue, C 85
Vogue's First Reader, B 11
Voices, C 112
"Voices of the Books," AA 1
Volkening, Henry T., B 21, C 100

Walker, Susan, B 47
Wallace, Margaret, A 2.1.a, A 3.1.a,
    A 5.1.a$_1$
Walpole, Hugh, A 3.1.a
Walser, Richard, A 1.1.b, A 28, B 21,
    B 28, B 44, B 46, C 173, D 14, E 41
Walter, Erich A., B 8
"Waters of Darkness," AA 1
Watt, Homer Andrew, A 17
Watts, Georgia, C 153
Wayne, Don, A 2.3, A 3.3 *Note one*
Wayne, Frances, C 90
"The Way Things Are," AA 3
"The Web of Earth," A 4, AA 6, B 3, B 50,
    C 20
"We Shall Not Come Again," AA 1
The Web and the Rock, A 7, A 8.1.a,
    A 8.2.a, AA 4, AA 7, B 27, B 35, B 51,
    C 21, C 34, C 71, C 72, C 74, C 75,
    C 85, C 104–C 108, C 110, C 163,
    C 164, C 175; Grosset's Universal Library, A 7.1.g; Harper Crest Library
    Edition, A 7.1.m; Harper Modern Classics, A 7.1.i; Laurel Edition, A 7.3;
    Penguin Modern Classics, A 7.5; Perennial Fiction Library, A 7.1.n; Perennial Library, A 7.4.b; Signet, A 7.4.a;
    Signet Modern Classic, A 7.4.a
Weber, William, C 158
"Welcome to Our City," B 30, C 151
Welcome to Our City, A 14, A 23, A 28,
    C 172, C 185
Wells, Frank, B 15, C 131
West, Herbert Faulkner, A 2.1.a *Note four*
West, Luke, E 34
Westall, Jack M., B 40, C 184
Westall, Mary Mitchell, C 184
A Western Journal, A 16, C 104, C 147
"A Western Journey," C 104
"The Western Journey: Prelude and Aftermath," C 166
"What Are We?" AA 3
What Is Man? D 1
"What Is This Memory?" AA 1
"What the Galley Proofs of Wolfe's *Of
    Time and the River* Tell Us," C 186
Wheaton, Mabel Wolfe, A 5.1.c *Note one,*
    A 8.1.a *Note two,* A 9.1.a *Note one,*
    B 26, C 137, C 148, E 22–E 24, C 140
Wheelock, John Hall, A 3.1.f *Note two,*
    A 3.2.a *Note one,* B 14, B 18, B 27
"Where Are We to Seek," AA 3
"Where Now?" AA 1
" 'Which of Us Has Known His
    Brother?' " E 34
White, William Allen, A 8.1.a, A 9.1.a
White Ladies, A 3.2.a
Whitson, Max, E 18
"Who Has Known Fury," AA 1
"The Whorehouse Rag," A 29
"The Whores," A 29
Wilhelm Meister's Apprenticeship,
    A 3.1.a, A 3.2.a
Wilkommen in Altamont! Herrenhaus,
    B 30
Willamette River Press, B 52
William Heinemann Ltd., A 2.2, A 2.7,
    A 3.2, A 3.5, A 4.1.a$_2$, A 4.2.a, A 4.4,
    A 5.1.a$_2$, A 5.1.a$_3$, A 7.2.a, A 7.2.b,
    A 8.2.a, A 8.2.b, A 13.2.a, A 18.2,
    AA 4.1.d, B 16, B 24
William J. Cocke, B 41

Index

William Targ, A 10
Williams, Betty Lynch, B 40
Williams, E. B., AA 2
Williams, Horace, C 144
Wilson, Edmund, B 13
"The Wind from the West," A 29
The Window of Memory, A 12, A 20.1.a, B 27
Wings (The Literary Guild), E 13
"The Winter Of Our Discontent," C 106
"Wir Sprachen Thomas Wolfe," C 57
The Wofford Journal (Wofford College), E 14
Wolfe, Benjamin Harrison, A 4.2.a
Wolfe, Fred, A 4.1.c *Note one,* B 26, C 186, E 14, E 34, E 36, E 37
Wolfe, Jim, B 46
Wolfe, Julia F., A 8.1.a *Note two,* A 9.1.a *Note one,* A 11.1.a, B 50, C 130, E 21, E 43
"The Wolfe-Bernstein Letters," C 180
"Wolfe Calls: Questions and Answers," C 179
"Wolfe Denies 'Betraying' Asheville," C 16
"Wolfe Described Teacher As 'Mother' Of His Spirit," E 23
"Wolfe Found Life Not All Bad, Not All Good," E 22
"The 'Wolfegate' Affair," C 175
"Wolfe Home With Avid Views of Life," C 69
"Wolfe Leaves After Summer Visit Here: Finishes New Story," C 75
"Wolfe Plans Novel Patterned After Swift's Famous Satire," C 77
"Wolfe Play To Be In N.Y.; Will Appear In Book Form," C 139
"Wolfe Revealed America's Soul," E 24
"Wolfe Revisits Student Scenes," C 62
"Wolfe's *Look Homeward, Angel* in the Library Marketplace," A 2.6.a *Note one,* A 2.6.b *Note one,* A 2.6.c *Note two,* A 2.10 *Note two,* A 3.1.z *Note two*
"Wolfe's Harvard Years," B 21
"Wolfe's Stonecutter Once Again: An Unpublished Episode," C 167
"Wolfe Tells Club Members He Plans To Return To City," C 67

"Wolfe the Reviser," E 47
Worcester Sunday Telegram Feature Parade Section, C 150
Works In Progress, B 37
World Distributors, A 4.3
"The World of First Light," AA 1
"Write Hard and at Home Advises Author at C.U.," C 45
Writer's Digest, C 109, C 153
"Writers Have Their Place In World, Says T. Wolfe," C 87
"Writing and Living," AA 8, B 50
"Writing Is My Life: Letters of Thomas Wolfe," C 131
"Writing is my life: Munich and New York," C 131
"Writing is my Life: The Novelist Under Fire," C 131
"Wyler Will Direct Motion Picture of Famous Novel," C 140

The Yale Review, C 83, C 171
..."The Years of Wandering in Many Lands and Cities," A 15
"Yesterday, Remember?" AA 3
"Ye Who Have Been There Only Know," E 3
You Can't Escape Autobiography: New Letters of Thomas Wolfe," C 146
You Can't Go Home Again, A 8, A 24 *Note two,* AA 4, AA 7, B 35, B 50, B 51, C 1, C 3, C 21, C 23, C 26, C 64, C 73, C 78, C 84, C 85, C 102, C 113, C 114–C 117, C 119, D 1 *Note one,* D 7, D 8 *Note one,* D 12 *Note one;* Grosset's Universal Library, A 8.1.q, Harper Modern Classics, A 8.1.m; Laurel Edition, A 8.3.a–e; Penguin Modern Classics, A 8.5.a–b; Perennial Library, A 8.4.b–f; *Perennial Library,* A 8.6; Signet, A 8.4.a
"Youghill Kang Distills Riches of Experience," C 17
Young, Francis Brett, A 3.2.a
"Young and Drunk, and Twenty," AA 1
"You Were Not Absent," AA 3
"Yuh Musta Been Away," AA 3

Pittsburgh Series in Bibliography

WALLACE STEVENS: A DESCRIPTIVE BIBLIOGRAPHY
J. M. Edelstein

EUGENE O'NEILL: A DESCRIPTIVE BIBLIOGRAPHY
Jennifer McCabe Atkinson

JOHN BERRYMAN: A DESCRIPTIVE BIBLIOGRAPHY
Ernest C. Stefanik, Jr.

RING W. LARDNER: A DESCRIPTIVE BIBLIOGRAPHY
Matthew J. Bruccoli and Richard Layman

MARIANNE MOORE: A DESCRIPTIVE BIBLIOGRAPHY
Craig S. Abbott

NATHANIEL HAWTHORNE: A DESCRIPTIVE BIBLIOGRAPHY
C. E. Frazer Clark, Jr.

JOHN O'HARA: A DESCRIPTIVE BIBLIOGRAPHY
Matthew J. Bruccoli

MARGARET FULLER: A DESCRIPTIVE BIBLIOGRAPHY
Joel Myerson

RAYMOND CHANDLER: A DESCRIPTIVE BIBLIOGRAPHY
Matthew J. Bruccoli

DASHIELL HAMMETT: A DESCRIPTIVE BIBLIOGRAPHY
Richard Layman

SUPPLEMENT TO F. SCOTT FITZGERALD: A DESCRIPTIVE BIBLIOGRAPHY
Matthew J. Bruccoli

JAMES GOULD COZZENS: A DESCRIPTIVE BIBLIOGRAPHY
Matthew J. Bruccoli

HENRY DAVID THOREAU: A DESCRIPTIVE BIBLIOGRAPHY
Raymond R. Borst

RALPH WALDO EMERSON: A DESCRIPTIVE BIBLIOGRAPHY
Joel Myerson

ROSS MACDONALD/KENNETH MILLAR: A DESCRIPTIVE BIBLIOGRAPHY
Matthew J. Bruccoli

EMILY DICKINSON: A DESCRIPTIVE BIBLIOGRAPHY
Joel Myerson

EMERSON: AN ANNOTATED SECONDARY BIBLIOGRAPHY
Robert E. Burkholder and Joel Myerson

NELSON ALGREN: A DESCRIPTIVE BIBLIOGRAPHY
Matthew J. Bruccoli

THOMAS WOLFE: A DESCRIPTIVE BIBLIOGRAPHY
Carol Johnston